Praise for *Th*

"Potent and provocative!"
—**Fiona Horne**, author of *The Art of Witch*
and *Witch: A Magickal Journey*

"I must admit, I didn't think a book entitled *The GLAM Witch* was going to be my thing. Just as the author Michael Herkes didn't quite resonate with traditional Wicca, I've never found myself drawn to glamour and fascination magick. So imagine my surprise when he dispels that notion right off and presents a profoundly rich tradition based upon the dark goddess Lilith. It's wonderful when expectations are smashed and you see things in a new light, and *The GLAM Witch* certainly does that. Filled with great research, firsthand experience, devotion, art, and of course still some glamour, he presents it in a fun, modern accessible style, but with a depth and sincerity that is often missing in modern popular books. I particularly liked the astrological approach to the three forms of Lilith."
—**Christopher Penczak**, author of the *Temple of Witchcraft* series and *Gay Witchcraft*

"Articulate, exciting, and fresh! A glorious work about Lilith and her goddess glamour!"
—**Deborah Castellano**, author of *Glamour Magic*

"Michael Herkes' debut book, *The GLAM Witch*, is a clever, well-written, and truly brilliant piece of work. I applaud the author's dedication to detail (no stone is left unturned), and his humble reverence toward the Great Goddess in her form of Lilith: an often misunderstood force of nature — and ourselves. This is a book for those seeking self-empowerment, self-love, and a knowledge of ancient and modern magical practice."
—**Raven Digitalis**, author of *Esoteric Empathy* and *Shadow Magick Compendium*

"The GLAM Witch is an unapologetic exploration of deep magic and spirituality. Michael Herkes creates an enchanted safe-space for us to explore our flaws, kinks, creative callings, and our truth. His coming of age story as a queer witch guided by the ancient wisdom of Lilith is a reminder that we're all on our own journey of discovery . . . magic is available for all of us no matter who you are, where you find yourself, or how you wish to show up! Herkes deep dives into the historical significance of Lilith, her evolving influence, and his personal initiation of empowerment through her tutelage. You can feel Herkes' wisdom and support throughout the book . . . encouraging you to live your truth and offering a practical foundation for putting magic into practice! This is a must read for the Femme mystic, the rebel seeker, and anyone wishing to walk the path of the self-made witch!"

—**Shaheen Miro**, author and creator of
The Lunar Nomad Oracle, co-author of
Tarot for Troubled Times

"I LOVE this book. Michael Herkes' voice is a dream. His passion is palpable, lifting out of the pages and into your hands and heart. It looks at how the goddess/archetype Lilith has for so long been worshipped and feared, and walks readers through how they can create a relationship with Lilith, as well. In fact, it's called *The GLAM Witch* because Herkes explores the Great Lilithian Arcane Mysteries (GLAM). Through luminous text, you'll find astrology, ritual, and a magic that is steeped in power."

—**Lisa Marie Basile**, author of
Light Magic for Dark Times

"A must for anyone interested in Lilith or the magic of glamour. Michael Herkes exudes new power into this feminine archetype and aids the reader on a pathway that leads to beauty, passion and her exotic temptations. He also did his research and offers us ancient wisdom that meets the present age. The book is fun, inspiring and filled with magic."

—**Brian Cain**, author of *Initiation into Witchcraft*

THE GLAM WITCH

A Magical Manifesto of Empowerment with the
GREAT LILITHIAN ARCANE MYSTERIES

MICHAEL HERKES

Foreword by Fiona Horne

WITCH WAY
PUBLISHING

Third Printing, 2021

Witch Way Publishing
9090 Skillman St, #182-A/203
Dallas, TX 75243
www.witchwaymagazine.com

Printed in the United States of America

ISBN 978-0-578-21202-9

Editor: Tonya Brown
Technical editor: Paul Flagg
Cover & interior design: Michael Herkes
Author photograph: Caitlyn Ridenour
Interior photography: Michael Herkes, unless otherwise noted.

Disclaimer: This book contains some intense rituals and ingredients, such as
toxic herbs, blood, bodily fluids, and sexual situations. Please be warned that
Witch Way Publishing and the author are not held responsible for what you
choose to practice. Intended for ages 18 and up.

To the outcast:
May you find your home…your place to rest.

CONTENTS

FOREWORD

by Fiona Horne

Michael Herkes has crafted something quite spectacular and unique in this book—the first deeply researched, and deeply lived, ode to Lilith and guide to living with her as a patron goddess and magickal inspiration.

When I formed my first coven many years ago, Lilith came to me in a vision—like the evening star in the dark night sky. To me, she embodied the enlightening beauty and profound wisdom that is found in the dark cauldron of creation. As my patron goddess, she challenged me. Being brought up Catholic, I knew from biblical stories that she was the first wife of Adam and refused to lay underneath him and was banished to the shores of the Red Sea, where she gave birth to 1,000 demons a day . . . or something like that. As a witch, contemplating her in a sacred way, Lilith forced me to face society's—and my own—misconceptions and presumptions about what my gender was capable of and who I could evolve to be. Turning these pages, what resonated very deeply with me is the passion and authenticity of Michael's path and this GLAM Witchery he offers.

I met Michael in 2006 at one of my book signings in Chicago. Very friendly and very magickal, those were early days for him on his path, and through our mutual interests—both practical and magickal—we forged a friendship that has allowed me to witness his growth and evolution into a powerful mage.

I completely love this book. It is dripping with well-researched scholastic information on Lilith, whilst being so cleverly creative, colorfully entertaining, and expansive as Michael shares his wisdom on GLAM ritual, spellcasting, and life crafting. *The GLAM Witch* ultimately elevates and liberates the reader to explore their magickal universe, fortified by the original feminine force.

Her time is now . . .

INTRODUCTION

My Witch Ways

"The first time I called myself a 'Witch' was the most magical moment in my life." —Margot Adler, *Drawing Down the Moon*

My introduction to modern witchcraft was fueled by the glamorization of witches in Hollywood during the '90s. As the New Age movement progressed, and more and more witches popped up in television shows and movies, I developed an affinity for them. But it was also a deep-rooted fascination with things—such as the moon, snakes, and femininity—that would lead me to my witch ways. These components combined and began to ebb and flow to the pounding beat of the Goddess' heart. Over time, I came to know this goddess as Lilith, a powerful archetype and representation of the witch. Saturated in her teachings from early childhood, I was propelled into an esoteric world of witchcraft that facilitated a spiritual awakening of personal empowerment and expression.

My first exposure to Lilith came in 1998, before I would embark on my magical journey as a witch. I had found her among the pages of a graphic novel, *Buffy the Vampire Slayer: The Dust Waltz*, by Dan Brereton. In it, she appeared as a mysterious red-haired woman who wore a flowing lavender gown and golden crescent moon earrings. Even though she was just a drawing on the pages, she had a presence unlike one I had ever seen—a rich glamour and electrifying magnetism. The book identified her as Adam's first wife, prior to Eve, and as the mother of all vampires. In the story, she was planning with her sister Lamia, a snake-haired Medusa-like character, to unleash evil into the world, and it was up to Buffy to stop them. Medusa was an entity that I had gravitated toward early on due to my love for snakes. Although I was well versed in who she was, I was spellbound by Lilith.

As shows like *Buffy* and *Charmed* progressed in the new millennium of Y2K, they began to serve witchcraft to the world on a silver platter. It was this that introduced me to the exotic word "Wicca," which was used synonymously with "witch" and "witchcraft" on both shows. This led me to my first book on witchcraft in 2000, titled *Teen Witch*, by Silver RavenWolf. In reading it, I found that Wicca was coined the religion of witchcraft and was a modern twist to ancient pagan practices—revering the divine in both feminine and masculine forms. It honored nature as sacred and celebrated the cycles of the moon and sun as representations of the Goddess and God. In Wicca, there weren't any demons or forces of darkness to fling at my enemies; however, there were spells and rituals one could do to effect positive change in their life. Spells were like prayers that were fused together with energy sources and correspondences that assisted in fueling the intent of a desired outcome. It was different from what I had anticipated, but I was interested, nevertheless. I particularly liked the idea of the Goddess, since I had always felt a deeper connection to feminine things. Additionally, I came to find that this spiritual path was very welcoming to the LGBTQ+ community, and at the time I was beginning to explore my sexual identity as a young gay man (and tormented regularly for it). I discovered "The Charge of the Goddess" in Starhawk's book *The Spiral Dance* which expressed universal acceptance of sexuality, affirming that "all acts of love and pleasure" are sacred to the Goddess. I started to feel empowered and welcomed. Witchcraft made me feel like I had found a place of belonging.

From here, I would persevere in my witch studies with additional books. I understood the material I was reading, but something was not fully clicking. It wasn't until I came across a dark blue square book in my library's metaphysical section that things changed. The cover of the book featured a blonde woman with a mystical gaze sitting on a pile of stones. Large, hot pink letters splashed across the top of the cover, reading *Witch: A Magickal Journey*. It was penned by a glamorous Australian rock goddess named Fiona Horne. I flipped the book over, and there was another photo of her holding a spotted brown snake. I saw this as a sign, connecting back to my initial love of the prehistoric creatures I had collected in the neighborhood fields as a child. As I continued thumbing through the pages, I came across a section on different goddesses. Here, I spotted Lilith again, with reference to her as Adam's first wife and as a "source of inspiration to witches". I checked out the book and instantly fell in love. Its tone was unlike all the other books I had been reading—the words felt more like I was having a personal conversation with Fiona rather than being lectured to. I found that there was a personality in this book that the others did not possess. I had found the missing link. It was here that Fiona unconsciously poured gasoline on the flickering flame of witchery within my soul, setting it fully ablaze. In doing so, she became my literary high priestess, inspiration, and *she*ro.

In some of the other books I started to pick up, I noticed references to a patron deity. While Wicca saw the divine as a balancing act of feminine and masculine, it was said that in your practice, one deity may pop up that would become your singular focus of worship. This would be a particularly intimate relationship with a divine force. The deity would become your mentor and teach you many lessons. In most cases, their archetypes would interweave with your life, and you would become a living extension of them. I became hungry to find mine and started digging more into Lilith, since she had initially piqued my interest when I first saw her in the comic. Sadly, information on her was even more limited than it is now. The internet was not like it is today, and the little I did find always referenced her as demonic and evil. I was desperately trying to convince people that what I was doing was not devil worship, so I ran for the hills and buried the thought of Lilith deep within the back of my head. Instead, I began to explore countless other goddesses. I had started deity speed-dating with Aphrodite, Artemis, Hecate, Inanna, and Medusa. To my dismay, I had no connection with any of them. Something was always missing.

During this time, Lilith would continue to make herself known to me. I would experience coincidences, such as opening a book and seeing the name Lilith (or a variation like Lily) or turning on the TV and seeing a character by the same name. With each discovery, I would become curious about her again. But, despite this, I ultimately continued to push her away out of my own ignorance and fear. The more I screened her spiritual call, the louder she became. Finally, she called out to me again through Fiona Horne.

In March 2004, the Sci-Fi network (now known as SyFy), debuted a reality show called *Mad Mad House*. The show consisted of ten contestants living in a house with five "alts," who were people leading alternative spiritual lifestyles. Fiona took up residency as the house witch and would enlighten the guests on the practices of modern witchcraft, introducing them to it with several rituals to empower and heal. In the fourth episode, though, Fiona called upon her patron goddess to assist in getting to the bottom of some manipulation by the contestants. As I sat there watching her chant out a series of ancient names, it was revealed that her patroness was no other than Lilith.

It was clear that I could no longer ignore her. Lilith was literally screaming at me like the screech owl she had been referred to in her mythologies. My magical mentor, who I wholeheartedly looked up to, had just expressed a personal relationship with the goddess who'd called out to me long before I began my studies in witchcraft. If this wasn't the epitome of a sign, I don't know what is. I felt, from this, that I had been called to serve Lilith. It was time for me to suspend my fears and start foraging a relationship with her. I finally answered her call and stepped into my calling.

In the post revelations of *Mad Mad House,* I also learned that Fiona's personal practice with Lilith was further fleshed out in a new book called *The Coven: Making Magick Together.* Available only in Australia at the time (it was re-released for America under the title *L.A. Witch: Fiona Horne's Guide to Coven Magick* in 2007), I was able to find a copy on eBay, and used it as a building block for my Lilithian ways. As more information on Lilith became available to me, I studied the analytic, psychological, and demonic folklore associated with her on a grander scale. I coupled my goddess studies as a whole with the Sumerian mythology from which she originated, and further anchored it with the intuitive guidance established through my meditations, dreams, and rituals with her.

As I slowly and respectfully started welcoming her into my life, I realized that the harsher energies I had initially read about her were nothing to fear. Instead, they were quite transformative. I found her essence to be very much like my flesh-and-blood mother. Lilith's love is strong . . . but tough. I came to see her not as a demoness, but as a creative expression of feminine consciousness—a ripe and powerful extension of the great Goddess who had been slandered by the patriarchy. I also came to learn how much of a connection she has to the moon and the serpent. I started to feel like I had been guided along for many years without realizing it.

Around 2009, my practice as a Wiccan became lackluster. At this point, I had been practicing solitarily for eight years, only learning from the books I was reading. I moved up to Chicago from the south suburbs and thought I would finally have the opportunity to meet other witches and maybe join a coven. My excitement halted when I realized that was not going to happen. I tried connecting with fellow witches in the city, but each road I took led to a dead end. The city was proving hard to navigate socially. The people I was finding were only interested in witchcraft as a fad. Even the ones that were serious would flake out.

Then I started to break away from the structured constraints of Wicca. While I still respect its values and beliefs, it just resonated less and less with me, particularly working with the masculine God energies. Even though I am physically male, I have never really connected to the gender. I found more comfort and empowerment in femininity. What I appreciated about Lilith was the omnipresence to her that combines the primal feminine force with harsh masculine energy, a duality surpassing gender identity.

I realized that one does not have to be Wiccan to be a witch and that there are many different branches and traditions of witchcraft one can practice. I started to see the power that came from being an eclectic solitary practitioner, one who worked alone and adapted their practice from various sources, paths, and traditions. It was time for me to stop living a spiritual life that I thought I should have and to start *witch*-crafting my own tradition. I had my deep-rooted core beliefs that I established through Lilith, and that was all I needed from a spiritual standpoint. So, I let go of the want and desire to join a group. In the end, Lilith was a representation of an outcast, solitary in her very nature. There was no shame in continuing down a road of spiritual solitude. I knew that, even when I felt alone, I had her deep within me as an extension of my true self. So, I stepped forward on my very own yellow-brick road and in doing so asked myself, *What would Lilith do?*

The book that follows is the documentation of my personal practice as a witch and a devotee of Lilith, which I refer to as the Great Lilithian Arcane Mysteries, or GLAM. It is my offering to Lilith and the world. My hope is that it may inspire others in the way I have been inspired on my path—either in working with Lilithian energies described here or in molding a personalized spiritual practice. My hope is, that in sharing Lilith's mysteries, one may grow spiritually and mentally by cultivating confidence, overcoming adversity, and achieving authenticity. This is my manifesto for spiritual survival and my testament for finding empowerment in what makes you uniquely you. With that said, I cordially invite you to reach for the glittering fruit of knowledge that hangs above you and to discover the magically delicious life of the GLAM Witch!

PART I

The Theory of

THE GLAM WITCH

1

EXILE TO GLAMVILLE:

Defining the GLAM Witch

"When I say witchcraft is a spirituality, I mean it is a spiritual path. You walk it for nourishment of the soul, to commune with the life force of the universe, and to thereby better know your own life." —Christopher Penczak, *The Inner Temple of Witchcraft*

Whether you're born with it, or it's witchery, glamour is something that we all long for, yet it can feel so far out of reach. Glamour is magical and enchanting but also subjective. It is an exotic word that penetrates the mind differently, depending on the individual. While in many ways a blanket connotation referring to a lifestyle of beauty and luxury may fit the bill, it is not necessarily a one-size-fits-all definition. For some of us, glamour may be a lifestyle of the rich and famous, whereas others see it more as a costume you put on when hitting the town for a night out with friends. Perhaps it is a trip to a day spa for relaxation and pampering or a trip to the local bakery for a decadent indulgence. It could also be the tranquil peace of complete solitude or the ecstatic hustle and bustle of socialization. Or it could be acts of witchcraft!

Historically, glamour was considered to be one of the first variations of a witch's spell—an ultimate act of magic. The first time I heard of glamour in this capacity was from the famous witch movie *The Craft*. In it, one of the young witches waves her hands over her hair and—poof!—she is instantly blonde, calling it a "glamour." Unlike the movies, the witches of the real world are not able to change hair color at the wave of their hands. We take a box from the local supermarket with us to the bathroom or make an appointment to see our stylist, just like everyone else.

Much of today's modern witchcraft is eclectic in nature, drawing upon a number of metaphysical philosophies and occult practices that the individual witch merges with their own unique style of witchery; therefore, there is not a one-size-fits-all definition for what a witch is anymore. That being said, there are a number of organized traditions of witchcraft that have their own particular styles and ideologies that define their paths. In the most general of cases, witches are individuals that have an affinity for nature and tap into and control spiritual energy in their life and in the world around them. Energy is an abundant force, both seen and unseen by the naked eye. We rely on energy for many things in life. Everything is made up of energy, and witches shape, mold, absorb, reflect, and deflect it through the art of magic.

The magic weaved by witches is done through developing relationships with sources of energy useful to the witch's goal. Some witches use energy sources, such as an element, while others tap into the phases of the moon, solar cycle of seasons, or other astrological phenomenon. Some witches opt for using entities like deities, spirits, ancestors, or even other people as sources of energy to draw from. Whichever energy source a witch chooses to work with, they do so by fusing the energy with intent. Every thought form, wish, desire, burst of creativity, or surfacing of negativity breathes life into intention, which in fact happens to be the most potent energy used by witches—the power of will.

Regardless, it is important to remember that witchcraft is a craft, a practice, and although it can certainly be religious, it does not necessarily have to be. While not all witches work with goddesses or gods, many do, drawing on the energy of polarity in the feminine and masculine forms of divinity. Over time, though, a witch may devote their practice to a single goddess or god, whom they connect with deeply. This connection is generally associated with drawing on the energetic symbolism of a particular deity. In my practice, this is Lilith, an enigmatic goddess who is often considered the first witch among other titular titles.

Lilith is one of the oldest known female spirits of the world. Her roots come from ancient Sumerian times, where she was considered a wind spirit and a sacred prostitute. She was later adopted by the Hebrews as Adam's first wife, who tried to oppress her. Lilith found the courage within to stand up for herself and fly away from paradise for a free life. In doing so, she was cursed by patriarchal society and referred to as a nocturnal night hag, sexual demon, and child killer. Despite the calculated attempts to shut her out and paint her as a horrific demoness, she lives on.

Wearing many hats over the centuries, Lilith is currently seen as a mysterious goddess in modern witchcraft—governing independence, sexuality, personal power, and occult wisdom. Best known for her voluntary exile from Eden, she has elevated herself in the eyes of witches, feminists, and rebels as the poster girl of unapologetic authenticity—champion of equality and freedom. Unfortunately, the negative aspects that have been placed upon her throughout history often deter people from working with her. Yes, Lilith has her dark side, but remember that age-old saying that it has to be dark to see the stars. Through that darkness, we experience light.

In Lilith's exile, she was said to take refuge in the desert caves on the coast of the Red Sea. There, she was graced with the luxurious glamour of freedom in the darkness of the wild night, under sparkling stars. And this cave, Lilith's cave of glamour, mystery, and witchcraft, is where our story begins. Welcome to Glamville—home of the GLAM Witch.

The Birth of GLAM

In the years of walking a path as a solitary witch and devotee of Lilith, it became clear to me that I needed to define what my practice was. I could lump it under being an eclectic solitary, but I felt that it deserved more than that. There is much power in names, titles, and labels. None of us like labels, in fact, growing up my friends would routinely say that labels were best left for soup cans and fashion brands. But labels can be seen as more than just restrictive, as they can assist in providing stability, structure, and identification.

So, I thought about different titles that would be suitable, connecting my witchcraft to Lilith. While revisiting early notes I made in my research on Lilith, I came across a quote from esteemed witch Doreen Valiente's book *An ABC of Witchcraft: Past and Present*: "The moon goddess Lilith is the archetypal seductress, the personification of the dangerous feminine glamour of the moon". And in that passage, the word "glamour" stuck out. My first job after high school was as a photographer at the infamous Glamour Shots, and as a colorful queer person, I had always been drawn to glitz, glamour, and beauty. Lilith possesses a dark glamour of her own, so I saw it as being a fitting representation and an ode to her.

But more than that, I see glamour as an enriching luxury and, to me, witchcraft is a spiritual luxury—the luxury of leading an enchanted and magical life. So, I looked at the root term of the word—"glam"—and thought about roots. Roots are the means of support, an underground, mysterious appendage that provides nourishment and stability, much like a name or label does. And this is where I would anchor my practice as a modern witch and devotee of Lilith—in the root term of "glamour." It is from this that GLAM took on the form of an acronym for the Great Lilithian Arcane Mysteries, my personalized path of Lilith-based witchcraft.

GLAM vs. Glamour

Despite similarity, it is important to understand that "GLAM Witch" and "glamour magic" are not necessarily synonymous. To help differentiate the two, when you see "GLAM" referenced in this book, it is referring to my overall spiritual practice of the Great Lilithian Arcane Mysteries. "Glamour" will refer to either society's definition of enchanting fantasy and luxury or, more specifically, glamour magic.

The GLAM Witch is a witch who embodies the essence of Lilith. One who cultivates confidence, sizzles with sensuality, and stands up to adversity; one that is authentically unapologetic in their life and spiritual path. This Lilithian approach to witchcraft means that one walks in the path of Lilith. The practice of the witch becomes concentrated on her many epithets and blossoms as a sensual flower in her garden of moonlight. One taps into the energy of Lilith for magical workings and strives to be a living expression of her. A GLAM Witch is a badass. They are complete unto themself. They are authentic and unapologetically themselves. They do what they like, when they like, how they like, and do not feel the need to answer to anyone—just like Lilith.

Self-esteem, pride, and vanity can often be construed as negative attributes, but they are empowering to a GLAM Witch; they give birth to inner confidence. The spiritual energy manipulated by a GLAM Witch first begins with opening yourself up to the call of the universe, accepting the magic of your life. This, as you will see, is ultimately anchored in the inner self. A GLAM Witch needs to break free of the confines of society and embrace all facets of themselves for who they truly are. Your pride and confidence must first glow. This allows you to shed your inhibitions and insecurities, subsequently allowing you to become a greater more powerful witch! If witchcraft is truly fueled by your intent, the more self-assured you are will only make your magic stronger. When you are confident in yourself and understand who you are on a deeper level, you can use the GLAM Witch tools to magnify your intentions and create a magical life.

Magic & Spells

Now, time for what you have all been waiting for—the spells! Truth be told, I came to witchcraft for the spells, but they aren't supernatural sprinkles of glitter and sparkle. Spells are essentially a witch's version of a prayer. Spells start with a need, and once this is established, it is combined with a variety of ingredients that energetically correspond to the initial intent. These are then propelled into reality with visualization and the power of the word (they are called "spells" because we have to actually "spell out" our wish!), thus manipulating energy.

Witches are practitioners of magic and do spells and rituals that align with our goals. There is no one universal witch goal. For some, this maybe an abundance of esoteric wisdom. For others, it is a means to control others, bending their will in matters of love, lust, or punishment. Still, there are those who utilize witchcraft and magic for spells and rituals to communicate with departed spirits, and others who use witchcraft as a spiritual act of service to the world, helping to heal and inspire. This book will touch on a variety of these applications; nevertheless, the overall goal of the GLAM Witch is inner transformation and personal empowerment.

It needs to be addressed, though, that somehow over time, witchcraft developed certain colors to define the type of magic one performs. In pop culture, it is commonly seen that those witches who are geared toward healing and peace are white witches, bathing in the white light of spiritual flufflepuff. On the flip side, those who work with the dead, curses, and other taboo forces are considered black witches, and practitioners of black magic. That said, witchcraft is truly a colorless practice. Since ours is more of a nature-based spiritual path, we work with the natural forces of life to help establish harmony, balance, and equality in our lives and in the world around us. Sometimes, this can be healing and loving. In other instances, it can be harsh and destructive—just like Lilith, just like the natural rules of nature.

A Note for the New Witch

Witchcraft is having a "moment" again. Pop culture is resurrecting the glamour of witches in television shows, movies, fashion, and social media. Some are even reclaiming the title of witch as a means of political rebellion. Regardless, each generation continues to add new elements to modern witchcraft. The practice evolves as we do. Some of the philosophies in this book may be new, and some are old. Some are going to be just flat-out different, and perhaps my style might not be suitable for you at this time, and that is ok.

If, by chance, this is your first book on witchcraft, I am honored to say the least but wholeheartedly recommend you check out some of the books listed in my references at the back of the book for further study. Also, remember that your witchcraft is a process and a spiritual journey. It is not an event where you wake up and—poof!—you have all of the wisdom and teachings down pat!

Many individuals turn to witchcraft for the frivolity of it. The ideology of casting spells and rituals has become a fad among spiritual junkies looking for the next adrenaline rush. Witchcraft is not fast-food spirituality. Don't expect to roll up to a magical drive-thru and order a lover, money, health, and protection and get it served to you in a cute box with a fun toy. While patience is a property that I often struggle with for mundane matters, when it comes to witchcraft it is essential. If anything, think of witchcraft as a good crockpot recipe. You have to throw in a bunch of ingredients like herbs, crystals, planetary correspondence, color magic, etc., and brew it in your mind's cauldron with intent. You have to let it simmer. You will need to let your knowledge of witchcraft steep a bit before you start the process. You cannot cut corners. A microwaveable meal might be faster, and it may still provide you with necessary nutrition, but it will not be as decadent or as rewarding as one that has been simmering for an extended period of time.

You see, the universe, spirit guides, goddesses, and gods all exist outside of our reality. Reality is a human construct. We have confined time to calendars and clocks and expect the laws of attraction to be on our terms. But they exist on different planes. These planes all mirror and layer on top of one another, yes, but we speak in a different time language—a different astral time zone.

A truly essential part of blossoming as a witch is to develop the confidence and "ego" necessary to achieve manifestation. Remember that this is not instantaneous either. This book alone will not answer all of your questions or solve all of your problems; it is a roadmap to developing confidence and authenticity in your craft as a witch. It is necessary to research, read, and continue to learn and grow on your path to experience the most from the material outlined within these pages.

Witchcraft is work, and GLAM Witchcraft is even harder work, because it truly is about constant personal transformation. It is going to get raw and ugly. It is a spiritual journey to enlightenment and empowerment. It is never too late to shed your skin and be reborn again. With each obstacle there comes a lesson, and through overcoming them we learn and grow. Like all crafts, practice makes perfect. As you board the bus for the world of witchcraft, focus less on the destination and more on the scenery of the ride. Trust me, it will only make your magic stronger in the long run!

Why Lilith?

Perhaps you are asking yourself "why Lilith?" I have noticed in the last few years that there is a growing popularity for Lilith, yet she remains an enigma wrapped in a riddle of occult wonder. Even still, she is not as mainstream as many other witch goddesses of today, such as Hecate, Aradia, Diana, or Kali. But Lilith is a very potent source of energy, whether she is viewed as a goddess, spirit, archetype, or astrological being. If you have heard her call, chances are there is a lesson that you need to learn from her. She is a socket of occult power. Once we thrust ourselves into her, we become enveloped in the magical electricity of authentic personal empowerment.

Many associate Lilith's role of equality only with feminism, but I see her encompass it on a greater scale. This can help explain why she continues to pop up more and more each year. The world is in desperate need of equality at the moment, with constant threats of terrorism, racism, sexism, the rebirth of neo-Nazis, and the ever-increasing hate crimes in the LGBTQ+ community, not to mention the environmental crisis. Race, gender, and orientations have divided us, though we are all created the same and equal with the earth. In these troubled times, Lilith is needed more than ever to help elevate us to new heights. Now is the time for Lilith's ascension. For these reasons, I feel it is time to shed some light on Lilith and share how I have woven her into my personal path as a witch.

How to Use This Book

The book you hold in front of you is the documented record of my theory, practice, and lifestyle as a witch and devotee to Lilith. It is split into four parts. We will first take a look at the theory behind the GLAM Witch. This will unfold through examining Lilith's *herstory* and what elevated her to the role of a goddess in modern witchcraft. It will help provide a contextual theology for better understanding her archetypes and epithets that further align to magical practice. From there, we will head into the second part, exploring a more spiritual practice of the GLAM Witch. This section will identify different tools and ingredients used to honor Lilith, how to make contact with her—including worship in ritualistic and ceremonial practices—and establish the five Lilithian Laws that make up the Great Lilithian Arcane Mysteries. The third section is devoted to the "crafts" of the GLAM Witch; these are the five channels of magic that a GLAM Witch uses in their practice. They are not inherently Lilithian and can be incorporated into any existing magical practice but do extend into Lilith's archetypes. The fourth and final section will detail several recipes from my personal collection to help manifest and achieve the results outlined in the previous chapters and also provide an outline for a weekend of witchy self-care.

As you continue reading, remember that anyone can take the material outlined in this book and merge it into their existing personal practice. In fact, I encourage you to! This is a snapshot of my way of doing things, but my way is definitely not the only way. What works for me might not work for you, and that is not a bad thing—it's just different. If you feel compelled to use another deity or spirit for the activates we discuss here, feel free. Working with deities can sometimes be like working with co-workers or bosses, or even like dating. Sometimes there is chemistry, and sometimes there is not. While you do not have to use Lilith, I encourage you to at least explore her archetype in these magics for maximum effect.

In many ways, Lilith can twirl into your life like a windstorm and turn it upside down. Scary as it may seem at the time, it is necessary for true transformation to take place. As you will find in due time, it is how one rebuilds their fallen tower that gains her attention and respect over those who grovel and point blame elsewhere or ignore what is right in front of them. So, if you are up for a challenge and ready to fearlessly march ahead on the path of the GLAM Witch, let's carry on. Remember that like the devastation of a wildfire, under the debris will emerge new life. You will emerge, like the phoenix rising from the ashes. You will transform into the GLAM Witch.

2

ALL ABOUT LILITH:

The GLAM Witch Goddess

"Lilith, the true Mother of All Living, must be acknowledged . . ."
—Janet & Stewart Farrar, *The Witches' Goddess*

L ilith's metaphysical resume is as complex as it is long. Even still, much of it is debated. Her ancient roots are fragmented and highly controversial among historians, but her Hebrew and subsequent mythologies are abundant and ever-growing. While the true origins of Lilith remain unknown, we at least have a reference point from the breadcrumbs she has left throughout history. By combining these and observing how outrageous her myths became over time, we can understand more of where she came from and what she represents presently.

A great deal of anthropological and historical analysis has been done on Lilith, much of which is listed in my references for further reading. The problem I found with these during my early work with Lilith, however, was that they are purely historical analyses that lacked the magical and spiritual depth I was after as a witch. So, this chapter will not only serve as a condensed overview on Lilith's *herstory* but will also include my interpretation of it as relevant to the Great Lilithian Arcane Mysteries. It is the foundation on which GLAM is built. In understanding the legacy of Lilith, we can assist in raising her to new heights in modern witchcraft, calling her from the wilderness and into our hearts. But before we move forward to the fun stuff, we must travel back—five thousand years to be exact—and learn all about Lilith. So buckle up for this crash course on Lilith 101!

Ancient Origins

The oldest possible association of Lilith goes as far back as 3000 BCE to the Mesopotamian lands of Sumer. This ancient ground, presently known as Iraq, has been considered the earliest known civilization in the region. Relics from this time detail hundreds of goddesses and gods that reigned supreme during the period, yet many are still unknown. Thanks to few surviving artifacts, myths have been uncovered and later translated to detail the legends of the gods.

In some of my early research, I found speculation of Lilith originally as a Sumerian fertility goddess. Through further investigation, I found this first incarnation to possibly be a beautiful maiden goddess named Sud, who ruled over grain and agriculture. In one story, Sud was raped on the banks of a sacred river by Enlil, God of air and atmosphere. Sud became pregnant and, in punishment, Enlil was sent to the underworld. Sud followed him there and encountered him on three different occasions, leaving each impregnated and giving birth to other gods. Over time, Sud's anger

13

for Enlil changed to love as he matured in the Underworld. From this love, they returned to earth where Enlil, who's name translates to Lord Air (*en*–lord, *lil*–air), gave Sud the name Ninlil, or Lady Air (*nin*–lady, *lil*–air).

It is here that Ninlil became the "lady of the open field," which I believe represents the fertility of agricultural pollination by wind. The story is symbolic of how wind rapes the grain, carrying it to the earth, where it matures underground and re-emerges in a new form. After Ninlil's death, it is said that she was reincarnated as the south wind, which brings us to Lilitu, the entity that scholars widely accept as the earliest form of Lilith.

Spirit of the Moon

Found in cuneiform throughout Mesopotamian regions of Sumer, Akkad, Assyria, and Babylonia, the Lilitu is commonly considered a class of female night demons. While some see Lilitu as a reincarnation of Ninlil, this leaves a major plot hole in the theory. Yes, both contain the root word *lil* and are considered rulers of the south wind, but if the theory is true, how did a beloved goddess become a demon?

In researching the Sumerian language, the etymology of Lilitu gives us additional clues as to who she is. We know that *lil* translates to "air" or "wind"; however, it was also used to describe "breath," the "spirit of place," a "back country" or "open country," and sometimes even "infection." Meanwhile, *itu* was a reference to "moon," "month," and "moonlight." It is worth noting that the Sumerian people were known for having established a calendar system based on the lunar phases, which would be why "month" and "moon" are used to describe the same word.

It is from this etymology that Lilitu was known as "a wind spirit of the night." Some scholars have used this to conclude that Lilitu was a demonic spirit that brought chaos and disease; a ruler of storms and night; an attacker of children; and a seductress of men. It is important here to note that the Sumerian views on demons were not the same as modern society's. They were not always considered evil, and in many cases were simply just another form of spirit.

While *Lil-itu* can certainly be translated to "spirit of the night," I favor the possibility of it being a reference to the "spirit of the moon," or perhaps even "breath of moonlight." Yet, there are negative associations with each root term. The wind can be destructive when it comes to storms, and if we look at the south winds, we see that these were how the summer storms originated. These storms brought bountiful rains and fertility to the lush Fertile Crescent but, like all storms, a bit of chaos is brought too. Meanwhile, the possible use of *itu* as "infection" certainly favors the disease detail, for which I have another theory.

A Handmaiden's Tale

One of the most important parts of Lilitu's story from this period is her role as the handmaiden to Inanna—a radiant goddess, widely worshipped in Sumer. She was seen as the "Queen of Heaven" and also known as Inanni and Ishtar, and later as Astarte, who would eventually align with Greek Goddess Aphrodite. Inanna was a goddess of beauty, sexuality, astronomy, astrology, prostitution, agriculture, love, and war. Being a goddess of sexuality, temple prostitution in dedication to Inanna was a customary practice. Sexuality was revered as a gift of the Goddess. Virginal women and, even homosexual men garbed as women, were responsible for carrying out the Goddess' divine sexual teachings.

In 1914, Assyriologist Stephen Langdon published *Tammuz and Ishtar: A Monograph Upon Babylonian Religion and Theology Containing Extensive Extracts from the Tammuz Liturgies and All of the Arbela Oracles.* Per the text, "a tablet redacted in classical Sumerian, and certainly a product of the Sumerian period, describes the female personification of lust as under the protection of

Innini [a/k/a Ishtar, f/k/a Inanna]. The text describes minutely the demon sent by Innini, a beautiful and licentious unmarried harlot, who seduces men in the streets and fields. And in a grammatical text she is explained as the hand of Innini." In the footnotes, Langdon further notes that the harlot was called Lilitu by the Semites.

This reference has been interpreted by historians as a way to disassociate the lustful acts from Inanna's "Mother" Goddess role by passing it into another entity, à la Lilith as her handmaiden. In this capacity, Lilith can be considered the great teacher of sexuality and tantric sex magic, as passed down from the highest ruling goddess of the time. Knowing that Lilitu was a sexual servant of the Goddess, and that the Mesopotamian regions were home to some of the first sexually transmitted infections, we can build the correlation between Lilith as a night spirit and bringer of disease. I believe that this, in connection to the natural fertility association of Ninlil as a goddess of grain and air, is why in the evolution of Lilith's myths she is frequently connected to sex, seduction, and temptation.

The Ḫuluppu Tree

Around 2000 BCE, the poems of Gilgamesh were being chiseled away into stone. In Tablet XII, titled *Gilgamesh and the Ḫuluppu-Tree*, Lilith resurfaces in connection to Inanna. In the tablet, an entity named Ki-sikil-lil-la-ke (or simply Lillake) causes the great Mother Goddess grief as she takes up residency in Inanna's sacred ḫuluppu tree with a snake and a bird. World-renowned Assyriologist Samuel Kramer translated "Ki-sikil-lil-la-ke" to "Lilith" in 1932; though, other historians have rejected this claim. Nevertheless, there are parallels between this story and the many forthcoming myths of Lilith. As a result, this is a noteworthy piece of her story today.

In Kramer's book, *Sumerian Mythology*, he translates the story. In it, Inanna found an uprooted ḫuluppu tree and planted it in her garden. Her plan was to eventually use the wood from the tree for a throne. Over time, Inanna was unable to cut down the tree because a serpent "who knowns no charm" was coiled at the base; an Anzû bird had built its nest in the crown; and Lilith, the "maid of desolation", took up residency in the middle. A distraught Inanna wept until the "great Sumerian hero" Gilgamesh overheard her and came to rescue the goddess. He killed the snake and caused the Anzû to fly away with its young. Lilith "tore down her house and fled to the desolate places where she was accustomed to haunting."

If you are anything like me, hearing this story is likely going to raise your eyebrows. Upon my early research on Lilith, it seemed very odd to me that Inanna was crying over her sacred animals and handmaiden being in her tree. It does not strike me as a logical com-

Bird, Snake, & Tree

In *Gilgamesh and the Ḥuluppu-Tree*, we see Lilith being linked to the bird and snake for the first time, in addition to running off into the wilderness. The bird and snake have long been associated with the Goddess and divine wisdom when it comes to mythological symbolism—birds with their abilities to ascend into the sky and the heavens above, while serpents burrow deep within the earth to the underworld. The bird represents enlightenment, and the whole tree takes on the archetypal representation as a tree of life. The representation of the snake entwined at the base of the tree also connects to the kundalini essence that resides coiled at the base of our spines. Meanwhile, the ḥuluppu tree is believed to be a white willow, a magical tree that is greatly associated with wisdom, water, and the moon.

plaint any deity would make. Nor does it seem logical that a deity of such stature and power, who ruled over war, would allow a half-god, half-man to come rescue her, no matter how handsome he may be!

I began to think that instead Inanna was crying not for the supposed invasion but rather for the death and exile that came with Gilgamesh. My research uncovered a similar theory in *Mysteries of the Dark Moon*, by astrologer Demetra George. In the book, the author provides an overview of Lilith and further suggests that in response to the patriarchy, Inanna "must sacrifice her virginity, that is, her new moon maiden nature as a Goddess who is free and autonomous. She must also submit to the new solar Gods and allow Gilgamesh to destroy the key symbols of her power: the bird, the snake, and the tree."

With the growing patriarchy, stories shifted and became dominated by the male perspective. Inanna needed to conform to this if she was going to stay visible. Think of the modern adage, "there is no such thing as bad press"; we currently see this aligned to celebrity status and, regardless of how a story plays out, as long as people are being talked about, they stay relevant. I believe the same is true for deities and spirits. Without worship, without the power of thought to keep them alive, goddesses and gods die. In this moment of time, Inanna was unwilling to die so she conformed in fear. If this were the case, the tears could represent the sadness of Inanna, or even general society as it conformed to the new masculine force. But as we see here, Ki-sikil-lil-la-ke did not conform. If this entity was in fact Lilith, it would represent the wisdom of the divine great Mother Goddess being poured into her high priestess to flee and re-emerge when ready.

Queen of the Night

In the 1930s, an artifact came to light that would prove to be another controversial article in the pages of Lilith's story. A terracot-

18

Photo: Personal photograph of the Burney Relief / Queen of the Night taken at The British Museum on January 8, 2018. This image has become one of the most popular depictions of Lilith and is heavily debated amongst historians and the magical community.

ta wall plaque was brought to The British Museum in three pieces by way of an art dealer named Selim Homey. Very little is known about the exact origins of the relic, since it was not excavated. It is believed that Homey may have picked it up during his recorded travels to Iraq in the 1920s. Because of how spectacular the image depicted on the plaque is, many questioned the object's authenticity. The piece entered The British Museum's records in 1933 and underwent an authentication process which verified it was originally created between 1792 and 1750 BCE. Despite this, The British Museum turned down the acquisition of the relief in 1935. It was here that Sydney Burney purchased the piece, subsequently resulting in its being called the *Burney Relief*.

From there, the artifact was passed around to various private collections until it eventually returning to The British Museum, which then officially purchased it in June 2003. In the sale, the relief was renamed to *Queen of the Night*. This image has become the most popular visual representation of Lilith over the years. Many historians reject the likelihood of this, favoring Inanna's counterpart Ishtar or her sister Ereshkigal, Goddess of the Underworld, due to the horn crown and the rod and ring. These are typically seen in high-ranking deities, and from the information available, Lilith in her forms as Lilitu or Lillake were not seen as prominent at the time. The British Museum currently describes the plaque as a depiction of Ishtar and has discontinued referencing Lilith.

In January 2018, I had the opportunity to visit the controversial artifact for the first time. In the brief moments I had with her, I was completely hypnotized by the glory of what was trapped behind plexiglass twelve inches from my face. Despite my love for Lilith, and metaphysical phenomenon for that matter, I remain healthily skeptical of things from time to time. Being in London and in front of the *Queen of the Night*, I can attest to Lilith's presence. While I completely accept the fact that this relief could very

Photo: The Queen and me at The British Museum on January 8, 2018. Regardless of the debates, the Queen of the Night has become such a staple in Lilith's modern story that there is great power behind using it in connection to her and is a welcomed depiction of Lilith in my practice. Experiencing her up close and personal was magical!

well have originally been any of the magnificent goddesses theorized, or perhaps even one that has been long since forgotten by time, I have a strong sense that it does represent Lilith/Lilitu in her role as the handmaiden of Inanna/Ishtar.

There are elements of both figures represented in the one image—a supreme deity's headdress and the rod and ring of justice, in addition to the wings and talons of a beastly spirit Lilith was known as. In certain situations, a grand devotee of a deity may take on the physical representation of that entity. In this case, the headdress and rod and ring showcase the possibility; the wings and the clawed owl feet illustrate that this remains Lilith in Ishtar's image, elevated to a place of power. Standing above Ishtar's lions, with Lilith's birds in forefront glory, perhaps represents what happened when Lilith fled the huluppu tree. Lilith ascended into a role of supremacy but remained hidden away. There is something to be said for hiding; it may be seen as a weakness, but it is also a surefire means of survival. So, perhaps this plaque is a representation of that—the goddess worship that went underground as Lilitu/Lillake fled to the wilderness. Maybe the *Queen of the Night* was a cult item once placed on a shrine for worship. The possibility of it being a secret object of worship would help explain how such an ancient piece remained in such good condition, despite the clean breaks that were able to be fitted back together. With the absence of proper documentation to accurately identify the *Queen of the Night*, the Queen herself remains an ancient Jane Doe. Regardless, this depiction has become such a staple in Lilith's modern story that there is great power behind using it in connection to her. And because of this, the *Queen of the Night* is a welcomed depiction of Lilith in my practice.

Into the Wild

On the flipside of the Gilgamesh poem, Lilith's stories took a twisted turn. In the 8th century BCE, Lilith would make a cameo in the Book of Isaiah, later being compiled into the Bible in verse 34:14 describing the fall of Edom. Depending on the edition, her appearance has been substituted with other names, such as Lilit (the Hebrew spelling of Lilith, as there is no "th" equivalent in the language) or her Greek counterpart Lamia, as well as a variety of animals—howling creatures, night creatures, a night bird, a night monster, a night owl, or a screech owl. To give a clear picture on the meaning behind the reference, see verses twelve to fifteen from the Common English Bible, which give's Lilith's name:

> [12] No Kingdom There, they will call it,
> and all its princes will disappear.
> [13] Thorns will grow up in its palaces,
> weeds and brambles in its fortresses.
> It will be a dwelling for jackals,
> a home for ostriches.
> [14] Wildcats will meet hyenas,
> the goat demon will call to his friends,
> and there Lilith will lurk
> and find her resting place.
> [15] There the snake will nest and lay eggs
> and brood and hatch in its shadow.
> There too vultures will gather,
> each with its mate.

This representation of Lilith is later reinforced with her appearance in the Dead Sea Scrolls, a set of ancient Jewish writings from between 408 and 318 BCE. In the fragment, titled *Song of the Sage*, we read:

And I, the Instructor, proclaim His glorious splendor so as to frighten and to te[rrify] all the spirits of the destroying angels, spirits of the bastards, demons, Lilith, howlers, and [desert dwellers] ... and those which fall upon men without warning to lead them astray from a spirit of understanding and to make their heart and their ... desolate during the present dominion of wickedness and predetermined time of humiliations for the sons of lig[ht], by the guilt of the ages of [those] smitten by iniquity – not for eternal destruction, [bu]t for an era of humiliation for transgression.

In both texts we see that Lilith is associated with the wild and other undesirable animals and spirits. It is possible that the bastards and demons in the Dead Sea Scrolls refer to those pagan people who did not convert to the new religions.

The Seductress & Child Killer

Drawing upon her ancient connections to sexuality, Lilith also became the personification of sexual evilness from the beginning of the Common Era forward. In her role as a seductress, Lilitu is said to have been the original succubus, with her daughters being succubi and sons incubi. These creatures were blamed for men's nocturnal emissions and were also used as a scapegoat for the rape of women.

The Talmud, a body of civil and ceremonial Jewish law, contains the text of the Mishnah and the Gemara. Written around 500 CE, the Gemara made several explicit references to Lilith, including one warning that: "One may not sleep in a house alone, and whoever sleeps in a house alone is seized by Lilith." She was the ultimate taboo and woman that men wanted but should never have. Her glamour, beauty, and sexuality made her powerful by way of man's animalistic impulses—and this power scared them—so they vilified her, ultimately deifying her as the representation of what women should never be, all the while suppressing womankind altogether for this very reason.

Lilith was also seen as a child-killing night hag who drank the blood of infants, subsequently leading her to being seen as the first vampire in several folkloric tales. Some historians speculate that this is a reference to Lilith in connection to another "L" goddess from Sumerian civilization named Lamaštu. This fearsome goddess was essentially responsible for population

Grecian Reference

In Greek mythology, Lilith is often compared to the Lamia. A once beautiful woman, Lamia was turned into a half-woman, half-serpent creature after Hera killed her children in an act of jealousy. As a result, Lamia became a child-killing monster that was also known to seduce men. Lamia is one of the names commonly substituted for Lilith in Isaiah 34:14.

control and would take the lives of pregnant women and children. Regardless, these myths on Lilith have been considered an attempt to better understand the death of mothers during childbirth as a result of medical complications and the crib death of infants.

As a result, Lilith came to be seen as a nightmarish spirit and was deeply feared. Numerous incantation bowls to ward her off—believed to have been created between 500 and 600 CE in Nippur—have even been found. Directly referencing Lilith, these bowls were believed to protect families from her powers. Ritualistically, the bowls are used like a magical mouse trap to "capture" Lilith. People would place the bowls upside down under the home in an attempt to trap her. Other records suggest that the bowls would then be smashed in an attempt to defeat the "demoness".

While not accepted as standard etymology, an interesting speculation from this period is the possibility of Lilith being the catalyst for the word "lullaby." Witch authors Janet and Stewart Farrar discuss this in their book *The Witches' Goddess*: "incidentally, the word 'lullaby' is said to be a corruption of 'Lilla, abi!'—a Jewish banishing spell meaning 'Lilith, avaunt [away]!'" This theory suggests that the lullaby was designed as a spell to tell the child that they must be quiet, or else the monstrous Lilith would come and eat them.

Overall, I feel that this representation of Lilith was intended to further deter people from the pagan practices. I do not associate Lilith as a child killing entity in the literal sense. Because of her sexual liberation, I think child killing comes from her representing sex for pleasure above procreation. The impulsive sexual nature that was associated with Lilith emphasized sex out of marriage and encouraged fantasy through masturbation – two acts that are routinely seen as sinful.

The Garden

Estimated in origin of 700 – 1000 CE, the text emerged which brought the most famous Lilith we know to life. The *Alphabet of Ben Sira* tells the tale of Lilith as the original female inhabitant of the Garden of Eden, defiant in her submission to man. The story goes that God created Lilith out of the earth, just like Adam. However, the two were quarrelsome and were immediately combative. Adam considered himself superior to Lilith and demanded that she lay below him during sex. Lilith argued that since they were both created from the earth that they were equals.

Fed up with the inequality, Lilith pronounced the ineffable name of God and flew out of Eden. She found refuge on the shores of the Red Sea where she was having sex with "demons." I feel this part of the story symbolizes Lilith's return to the outcast pagans who were still honoring the Goddess through sexual rites.

Adam was depressed over Lilith's disappearance. He couldn't seem to wrap his head around the idea that *his* woman that was created for him would run away. In a prayer to God, he asked that she be returned. God sent the three angels Senoy, Sansenoy, and Semangelof to find her, telling them that if she does not return one hundred of her children will die each day.

When the angels found Lilith at the sea, they demanded that she return. She wanted nothing to do with that and confessed to them that she was created to cause illness in infants—having domain over males for their first eight days of life, and girls for twenty. She agreed to having one hundred of her "demon" children murdered each day and added that if she sees an amulet hanging by a child with the angels' three names she would retreat and not cause harm.

Queen of Sheba

In the 7th century CE, stories of Lilith's seduction were connected to King Solomon. In one tale, Lilith takes the form of the Queen of Sheba, attempting to seduce the king. Under her dress, however, he spots her hairy legs and clawed feet, identifying her as Lilith. As the seductress, Lilith was man's biggest fear—a woman in power, for the carnal appetite of mankind proved to be their biggest downfall.

All in all, this story is essentially a metaphor on the result of feminine disobedience to male power during the time. It is also believed to be an explanation to the contradiction made early on in Genesis 1:27, which states, "So God created man in His own image; in the image of God He created him; man and female He created them." In the next chapter, we see the creation of Eve: "With the rib taken from the human, the Lord God fashioned a woman and brought her to the human being.

Photo: Adam, Eve, and the (female) serpent at the entrance to Notre Dame Cathedral in Paris. - March 1991 by Rebecca Kennison. Dual-licensed under GFDL and Creative Commons. This image showcases Lilith as the serpent in Eden as she tempts Adam and Eve with the forbidden fruit.

Photo: The Sistine Chapel - The Original Sin and the expulsion from Eden. Dual-licensed under GFDL and Creative Commons.

The human said, 'This one finally is bone from my bones and flesh from my flesh. She will be called a woman because from a man she was taken'". Did anyone else catch that interesting plot hole? The flaw between the first two chapters of Genesis suggest there was a woman prior to Eve. So they enlisted Lilith as a scapegoat, since she was already seen as a terrifying female spirit of the time, thanks to the slanderous stories that were being told of her as a sexual wanton and child killer. Despite this, I love the parallel that this narrative makes to Lilith as the first wife of Adam, as she is also a representation of the original Mother Goddess who predated the patriarchal religions. Lilitu was known as the sexual priestess of the Goddess, the evil child-eater, and seductive night spirit—all elements of her representation in *Ben Sira*. Consequently, she was the perfect package to insert into their stories.

It is also worth noting the strong connection between this story and the Gilgamesh poem. In both stories, the archetype of Lilith will not fall victim to male dominance and flees into the wilderness. The huluppu tree and the tree of knowledge are the same, Inanna's garden can represent Eden, and Ki-sikil-lil-la-ke is Lilith. Most importantly we see that with each variation, Lilith has the power of choice, and she chooses to leave!

29

Evolution Post Eden

From the late Middle Ages through the Renaissance period, Lilith's legacy expanded with a variety of new stories coming to light. The Zohar from 1200 CE taught that Lilith returned to Eden in the guise of the serpent that seduced Eve. It goes on to further detail Lilith's role as a succubus, including the mythology of her returning to Adam and stealing his sperm to create her demonic children. This connection between Lilith and Adam was very popular during the 14th to 17th centuries CE where she was continuously feared for haunting the dreams of men.

In the 13th century CE, the Spanish Kabbalah reclaimed Lilith by creating several alternative stories about her origins. Perfectly captured in *The Hebrew Goddess* by historian and anthropologist Raphael Patai:

> Her creation is described in many alternative versions. One mentions her creation as being before Adam's, on the fifth day, because the "living creatures" with whose swarms God filled the waters included none other than Lilith. A similar version, related to the earlier Talmudic passages, recounts how Lilith was fashioned with the same substance as Adam was, shortly before. A third alternative version states that God originally created Adam and Lilith in a manner that the female creature was contained in the male. Lilith's soul was lodged in the depths of the Great Abyss. When God called her, she joined Adam. After Adam's body was created, a thousand souls from the left (evil) side attempted to attach themselves to him. God drove them off, however. Adam was left lying as a body without a soul. Then a cloud descended and God commanded the earth to produce a living soul. This God breathed into Adam, who began to spring to life and his female was attached to his side. God separated the female from Adam's side. The female side was Lilith, whereupon she flew to the

Cities of the Sea and attacks humankind. Yet another version claims that Lilith emerged as a divine entity that was born spontaneously, either out of the Great Supernal Abyss or out of the power of an aspect of God (the Gevurah of Din). This aspect of God, one of his ten attributes (Sefirot), at its lowest manifestation has an affinity with the realm of evil and it is out of this that Lilith merged with Samael.

Additionally, the Kabbalistic text known as the *Treatise on the Left Emanation* goes on to discuss Lilith and Samael as a conjoined androgynous twin couple to Adam and Eve. From here, Lilith's terrifying image would become enhanced with other mythologies as Samael's wife, and ultimately the Queen of Hell.

Romantic Era

During the Romantic period, Lilith became a staple of fascination, taking residency in poems and paintings that emphasized her dark and seductive glamour. This period in Lilith's legacy remains a favorite of mine where she began to change into the object of creativity. She started to infect the minds of artists, painters and poets alike, illustrating the seductive quality of danger. In 1808, the infamous play *Faust*, by German writer Johann Wolfgang von Goethe, features a cameo of Lilith where Faust discusses her story with Mephistopheles insisting "her beauty's one boast is her dangerous hair. When Lilith winds it tight around young men. She doesn't soon let go of them again." Later, Faust has a brief encounter with Lilith in the role of "The Pretty Witch" where they discuss man's fascination with apples.

Goethe's portrayal of Lilith in *Faust* would later become the inspiration of the British artist Dante Gabriel Rossetti's famous oil painting called *Lady Lilith* (see page 175). Released in 1866, the artwork portrays Lilith sitting in a chair, fixated on her reflection in a hand mirror while she brushes her flaming blonde mane of hair.

She wears a white dress, said to represent sterility, that has seductively fallen off her shoulder. She is surrounded in a sea of flowers, including a floral crown resting on her lap. Next to her is a vanity, topped with a perfume bottle and another mirror reflecting a lush garden, perhaps as an ode to Eden. In conjunction with the painting, Rossetti released the following poem, entitled "Body's Beauty":

> Of Adam's first wife, Lilith, it is told
> (The witch he loved before the gift of Eve,)
> That, ere the snake's, her sweet tongue could deceive,
> And her enchanted hair was the first gold.
> And still she sits, young while the earth is old,
> And, subtly of herself contemplative,
> Draws men to watch the bright web she can weave,
> Till heart and body and life are in its hold.
> The rose and poppy are her flower; for where
> Is he not found, O Lilith, whom shed scent
> And soft-shed kisses and soft sleep shall snare?
> Lo! As that youth's eyes burned at thine, so went
> Thy spell through him, and left his straight neck bent
> And round his heart one strangling golden hair.

The sonnet emphasizes Lilith's dangerous glamour and is said to represent a modern woman channeling Lilith's taboo beauty. Shortly thereafter, in 1887, John Maler Collier painted a similarly blonde image of her simply called *Lilith* (see page 216). It showcases her nude in the garden with an enormous snake entwined around her body. In both paintings, Lilith appears with an alluring coyness, not making eye contact with the viewer, alluding to a cat-and-mouse game of seduction.

Lilith's Rebirth

By the 1900s, Lilith had begun rebirthing herself into society. In 1904, Lilith was reinvented as the Goddess Babalon, in the occult system of Thelema. Thelema was established by the world-famous occultist, Aleister Crowley, and Babalon was considered to be the representation of primal feminine sexuality. In a footnote to Crowley's *The Vision and the Voice* (Liber 418), it states, "Here also is the mystery of mysteries, Lilith is truly Babalon."

In the early part of the 20th century, three astrological phenomena were identified and named after her: Asteroid Lilith, Dark Moon Lilith, and Black Moon Lilith. Each of these appear within our natal charts, drawing Lilith's energies into us on a personal level. We will discuss these at greater length in Chapter 7.

The mid-1900s also saw the birth of Wicca as an alternative Neopagan religion, later being considered the religion of witchcraft. Lilith's reclamation may be directly aligned with this New Age spiritualism as many saw her as the first feminist with regard to her voluntary exile from Eden. In his book, *Lilith: From Ancient Lore to Modern Culture,* occult author E. R. Vernor also claims that "a good many writers identify with Lilith such as Crowley and Gerald Gardner, the 1950s Wicca founder, who asserted that there was continuous historical worship of Lilith to present day".

From a pop culture standpoint, in 1996, singer/songwriter Sarah McLachlan brought Lilith into the fold by organizing a feminist music festival called *Lilith Fair*. The festival gained much popularity and support by promoting female-only musicians and standing up to the male-dominated recording industry. The 1990s also saw Lilith's introduction to Hollywood as a popular antagonist in many television shows and movies, often represented as the mother of vampires and demons.

The Meaning of Lilith

Today, Lilith has fully re-emerged as a dark goddess in occult practices; dark not in a negative sense but in that she represents the taboo areas of life that contradict society's expectations. She also represents darkness as the unseen and intuitive magic at the heart of all witches. Considering the extravagant legacy that Lilith has led, it is clear that she represents an impeccable force. She is the rebel, the wanton, and the lady of the beasts. She is the witch's Goddess and is the exemplification of personal power.

I see her demonic accounts to be the results of slander and hypocrisy attached to women and pagan practices of the time. German author, Rufus Camphausen said it best in his book *The Encyclopedia of Sacred Sexuality: From Aphrodisiacs and Exstasy to Yoni Worship and Zap Lam Yoga:* "Be aware that the demons described and maligned by one religious system or culture frequently are—or were—the deities of another one—a process that can easily be discerned from cases such as that of Lilith."

As the other forms of divinity died out, Lilith survived. She rebelled. She remained true in her nature and was called many nasty names in the process. By not conforming, she became demonized, and through this demonization, she was worshipped with relevancy. She took on horrible titles, but she survived, inadvertently worshipped, and given power by those who opposed her the most. We sometimes think that our deities and spirits need incense and candles or elaborately decorated rituals to survive; I strongly believe that the only thing a spirit needs to survive is belief. Belief gives any spirit power, and this is how Lilith survived. If there is only one thing you can take away from her mythology, it is the art of survival and the essence of thriving in your truest nature.

While I do not reject any facet of Lilith and feel as though all variations of her worship are worthy in their own right, I tend to disregard her Kabbalistic and Luciferian correspondences. This is not done out of ignorance. Instead, I feel that these veins pay tribute to her demonization, rejecting her original splendor and glory. Because of this, my work with Lilith is done through her older, ancient Sumerian associations. While these remain blurred and fragmented by the erosion of sandy desserts, I trust in my spiritual path and the signs and synchronicities that have brought me to where I am. If anything, I can turn to nature and the wild, primal instinct of Lilith for guidance.

As you begin to embark on your relationship with Lilith, take the information from this chapter and reflect on which ways her mythologies might mirror your life. Which epithet of Lilith do you relate to most? Which do you relate to least? Ask yourself why this is and what can be gained from exploring the characteristics that you relate to least. What can Lilith's story teach you about an obstacle that you are dealing with in your life right now? Your answers will start the process of furthering your relationship with her. Considering this, let us examine how the material from this chapter can be reflected into your life by way of witchcraft, as the rooted theology of the GLAM Witch turns to practice.

PART II

The Practice of

THE GLAM WITCH

3

TOOL TALK:

The GLAM Ingredients

"In the Craft, we do not believe in the Goddess—we connect with
Her; through the moon, the stars, the ocean, the earth, through
trees, animals, through other human beings, through ourselves."
—Starhawk, *The Spiral Dance*

After establishing the legacy of Lilith and how she has elevated
herself in modern witchcraft, our next step is to find where
her energies manifest in the world around us. This approach is
what I consider to be natural magic, the organic components that
become the ingredients of witchery in the Great Lilithian Arcane
Mysteries. Before connecting and foraging a relationship with Lilith, it is important to understand what objects are sacred to her and
can be used in our magic as offerings, as well as supplementary
representations of her. Most deities are known to have associations

with particular animals, flowers, and other symbols that have been used in their ancient worship. Because there are no recorded ancient ways of worship associated with Lilith, modern-day followers can sometimes feel as if they are at a disadvantage in working with her. While growing into my spirituality, one of the major hesitations I encountered when first starting to work with Lilith was the lack of texts dedicated to her mysteries and worship. As a result, I had to do a lot of legwork to come up with correspondences that mirrored her archetypes. This next section explores some of Lilith's correspondences as they relate to animals, colors, crystals, elements, herbs, moon phases, days and times, and other offerings that connect to her.

Lilith's Magical Correspondence

Animals

Animals are one of the most frequent associations used with deities. Almost every deity worshipped throughout time has had a connection with at least one animal. There are several animals that can be incorporated into your magical workings to represent Lilith through photographs, drawings, sculptures, and even body parts like hides and bones, which will further emulate the physical energy once associated to the animal. Also, to come across these animals in your daily life or dreams can be interpreted as a message from her.

�֎ *Cats*—The only existing parallel you will find between Lilith and cats from ancient times lies with the imagery in the *Queen of the Night* relief, showcasing Lilit`h atop two male lions; yet, examining cats on a biological level, they are very much Lilithian creatures. Cats are solitary and exceptionally independent. They also know when to retreat and are masters of the great escape. Cats are not easily manipulated into doing something—much like Lilith! Additionally, cats have routinely been linked to witches and seen as their familiars or animal spirit guides. Metaphysically, cats represent the intuition associated with instinct, and their biological eyesight and attentive hearing skills associate them with unseen knowledge.

✴ *Owl*—Lilith has been called the owl and connected to them in many stories. The Anzû bird in the Gilgamesh poem was translated by Samuel Kramer as owl and has further been linked to Lilith through the *Queen of the Night* and her name's synonymous translation of "screech owl" in the Book of Isaiah.

Owls are nocturnal beings who represent occult knowledge. They are deeply connected to the moon and to intuition, as is Lilith. As a bird, owls are messengers and were routinely seen as harbors of bad omens in many cultures due to their nocturnal natures. Owls possess excellent eyesight in the darkness of night to help them hunt prey. This biological link might uncover their representation of knowledge through foresight. Metaphysically, their ability of sight in dark times supports their representation of Lilith as the exiled outcast.

✴ *Snakes*—Snakes encompass an array of metaphysical qualities lending to power, wisdom, life/death/rebirth, and sexuality. Snakes have long been a sacred animal of the great Goddess, and many cultures have worshipped these creatures as powerful beings. Lilith has been connected to the snake through the Gilgamesh poem, as the serpent tempting Eve in Eden, and also as her Greek counterpart, the Lamia (described to have the lower body of a snake). Snakes connect to wisdom through their species' age. As ancestors of dinosaurs, they have essentially survived from the dawn of time and seen as keepers of knowledge. They can also bury themselves below the ground, metaphorically making them guardians of the Underworld.

Snakes are also symbolic of life and death. Of the thousands of different snake species in the world, around five hundred are venomous. Their venom is extremely toxic and can kill but has also been synthesized in medicine to heal; therefore, snakes are representations of life and death as both healers and killers. This dichotomy is represented through the destroyer aspect of Lilith—with life comes death, and through death, life is created. Some snakes are constrictors, meaning they crush their prey with powerful coils rather than with venom, showcasing their innate strength and power. Between this dualism, snakes also take on the representation of transformation and rebirth. This comes from their biological ability to shed skin, which Lilith has done several times in the course of history.

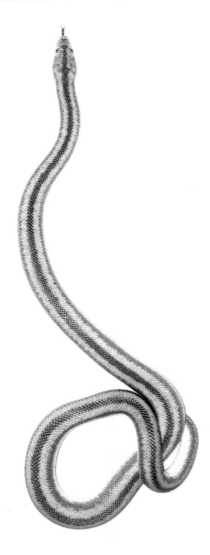

Snakes are also very sensual creatures in their phallic appearance, seductive movements, and in the Eastern philosophy of kundalini energy. The kundalini is the sacred serpent that lies in rest at the base of your spine and extends through the chakras to enlightenment. In this capacity, snakes can be used to assist sex-related

Photo: My rosy boa, Rosé.

magic. Since serpentine energy

is the most abundant animal energy associated with Lilith, it will be explored further later in this book.

Colors

Color is a potent ingredient of symbolism and witchcraft. From altar cloths and flowers to candles, colors exhibit their own form of energetic associations in magical workings. Here are a few of the colors that exude the most positive response from Lilith:

⊛ **Black**—Black has long been associated with witchcraft and the occult. It is the color that is stereotypically considered evil; but, no color is inherently evil. When it comes to Lilith, black is a powerful color that illustrates her connections to night, the dark moon, and the shadow.

⊛ **Pink**—Pink has been considered the ultimate "femme" color over the years. Because of this, it connects with Lilith's association as the primal feminine force. Pink is connected to self-love and attraction which deepens the connection to Lilith's independence and allure. Pink is also a tint of red, her primary power color.

⊛ **Red**—Red is the color most often associated with Lilith. Red has a long history of being considered the color of passion, lust, and sexuality, as well as rage, war, and wrath. By now, we know that all of these characteristics fit into the Lilithian archetype. Red is also the color of our blood. As a supreme spirit of femininity, it connects her to the monthly blood shed by women. Lilith's connection to equality is seen here too in that we all bleed red. Additionally, scientific analysis taken from the *Queen of the Night* relief has proven that red ochre was used as the original color for the figure's body.

Crystals

Crystals are one of many natural substances that witches can utilize to amplify, direct, and transform energy. Often seen on our altars, used in spellcraft, and adorned on our jewelry, crystals hold an abundance of energy and are just as potent as they are glamorous. They help align witches to earth energy. There are a number of crystals that you can work with when it comes to Lilith. I use the following crystals to help magnify her energies in meditations and rituals:

⊛ *Amber*—Since amber is a prehistoric resin, I link this stone to the primordial ancient Goddess. A substance with many attributes, I feel that it connects to Lilith most in its association with beauty and wisdom.

⊛ *Bloodstone*—Bloodstone yields courage, protection, and wisdom. It is a stone associated with sacrifice and the courage to let go of what no longer serves. This taps into Lilith's strength and the freedom that comes from removing yourself from negative situations.

⊛ *Garnet*—Garnet is a deep red stone that embodies an abundance of strength, courage, passion, and sensuality. Garnet is a vital representation of Lilith and is her ultimate stone of power.

⊛ *Geode*—These are rock formations that contain a hollow cavity lined with tiny crystals. Due to their shape they are generally seen as a representation of the goddess. They can also be utilized in work with Lilith as a representation of caves.

✸ **Indigo Gabbro** *(aka Mystic Merlinite)*—This stone relates to the balance of light and dark sides of our nature, as well as transformation. It connects to Lilith through her representation of equality, the shadow self, and enchantment.

✸ **Labradorite**—Dubbed a stone of magic, this crystal shows flashes of color that range from blue, green, and yellow to orange, and sometimes even purple. Because of its changing color, labradorite is considered a stone of transformation—Lilith is thought of as a shapeshifter, morphing into different forms throughout the progression of civilizations. Labradorite is also a powerful stone of intuition and psychic gifts. It helps instill the occult wisdom that Lilith weaves.

✸ **Moonstone**—As a spirit associated with the night and moon, moonstone is a perfect stone to use with Lilith's energies. Moonstone is connected to lunar energy, feminine mysteries, and intuition. There are many different shades of moonstone, such as white, rainbow, peach, green, and black. Black moonstone is an even more potent source of Lilithian power and protection. Peach moonstone supports soft lovely energies, combining magic with beauty and the instinct of following your heart. White or rainbow moonstone connects with the full moon, while black moonstone is connected more to the dark or new moons.

✸ **Red Tiger's Eye**—Red tiger's eye is a variant of the traditionally golden tiger's eye. It is known to rouse the kundalini (snake) energy within us, linking it to sacred sexuality. In this red form, it combines the essence of cat and snake power. Additionally, tiger's eye is a stone associated with strength and courage.

⊛ **Rhodochrosite**—Considered a stone of love and abundance, this one might seem like an odd crystal to connect to Lilith; regardless, rhodochrosite is a powerful stone for healing and transformation of emotions. It helps to heal past inflictions and allow for compassion to ebb and flow freely when incorporated into your life. It is also great for creative expression, helping creativity flow from the passion of the heart rather than the head.

⊛ **Rose Quartz**—Another love stone, rose quartz is also associated with beauty, grace, and self-love. Since Lilith is considered an attractive and self-reliant witch, this is a wonderful crystal to incorporate into Lilithian practices for beauty rituals and glamour magic.

⊛ **Ruby**—Mined from various locations around the world, rubies are found near the geographic origins of where Lilith was first discovered. It is a precious stone, highly valued and sought after. Its dark red color exudes passion, desire, strength, and royalty—all qualities which ooze from Lilith's archetype in relation to her being a Great Goddess. Wear ruby to project Lilith's primal and radiant powers.

⊛ **Smokey Quartz**—This is a variation of quartz that comes in dark gray, brown, or black forms. Smokey quartz is a protective grounding stone. It helps anchor negative energies and dispel of them. In some instances, an orange color of garnet called spessartine will form on smokey quartz. These combinations are usually mined out of China and symbolize sexual awakening, attraction, and manifestation. These are immensely powerful Lilithian stones.

Elements

Witches honor nature as sacred and frequently work with the elements. Each element has its own subset of qualities, which provide more context on their representation. She is unique in that each element can be linked to her both through her mythology and energetic connotations.

✸ *Earth*—Lilith aligns with earth through her connection to trees, first in the story of Inanna's ḫuluppu tree and later with the tree of knowledge in the Garden of Eden. In addition to the tree, and Eden itself, her Hebrew origins say she was created by earth. Also, the appearance of caves in Lilith's mythology represent earth energy.

✸ *Air*—The etymology of Lilith's name is derived from the Sumerian word *lil*, meaning "air" or "wind." It is suggested that she was a winged wind spirit in Sumer, aligning her with the element of air. Air also connects to our mind, clarity, and thinking—Lilith represents the freedom of choice and the ability to make difficult decisions effortlessly.

✸ *Fire*—Lilith is connected to fire through her associations with the wild desert and fire energies like sexuality, creativity, desire, passion, destruction, manifestation, and transformation.

✸ *Water*—Through the moon, blood, shadow self, and Red Sea, Lilith connects with the elemental properties of water. Water is representative of our emotional body and sensitivities. It is soothing and restorative, relating to the healing and transformative nature to which Lilith has experienced with survival.

✹ *Spirit*—Spirit is generally the representation of *us* and connects to Lilith being the internal representation of who we are. It also connects to ascension and inner knowledge gained from intuition. Lilith aligns to spirit in both her fall and in her elevation, showcasing her "as above, so below; as within so without" identity.

Herbs

Plants are another earth representation and are used in witchcraft for incense, healing remedies, and essential oils. Each herb has its own set of properties that can aid in and enhance a witch's workings. When making incense or oil blends for Lilith, the following connect with her:

✹ *Apple*—Apples are a magical ingredient for witches because of their inner pentagram. They are linked to knowledge and wisdom, in addition to courtship and romance. The fruit of the tree of knowledge, which Lilith used to tempt Eve, is commonly referred to as an apple; though, apples were not native to the origin lands of this biblical tale. Several other fruits, such as the fig and pomegranate, are more likely to be the original inspiration. Regardless, since many believe it was an apple and since the fruit has a connection with witchcraft, apples are still used as offerings and ingredients for Lilithian Witchcraft

✹ *Cardamom*—This rich and spicy herb can help manifest Lilith's fiery and seductive charm.

✹ *Cinnamon*—Cinnamon is a good alternative for cardamom, and is more readily available. In addition to its sensual aspects, cinnamon adds attraction, luck, and spiritual qualities to magical workings.

✸ **Datura** *(toxic!)*—This beautiful yet lethal flower is filled with intoxicating attraction and enchantment. It also helps stimulate intuition, magical power, offer protection, and can aid in protection by breaking curses. All of these properties are certainly within the realms of Lilith. Never eat Datura or burn in a place that is not well ventilated. Datura fumes are not toxic but can cause adverse reactions, such as a stinging burn to the eyes or hallucinogenic experiences. Use at your own risk.

✸ **Damiana**—Damiana is an aphrodisiacal herb. It is generally used in love and lust potions to awaken eroticism. This herb can connect to Lilith through attraction and sexuality.

✸ **Dragon's Blood**—Contrary to its name, this is not the blood of a scaly reptile. It is actually a resin from the tree named *Dracaena cinnabari*. Dragon's blood is a very universal ingredient in magic and connects to Lilith's energies mostly through protection, purification, and sexuality. It is also a good representation for blood in rituals.

✸ **Jasmine**—Jasmine is a night-blooming flower that oozes an incredibly sweet floral fragrance. It connects deeply to the essence of Lilith as a night goddess, while also adding glamour and enchantment to spellwork.

✸ **Jezebel Root**—This root comes from the Louisiana Iris. It acts as an herb of Lilith by symbolizing her role as a sacred prostitute, and helps to attract wealthy men. It is a great herb to add to spells involving attraction, wishes, and luck.

✸ **Lavender**—Lavender is an herb that is widely used in magic. It aids in sleep, love, luck, and protection. It is a good herb to incorporate into dream magic for Lilith.

✹ **Lily** *(all variants, including Calla Lilies and Lily of the Valley)*—These beautiful flowers are connected to Lilith by name. Lilies release a pretty yet pungent odor that I find very reminiscent of her energy. They are a representation of beauty, sexuality, and creativity in connection to goddess power. These make terrific offerings for Lilith, particularly those in shades of black, pink, or red.

✹ **Lotus**—Lotus flowers and roots are very spiritual and represent personal growth. The lotus grows out of the dark, murky soil and emerges atop water, floating in tranquility and peace. These connect to Lilith as representations of the beauty that arises from dark times.

✹ **Mugwort**—Mugwort is known for its ability to induce restful sleep and promote vivid dreams. Making a cup of mugwort tea before bed is a great way to invite Lilith into your dreams.

✹ **Orchid**—Orchids are beautiful tropical flowers that grow all over the world and are commonly seen to represent female genitalia. No wonder why the orchid is such a wonderful representation for the divine feminine, connecting to Lilith's beauty, glamour, and self-love.

✹ **Patchouli**—A fragrant and heady plant, patchouli has a distinct aroma that attracts or repels, much like Lilith herself. It is customarily used in spells and workings for love and lust.

✹ **Pomegranate**—Lilith loves pomegranates! This luscious red fruit is connected to passion, and its juice represents blood. It has been considered a fruit of the Underworld and one that can help in lowering the veils between the everyday and astral realms. Additionally, it has been thought to be a possible alternative fruit from the tree of knowledge, further connecting to Lilith's mythology.

⊛ *Poppy*—Rossetti's painting and subsequent poem of Lilith denotes the poppy as her flower. Poppies are used in magic and spellcraft for love, sleep, attraction, and luck. The opium poppy is the main source of opiates, a drug that is known for its sedative and sleep-bringing properties. Poppy is another potent source for Lilith dreamwork.

⊛ *Rose*—As the queen of flowers, the rose represents grace, love, honor, sex, beauty, and power. I live right next to a supermarket that has a tremendous fresh-flower section and decorate Lilith's shrine with roses on a weekly basis. Red roses make great offerings to her, but I have found that hot pink roses are her favorite floral offering. Whenever I have used this shade, the lower petals have always shriveled and died at an accelerated rate despite the expiration date.

Floral Color Magic

Additional magical qualities can be found in a flower's color. The correspondence for each color are:

- *Red*—love, power, beauty
- *Pink*—appreciation, honor, joy
- *Orange/Coral*—desire, courage, enthusiasm
- *Lavender*—enchantment, magic
- *Yellow*—new beginnings, joy, happiness
- *White*—purity, innocence, rebirth

⊛ **Sandalwood** *(particularly red)*—Sandalwood is frequently used in incense and oil blends for its pleasant woody sent. It connects with spirituality and manifestation of wishes.

⊛ **Vanilla**—The vanilla bean comes from a type of orchid. It encompasses the orchid's properties of enchantment and beauty but also stimulates a sweet luxuriousness that makes it a wonderful offering to Lilith.

⊛ **Willow**—Remember that the huluppu tree was considered a white willow, and this tree is considered a sacred tree for many goddesses. It inspires wisdom, magic, and divination.

⊛ **Wormwood**—Wormwood is known for its ability to induce visions. Wormwood helps in magic that involves divination, trusting your intuition, warding off, and hexing; it is also known to call spirits. It can be used to help bring Lilith into your space as she makes herself known in vision-related magics.

Moon Phases

Lilith is a goddess of the moon and night. In witchcraft, the moon is the representation of feminine divinity and much witch work is centered around the phases of the moon. Most connect Lilith to the dark moon, but I see her visible in each phase. Since Lilith is the embodiment of the moon, here is a snapshot of what each phase represents in metaphysical terms.

⊛ **New Moon**—The new moon marks the time of new beginnings. It is a powerful time for healing—a time to wipe the slate clean and start fresh.

✡ *Waxing Moon*—As the moon waxes from new to full, magical workings for attraction are at their best. This is a time for spells that initiate gaining or growing.

✡ *Full Moon*—The full phase is the orgasm of the moon's cycle, symbolizing robust abundance. It is a great time for magic involving manifestation and power.

✡ *Waning Moon*—As the moon wanes back from full to new, it is a time to let go. This is a time for spellwork that connects to protective magics like banishing and hexing.

✡ *Dark Moon*—The dark moon is the period between waning and new, where there is no moon visible in the sky. It is complete blackness. The dark moon is heavily associated with Lilith and is considered a time of deep introspection, divination, and accessing occult knowledge.

Timing

Lilith is a goddess of the moon and the night. She is also a goddess of transformation and can be observed at times of change, such as during the equinoxes and solstices, dusk and dawn, midnight and noon, all the phases of the moon, and eclipses. I have also found her energy to be strongest on Mondays, Tuesdays, and Fridays. This is probably due to Monday being associated with the moon, Tuesday's association to the aggression and passion of Mars, and Friday's attraction, beauty, and luxury extended from Venus.

Other Offerings

In addition to the substances we have already touched on, the following list represents additional offerings that can be utilized in Lilithian worship.

✸ ***Absinthe***—This is an alcoholic beverage that is traditionally made with wormwood. Most absinthe available in the United States is missing this ingredient. It increases vision and is nicknamed "the green fairy." With its bright green color, high alcohol content, and intense herbal taste that mimics black licorice, it makes for a fantastic Lilithian libation.

✸ ***Blood***—Blood is the source of our lives. It is our energetic fingerprint and a direct alignment to us. For this reason, many cultures have used blood as part of their rituals and worship. With witchcraft, and particularly in certain laws of magic, blood helps the universe pinpoint the desired magical manifestation. When working with blood, it is important to remain practical and safe, taking into consideration the health risks that are associated with it. When incorporating blood into your practices, it is not suggested to slice yourself up and gather gallons of it. Blood is often drawn using a lancet. These are safe and hygienic ways to prick yourself. Blood-stained bandages from natural cuts and scrapes work as good alternatives, as does menstrual blood.

✸ ***Bones*** *(from cats, owls, or snakes)*—Any bones that are associated with Lilith's sacred animals can be incorporated as ingredients for worshipping her. These help to focalize her energies with direct representations of her animal associations.

✸ ***Eggs***—Eggs are readily available at your local supermarket and make great offerings for Lilith. They represent her association with birds and are also as a symbol of the Goddess.

✸ ***Feathers***—Like eggs, these connect with Lilith's bird representations and make grate offerings to her in ritual.

✸ *Meat*—I have found Lilith to enjoy red-meat offerings. Considering how old Lilith is, and the fact that sacrificial practices were an act of worshipping various goddesses and gods, presenting her several slices of flesh is fitting. From an animalistic point of view, the owl and snake are also carnivorous, thus meat makes for an appropriate offering. When I offer meat to Lilith in ritual, I will try to get a cut of meat that is not commercially sold, such as a heart (from a cow or chicken); this way all parts of the animal are being used and not discarded behind a butcher shop. Hearts represent passion and are very suitable for Lilith. I usually offer this during moon rituals and discard it afterward by placing it in nearby vegetation to decompose into the earth or feed the carnivorous creatures of the wild.

✸ *Mirrors*—Folklore exists connecting Lilith to mirrors. She is said to live inside them, causing onlookers to have thoughts of vanity and narcissism. We will work with Lilith and mirrors later in this book. Having a mirror or reflective surface on your shrine is a good way to see Lilith through yourself.

✸ *Musk*—Not an herb but a pheromone that comes from the sex glands of certain animals, musk is mostly found in synthetic form but remains a popular fragrance for oil and incense blends. Musk is used to increase confidence and attraction while stimulating lust.

✸ *Nag Champa*—This is a fragrance blend in either oil or incense form consisting of frangipani flowers and sandalwood. Depending on the maker, several other ingredients like frankincense may be used as well. The name translates to "snake flower" in English, making it a wonderful representation for Lilith.

55

✸ **Red Beverages**—Dark red beverages are favored by Lilith. The color also resembles the life essence of blood. Earthy, peppery, or rich wines offer the decadent luxury associated with Lilith. I will leave this out on for her on my shrine until it molds to symbolize the perpetual art of transformation that resonates with her. Alternatively, pomegranate, cherry, or cranberry juices can be offered in rituals for those who prefer not to use alcohol.

✸ **Sand**—Desert sand combines earth and fire elements and connects to the desert where Lilith lived post-Eden.

✸ **Sex Toys**—Sex toys, leather, lace, and condoms are great items to work with to stimulate Lilith's lustful energy and sexual glorification. These are all especially good to place on her shrine for a good charge up before any type of lustful deed!

✸ **Sexual Fluids**—Like blood, sexual fluids are liquid life energy. Acts of sexuality are potent sources of Lilithian energy and may be used as offerings in sex magic rituals to Lilith. We will look at this in greater depth in Chapter 9.

✸ **Snakeskin**—Snakeskins are fantastic offerings to Lilith, as they not only represent her but are the physical remains of serpents. These can be ground in a mortar and pestle and added to incense blends or other powders to magnify Lilith's energy.

Basic Witch Tools

Artists use a variety of tools, such as paintbrushes, pens, pencils, and even computer programs to manipulate their chosen mediums and create art. Chefs have their cooking utensils and ingredients from which they craft their culinary delights. Through this same application, the arts and crafts of a witch are fashioned through a variety of tools used for magical recipes and forms of worship. Early in my studies as a teen witch, I used all the money I earned from summer jobs to purchase the tools I had read about. At the time, I believed these tools were mandatory and that, in not having them, I was unable to practice my witchcraft. It is important to note that tools do not make the witch. The only tools you will ever need, you already possess—yourself, your will, and your willingness to be of service. Your witchcraft is fueled by your spirit, mind, and intent—not a tool. That being said, I do enjoy working with some of the traditional tools of witchcraft but have learned not to rely heavily on them. Tools have their place and can assist in a variety of ways, especially for novice witchlings. Since I will be referencing several of them in ritual throughout the remaining chapters of this book, let us examine some of the most common tools seen in witchcraft.

✸ *Athame*—The infamous witch blade! An athame is a double-edged knife that has been magnetized and used as an energy conductor in ritual and spellcraft. It is designed to channel energy from you into items and create boundaries between our world and the astral planes. It slices the ether—not material matter nor yourself.

✸ *Book of Shadows*—Many witches keep a book that is dedicated to their magical practice. This will include instructions on the practitioner's witch practices such as rituals, spells, and other documentation as relevant to their studies. It can be very aesthetically pleasing to have a nice leather bound tome to collect all the materials to your practice. In our modern world many witches have opted out of this tool and instead keep an electronic folder on their technological device. Others use a three-ring binder to insert and arrange as necessary.

✵ **Cauldron**—I think of the cauldron as the witch's crockpot. A glorified symbol in witch imagery, the cauldron represents the fertile mother's womb. It can be used in a ritual for holding fire, herbs, water, candles, or any other magical ingredient that is the focus of the working.

✵ **Chalice**—A chalice is a drinking cup and a representation of the feminine. It can be used as a ritualistic offering vessel, housing wine or juice in ceremonial practices.

✵ **Divination Tools**—There are several different kinds of divination tools a witch may have in their practice. These could take the form of a black scrying mirror, crystal ball, runes, or tarot/oracle cards. Each of these are vessels for a witch to use intuition and psychic ability to see future events or otherwise better understand supernatural knowledge. We will touch on some of these specific items in Chapter 6.

✵ **Elemental Representations**—These are placed upon the altar to further represent and harmonize the space with the natural energies of the world. There are a variety of representations for each of these, and you can decorate them as you see fit!

- **Earth**—crystals, flowers, plants, salt
- **Air**—feathers, incense, oil burner, wind chimes
- **Fire**—candles, desert sand, obsidian (volcanic glass)
- **Water**—seashells, coral, bowl of water, beverage offering

✵ **Mortar & Pestle**—The mortar and pestle are devices used for crushing and mixing herbs or other ingredients of spellcraft into powder forms for baths, incense, or magic bags. In lieu of a mortar and pestle, a designated witchcrafting food processor is a good alternative.

Photo: Several of my witch tools. From the top: silver pentacle disc, book of shadows, tarot cards, cauldron, athame, and chalice.

⊛ *Offering Bowl/Plate*—The offering plate will be used in any ritual format for Lilith or any other deity, ancestor, or spirit you might work with.

⊛ *Pentacle*—A pentacle, in this regard, is a disc-like object that features the witch's star. This disc will generally sit in the center of an altar, where special items are placed upon for blessing, consecration, or offering. It can be fashioned from wood, clay, metal, or another earth-based form.

⊛ *Wand*—Like the athame, wands are used to direct energy and manifest. Wands may be fashioned from a piece of wood, deer antler, or even carved crystals. A lot of witches use athames and wands interchangeably.

Cleansing your Magical Goodies

It is common practice in the witch world to cleanse any of your new tools, and other ingredients, before working with them. Remember that everything is made up of energy and anything material can accumulate residual energy picked up by others. Cleansing your tools helps to remove any of this energy and further link the tool to you.

Using Crystals

Certain crystals are known not to hang onto residual energy and thus never need to be cleansed. Instead, they become a source for cleansing other objects. Smokey quartz is one crystal that will do this; they are known to absorb and neutralize unwanted energies. Rock salt is another mineral that can be used, due to its physical ability to dissolve. For this reason, it is considered a source of purification and can be combined with smokey quartz for a megawatt cleaning! To do this, create a circle of salt big enough to hold the object you are cleansing. Place a piece of smokey quartz in four positions around the circle, making a square-like shape. From there, place the object you are cleansing in the center and say:

Rock of earth, and mineral of sea,
cleanse and empower this tool for me.

Visualize the earthly energies engulfing the space of the circle and dissolve any negativity from the item. I will leave the tools in the circle for six to twelve hours to maximize the effects.

Using the Elements

Your items may also be cleansed by the elements. A fast and simple cleansing you could do is pass any new magical item through each of the elements, asking that each cleanse and empower your object for use. Be mindful with this approach, as certain items may catch fire or dissolve in water. For cleansing by fire, a good rule of thumb is to hover your object above the flame so that it can absorb a its warmth without actually touching the flame. Be sure to use motion so the heat does not start to burn away at the material. For dissolvable items, follow this same approach rather than submerging the object in water.

Using the Moon or the Sun

Objects can be placed under the light of the sun or the full moon. Because certain objects fade in direct sunlight, most witches stick to the light of a full moon instead. Simply place your object outside (if applicable) or in a windowsill that will catch the moon rays and ask the moon to cleanse and empower it.

Using Your Bed

A technique I started to work into my practice for establishing a connection to any tool or object of significance in my magical supply cabinet is to sleep with it. By sleeping with the object, I am able to merge our energies for several hours. Depending on the object, you can place it under your mattress, pillow, or just in close proximity to your bed.

Altars & Shrines

Creating altars and shrines can be a very fun, creative part of witchcraft. Altars act as the workstation for a witch's magic during ritual practices. They are the focal point that directly align the practitioner with the energetic source they are drawing from. They ultimately become the home for your tools and other ingredients needed in your spells or rituals. Some traditions have detailed instructions on altar setups, but if working alone, you have the flexibility to create an altar that is as complex or as simple as you wish.

Shrines are similar to altars in that they are energetic focal points to an individual witch's practice; however, shrines are dedicated to one specific spirit or entity and are tended to more frequently as a place of worship. Where altars can be permanent or just erected for a specific working, shrines are best left assembled at all times.

When constructing a shrine to Lilith, it is important to feature imagery and objects that resonate with her energies. In my years of working with her, I have

Photo: My Lilith shrine.

accumulated several statues that represent her and have used them all on her shrine at one point or another. Your central image of her does not have to be an elaborate statue, either—it could be as simple as a magazine cut-out of someone you feel emulates her vibe, or a framed photograph showcasing one of her various artistic renditions. Your shrine to her should be a representation of your connection to her and decorated in whatever manner is fitting to you.

Since Lilith is the only form of deity that I work with, my altar and her shrine have merged into one space. I do my daily devotions and worship here and will often do my spellwork here as well; if I need more room for spellwork, I will set up a large space in the center of my living room. My athame, chalice, pentacle, and elemental representations are on my altar/ shrine, along with a statue of Lilith, an offering plate, and a variety of representative objects to further instill her energies; I also include a mixture of fresh flowers and dried roses to represent the balance and beauty in life and death.

4

REVERANCE WITH RITE:

The GLAM Witch Worship

"Ritual's purpose is to turn all areas of the mind—the subconscious, conscious, and superconscious—in a specific direction to achieve a specific desired outcome."
—Edain McCoy, *If You Want to be a Witch*

Rituals are commonplace in our waking lives and are comprised of the habitual actions we take. These are as simple as getting ready in the morning, preparing a meal, or settling into your daily workspace. Witches use ritual to commune and work directly with our deities and spirit guides. One of the great privileges of witchcraft is that we each are our own priest(ess). Instead of going to a church, we create our own with our tools and personal altars. It is here that we personally connect to our divine sources through contemplative meditations and ritual practices. Up to now, we have been learning the "why" of GLAM, identifying the theologies of Lilith and several tools that can be used to build your knowledge of GLAM Witchery. In this phase of practice, we will put this information into action by connecting with Lilith through ritual and worship.

Making Contact

By now, you should be familiar enough with Lilith to begin connecting with her, if you have not done so already. I recommend that, in the beginning, you establish your relationship with her through meditation and visualization practices. These introductory exercises are best done at night and are not reliant on any particular moon phase. To start, create a relaxing and inviting space that helps you shut yourself out and disconnect from the distractions of the world around you. Dress in something that is loose and comfortable. When setting up your space, I recommend getting a large pillow or cushion to sit comfortably on. You may also sit in a chair if you prefer, so long as your feet can rest flat on the ground and are not left to dangle. To help invite the symbolism of Lilith into your room, include any representations of her (as outlined in the previous chapter) and burn candles in her sacred colors or incense that will draw upon her energies.

Once you are settled, ground and center yourself in a comfortable position. Close your eyes and focus on your breathing. Take ten slow, deep breaths—in your nostrils and out of your mouth. Focus on your breathing and allow yourself to relax into a meditative state. If you find yourself getting distracted, do not fret. Just shift back to focusing on your breathing. As you drift off to an ethereal meditative land, focus on her essence. Let Lilith burn herself into your mind's eye. Use your knowledge of her mythology to concentrate on one of her many representations. In this exercise, we are simply contemplating her. You can try to visualize her if it helps, but it is not necessary. For these types of meditations, I simply focus on her name and the power associated with it. When doing this, I feel a pulsating, tingling sensation around my third eye.

Once you have had enough, slowly drift back into consciousness, and write down any revelations or experiences you had; this will help strengthen your connection to her divine presence. During these initiatory exercises, it is very important not to force anything. Start small and build up. In the beginning, these sessions can be as few as ten minutes long. As you connect more and more with her, increase the time little by little.

When your connection to Lilith has been reinforced by these contemplations, you can begin pathworking with her. Pathworking is a different expression of meditation in that it allows your mind to tell a story. These are mental and spiritual journeys in which you allow your mind to drift as it wanders through Lilith's landscape. For this approach, begin in the same manner as you would for the earlier contemplations. As you relax and settle into your state of consciousness, you will be creating an active visualization. Instead of solely focusing on one of Lilith's themes, focus on meeting her while on a journey. Where you meet Lilith is entirely up to her, so relinquish any attempt at trying to control the landscape—let it organically form in your mind's eye. You may find yourself in a lush garden overflowing with tropical foliage, a desert wasteland, a shore by the sea, a dark cave, or even a place you visit frequently.

I have noticed that some tend to get hung up on appearances during meditation practices. As a shapeshifter, Lilith can take on a number of forms. Thus, there is no clear-cut explanation on what she looks like. In my early pathworking exercises with her, she appeared similarly to John Collier's painting of her—she was in a garden with long blonde hair and surrounded by a sea of snakes and flocks of birds—but for you, she may appear quite differently. Some only experience Lilith in animal form. Perhaps for you she will appear as a giant jungle serpent that slithers from a primordial swamp or hangs from a luscious tree. She may appear as a mysterious owl with a cryptic message. Others have recorded seeing her as half-beast, half-woman, appearing similar to a centaur or dragon. Some see her as a beautiful dark-skinned queen, while others see her as a blood-red-haired vixen. And even still, I have heard of some instances in which she does not take a form at all, just an ethereal shadow or cloud of colored smoke.

Lilith also has a knack for exposing herself in the form of another goddess, all the while making it even trickier to pin-point her. She is a trickstress, and part of her mysterious riddle is her identity. I have found that whichever visual form she decides to reveal herself in will resemble an important element of the seer's life. For example, if you aspire to be the next pop music sensation, she might appear to you as your supreme pop icon; I see this as a tactic she uses to reveal herself as your muse. With this in mind, it is also quite possible that she may take on the image of something that terrifies you too. Remember, though, that this is not done out of maliciousness but rather to assist you in getting to the bottom of, and resolving, the fear itself.

The Power of Name

Chanting is a powerful way to help alter consciousness in meditation and in ritual practices. It involves the repetition of powerful words, generally names or phrases that aid in the overall intent of your action. Chants can be lyrical, flowing statements or even a single word repeated over and over, helping to focus and align the energies with your consciousness. Crafting your own chant to Lilith for your meditations and other spiritual work can help focus and align your energies with her. This could be as simple as repeating her name until it becomes a blurred hum of "Lili-Lili-Lili-Lili." Alternately, you could craft one out of her other names.

Over time, Lilith has accumulated many names and associations to other figures. There is one story about an encounter between Lilith and the Prophet Elijah, during which Lilith is said to divulge several of her secret names that, when said, would lessen her malicious behaviors as a demoness in Hebrew folklore. These have been translated in several folkloric stories, in many variations, and were etched into protective talismans. Though these names were traditionally used to ward her away from those who feared her, I feel that they can be incorporated into the practices of those who work with her. Aside from these, Lilith has collected some other incarnations as well.

Names of Lilith		
Abeko	Gelou	Lilitu
Abito/Abitu	Gilou	Lillake
Abro	Hakash	Matruta/Matrota
Abyzu/Abizu	Ik	Makeda
Ailo	Ils	Ninlil
Alu	Ita/Ito	Odam
Amiz/Amizo/Amizu	Izorpo	Partasah
Ardat Lili	Kakash	Partashah
Astriga/Striga	Kali	Patrota
Avers Hikpodu	Kea	Petrota
Avitu	Kema	Podo/Pods
Ayalu	Keo	Raphi
Babalon	Kokos	Satrina/Satrinah
Batna	Lamassu	Talto/Tilto
Bilqis/Bilquis	Lamashtu	Thiltho
Bituah	Lamia	Zahriel
Elio	Laylil/Laylah	Zefonith
Gallu	Lilith	

I have met some devotees who will call out all of these names in a chant, but I personally feel that this can be an overwhelming task. In her album *Witch Web*, Fiona Horne sings a song dedicated to Lilith called "Dark Goddess." The song opens with a chant that lists several of Lilith's names. I have come to use it in my personal practice: *"Abro, Batna, Alu, Ita, Kokos, Kali, Odam, Kea!"*

The GLAM Sigil

Sigils are symbols used within witchcraft and magical practices that parallel with a specific desire. The symbol acts as a seal, furthering the intent. There are several sigil designs for Lilith available online, including one that uses the letters of her name (excluding vowels) to form a shape. Often, people will create sigils like this, using the power of the word emulating through the design. There is no right or wrong way to design a sigil, though. Some prefer to create a visual representation that reminds them of their overall goal. I am personally more partial to imagery than to letters and prefer this approach.

I developed an intricate sigil (to the right) that I use to represent the practice of GLAM Witchcraft. This sigil showcases enlightenment achieved through empowerment, confidence, authenticity, and sensuality. It starts as a pentagram acting as a representation of the practitioner; it also connects to each of the four elements and spirit. From the top point of the pentagram, a clockwise motioned spiral takes form as it lifts into an ascending, looping line. There are six loops representing each letter in Lilith's name; it resembles a cursive capital "L" and is inspired by the Buddhist Unalome, which symbolizes the path of enlightenment and the twists and turns one must take to get there. I also see it as an ode Lilith's serpentine kundalini energy—expanding from the practitioner, encircling the body, and weaving up into Lilith's astrological glyph. The base of this glyph presents an equal-armed cross that represents the equality magnified by Lilith. It also represents the concept of "as above, so below; as within, so without." The waning crescent moon sits atop this, symbolizing lunar energy, as well as the healing and transformative essence associated with this phase. The top features a pointed crown, a symbol of divinity and supremacy in regard to Lilith.

You may use this sigil (or countless others) in your work with Lilith, or you can develop one of your own. One way to use the sigil is as a contemplative visual representation during meditations. Simply focus on the sigil and its relationship to Lilith. The sigil can be used to decorate your altar or shrine—as a framed image or even carved into the wood. You can also etch it into a candle that is dedicated to Lilith and your GLAM Witch practices!

Witchcrafting: *A Devotional Candle*

It is a good idea to have a dedicated candle for Lilith, or for any spirit that you work with for that matter. This can be lit for daily devotions, meditations, and rituals as a symbolic offering to your chosen spirit. If you are so inclined to mold your own from scratch, even better! However, you can also simply use a store-bought pillar candle and dress it accordingly. Dressing a candle involves the for a specific working, shrines are best left assembled align the candle's power with your intent and/or chosen entity.

To craft your Lilith devotion candle, obtain the following ingredients:

Materials Needed
- Pillar candle in black, pink, or red
- Sharp knife for carving
- Pinch of cinnamon, dragon's blood, and rose petals
- 1 piece of snakeskin shed
- Eco-friendly glitter in black, pink, or red (alternate the candle and glitter colors if you so desire!)
- 3 drops Lilith oil blend (see page 273)

To start, carve a sigil—or even Lilith's name—into the wax. Next, combine the cinnamon, dragon's blood, rose petals, and snakeskin shed into a mortar and use the pestle to grind the mixture into a very fine powder. Once this is achieved, add eco-friendly fine glitter to the mixture and blend evenly. Pour your oil into the carving on the candle. While holding the candle, sprinkle your herb and glitter mixture into the crevices of your design, filling it completely. Do this over a plate or bowl to collect any excess glitter and powder to recycle and prevent a mess. When finished, place your candle in a fireproof container and drizzle a small amount of oil on top. Top this off with a light sprinkle of your residual glitter powder blend. You now have a candle that can be used in direct connection to your work with Lilith.

Ritual Anatomy

Once you feel confident in the relationship you have begun building with Lilith and have acclimated to her energies in your meditations, the next step would be to hold rituals for her. A common practice for ritual work among witches is the act of casting a circle. This is done by creating a dedicated sacred space with an energetic boundary between the worlds. This acts as a meeting ground to connect with deities, elementals, and other metaphysical forces. Symbolically, a circle signifies protection, unity, wholeness, and infinity. Some choose to outline the perimeter of their circle space with candles, flowers, or other décor, adding aesthetic and extra energy to the working.

There are many different ways and preferences for ritual work, and if you already have your own system in place, feel free to incorporate whatever elements of my practice into yours. The basic formula of casting a circle consists of purifying the space, grounding and centering, casting the circle, calling the quarters/elements, invoking/evoking deity, declaration of intent (i.e., the ritual's purpose), rising energy, cakes and ale, thanking deity, releasing quarters/elements, closing the circle. I will generally hold this type of ritual on the occurrence of a full moon or other astrological phenomenon that aligns to Lilith. For me, the moon is an extension of Lilith, and with the full moon representing the peak of lunar energy, it makes sense for me to utilize it in connection with honoring Lilith. However, you can perform this whenever you feel the need to do so.

While not necessary for all instances, I like to begin my rituals with a candlelit bath to cleanse my physical body. I'll also add bath salts or tea blends, crystals, or flower petals to help bond and focus the energies I intend to work with in the ritual.

If your shrine does not have enough room to support a ritual, create a temporary altar for the specific ritual need, with the tools and any other corresponding magical ingredients necessary. At this stage, it is appropriate to purify the space. There are various ways practitioners do this, but I prefer to walk the perimeter of the circle with a dragon's blood sage stick and say, "I cleanse this space in preparation of my rite." Once finished, return to the center of the circle or in front of your altar space. Relax your body and mind, and start to let go of the daily dramas that have occurred. Using the meditation techniques suggested earlier, ground yourself in the moment and focus purely on the task at hand.

Once you have grounded and centered, hold your athame in your hands and begin tracing a circular boundary around your space in a clockwise direction. You can do this by either walking the perimeter or standing in the center, turning as you go around. While doing this, say the following:

> *I conjure thee circle,*
> *A gate between the worlds I do trace,*
> *A meeting ground and sacred space.*
> *Now is the time, here is the place,*
> *A temple created, full of grace!*

While doing this, visualize your circle materializing in a spray of energetic light that forms in an egg-like sphere—above, below, and all around you. Focus on this energy. Your intent will shape it. The space is not yet finalized. It is customary to call the corners, also known as the elements. Each element is aligned with a cardinal direction—air to east, fire to south, water to west, and earth to north. Your ritual format here can be as simple as "I call upon air in the east; I call upon fire in the south . . ." or something more elaborate and hymnal. The words are not as important as the intent you fuel them with. Some witches prefer to use long, elegant invocations, while others don't. It is purely up to you. If holding a public ceremony or working with other witches, I tend to stick to this more basic approach. For my personal Lilithian rituals, I add each elemental association of Lilith into my call.

Starting in the east, the cardinal direction in which the sun rises, I state the following while I hold my corresponding air representation:

> *Gusts of wind that blew Lilitu,*
> *And wings that flew you,*
> *By the power of Lilith,*
> *I conjure thee, element of air!*

Next, I would move to the south and hold my fire representation, calling upon the fiery aspect of Lilith:

> *Sensual serpent, succubus of the south,*
> *Priestess of passion and lust,*
> *By the power of Lilith,*
> *I conjure thee, element of fire!*

Moving to the west, I would invite the water facet of Lilith:

> *Blood that flows like the Red Sea,*
> *And waves of unconsciousness inside me,*
> *By the power of Lilith,*
> *I conjure thee, element of water!*

Finally, I would call on Lilith's link to trees, holding my embodiment of earth in the north:

> *Guardian of knowledge in the tree,*
> *And dweller of caves once freed,*
> *By the power of Lilith,*
> *I conjure thee, element of earth!*

Once you have called the energy of the natural elements to join your ritual, come back to center. Plunge your athame into the sky, then tip it down to the ground and recite:

As above, so below,
The circle is cast high and low.

The circle is now bound and sealed. Now, standing in front of your ritual space, hold your arms out, palms to the sky, and invite your divine expression into the space. In this moment, you will choose to invoke or evoke Lilith; invoking involves calling up the merger of energies between you and who you are calling, whereas evoking is simply asking for an entity's presence—it is an invitation to join you within the circle. In my workings, I choose to *invoke* Lilith. Since this may be a new process for you, I would recommend evoking in the beginning. Light a candle dedicated to Lilith and recite this invocation of Lilith (just swap out "invoke" for "evoke" when reciting the next verse if you prefer):

She who was first, the Red Goddess,
Descend from the stars, the black abyss,
Queen of the moon, dark mistress,
Primitive mother, and great lioness!

I call on thee, Lilith!
On this night and in this hour,
I call upon your ancient power
And worship thee, sweet sacred flower!

From your cave by the Red Sea,
I ask that you please join me.
Serpent's fork and owl wings,
Sparkled jewels, your sacred things,
Curved horns and clawed feet,
On this night, we shall meet!

I invoke thee, Lilith!
This carnal flesh and fragrant bloom,
Offerings to you on this great moon.
Your magical presence makes me swoon,
As you cloak my circle and fill the room!

Open the gates between the worlds,
Show me the heavens above and hells below,
The wisdom within, the ebb and flow.
Be my guide, I will follow.

Winged Queen, Dark Goddess of the Night,
Illuminate my temple with your dark moonlight,
Share your wisdom and insights,
Your primal power and sensual delights.

Close your eyes and connect with Lilith. It is here that you will state the intent of the ritual by performing any meditation, spell-craft, divination, or worship desired. In whichever form of working you do, it is important to follow this with raising energy; this acts as the slingshot that pushes the intent into the universe. Energy raising can be done in a number of ways, such as chanting, danc-ing, masturbation (sex magic), or other activities that create a wind-up and release.

Once this stage is complete, it is time to make your offering. Traditionally, this stage of the ritual is considered the "cakes and ale," or "great rite," during which the athame (male) will be plunged into the chalice (female) as a ceremonial representation of the sexual union between the Goddess and God; this is then typi-cally followed by the blessing of food that will be snacked on to ground the energy that was previously built up. In my practice, though, I do not work with God energy, so I will usually present an offering to Lilith (from the list discussed in the previous chapter) and make a toast to her:

Thank you, Lilith.
I thank you for the gifts and lessons that you have granted me
In the past, and that which are to come in the future.
I raise this glass in toast to you
And celebrate you on this night!

I then take a sip and place the chalice back on the altar space. I sit for a moment in silence, reflecting on any messages or experience from the ritual.

Now, you may begin the closing process. In a very unscripted manner, I work my way backward, giving my thanks to Lilith and each element for assisting me in the working. From here, I take my athame and motion in a counterclockwise direction to release the circle and state a common phrase:

This circle is open but unbroken,
Forever carried within my heart.
May the veils between the worlds part,
And the magic I conjured begin to start.

And with this, your ritual is complete! Next, I take a moment to ground and center myself again before getting up. This helps prevent dizziness and adverse reactions from shifting consciousness too quickly. Once grounded, I take any perishable offerings outside and pour the leftover beverage on top of it as an offering to the land and wilderness in connection to Lilith.

To Cast or Not to Cast a Circle

As you expand in your practice, you may find that certain magics and forms of worship do not require a circle. General meditations or daily devotions to Lilith do not require these. I tend to cast a circle for major ritual events and honoring ceremonies like observing full and new moons but rarely for spells. My experience has taught me that it is better to work within the confines of a circle during these rituals because the circle creates a space between the physical and astral worlds, serving as a protective meeting ground from both benevolent and malevolent spirits that can affect your workings.

Spells are essentially manipulating energy to result in an outcome you desire on this plane of existence using mental intent and will. They may include colors, candles, herbs, crystals, and other objects we have discussed. Nevertheless, they are stating to the universe what you want changed. In these instances, I opt for a simple grounding to help me focus rather than calling a circle; I have experienced better outcomes with spells this way. The energies I am influencing with my spells are freely exposed to manifest more organically in the universe rather than starting in the boundaries of a circle. It is purely up to the practitioner to determine what works best for their individual needs.

5

LAYING THE LAWS:

The Laws of GLAM & Magic

"The Path is a way of life and on it the whole being must co-operate if the heights are to be won."
—Dion Fortune, *The Training & Work of an Initiate*

Nearly all spiritual paths have a set of rules to live by. Spiritual laws, principles, or truths help establish the lifestyle of any practitioner and further identify their path. There are many paths and traditions of witchcraft, each having components that set them apart from others. Witches who are members of a coven will traditionally have a set of rules by which they must orchestrate their magical and mundane lives to better reflect the overall goal(s) of the coven's work; however, solitary witches generally have the flexibility to choose their own code of ethics and blend it into their witch life. In developing my path as a solitary witch and devotee of Lilith, I created a set of laws that center on the empowerment yielded by her archetypes.

Lilithian Laws

The Great Lilithian Arcane Mysteries are a series of esoteric philosophies and magical practices that take shape through Lilith's Laws—a code of ethics that I have created in my practice of GLAM Witchcraft. But laws are imposing and become tricky when working with her. Lilith does not answer to anything but the universal forces of nature. Her law is wild and visceral; it coaxes the primal, instinctual, and creative natures that challenge society.

Buried deep within each of us are instincts that help shape who we are as individuals. These innate behaviors are the instinctual factors that motivate us. However, in many instances we have been conditioned to withdraw and hide certain aspects of ourselves due to the pressures placed upon us by society. Much of our makeup is the result of social stimuli that have been passed down through a series of learned behaviors. Lilithian Laws are based on the instinct of thriving in our own personal natures in the same way Lilith has. They illustrate how instinctual responses create empowerment through expression. The laws are also generic enough so as not to be confining; they provide intellectual, spiritual, and emotional freedom from society's limits, so they can be easily adapted to any preexisting personal codes of ethics. The laws are defined through a form of hedonistic individualism and the untamed, unapologetic nature that Lilith exudes. The Lilithian Laws of GLAM are to *see it, own it, flaunt it, indulge in it,* and *defend it.*

Law I: See it.

The power of sight, magical or mundane, is an influential motivator. When you see something, it helps reality set in. This law encourages you to be present for all moments of your life. It is about letting go of the distractions and flourishing in the enjoyment of the now.

As witches, most of us will practice some sort of divination, whether reading cards or runes, scrying, pyromancy, hydromancy, etc. Seeing it calls upon the innate power of intuition and psychic development. It is also a means of exploring the synchronicities of life and keeping your third eye open at all times.

Law II: *Own it.*

The idiom "own it" has become a popular catch phrase that is thrown around from time to time as a means to make someone take ownership of their (traditionally negative) actions. Taking ownership of something is an essential key to humbleness and is the first Lilithian law. By owning it, we embrace our true nature in all of its many forms. We acknowledge and welcome the good, the bad, and the ugly parts of us that are rooted in our very beings. Because the shadow represents the part of us that is not warm, fluffy, cotton candy clouds, it is regularly seen as negative, dark, twisted, and evil. To truly own it, though, we must not suppress our shadow and instead work with it to balance ourselves. As the ruler of the shadow self and the astrological black moon, Lilith is the embodiment of owning it.

Like Lilith, our shadow can be unpredictable. It can show up and cause a tsunami of chaos; however, when we hold the shadow back by burying it deep within, we can stunt personal and spiritual growth. This law encourages you to take a deep, hard look within and embrace your inner darkness. We must identify it and come to terms with it so that it does not rule us. Owning it inspires the suspension of fear and cynicism that come from self-loathing and doubt. By owning who we are, we ultimately heal our emotional wounds and emerge with an understanding that the dark parts of life are necessary for us to truly shine our brightest.

Law III: *Flaunt it.*

Vanity can also be considered one of the negative labels of society. We are trained that flaunting our best qualities can be chaotic, frivolous, and stuck up, or even slutty and arrogant. We are told that flaunting is not graceful and that confidence is synonymous with conceitedness. But vanity is not necessarily cocky. It can also be seen as self-expression, further exemplifying the self-love we've manifested by owning our nature from the previous law.

With flaunting it, we reflect our most unique intrinsic qualities outward for the world to see. This is the law that inspires us to shine, connecting to confidence and the way we carry ourselves. It is through Lilith's glamour as an enchantress that this law links to our external personification. Flaunting it inspires self-love to the fullest extent. Your body, your beauty, your passions, talents, and wisdoms—flaunt them. Seek out the beauty in life and advocate glamour. Not just the physical but all the beauty, arts, and creativities of the world as they reflect off of your glow.

Law IV: *Indulge in it.*

On a lot of levels, GLAM Witches are pleasure-seeking, and indulgence is essentially pleasure; it is gratification and satisfaction. Indulgence is luxury, and witchcraft is a spiritual luxury. This law encourages you to explore your desires and creativity. What makes you happy? What are you passionate about? What gives you pleasure? How can you pamper and nourish it? To indulge in it requires you to ask yourself all of these questions and put them into action.

Indulgence is also the ecstasy of orgasm. Our sexuality is an extremely powerful energetic force and aligns to Lilith's untamed carnal nature. Indulgence and sexuality are primal and lead to ecstatic pleasure. Pleasure is a influential motivator, and through sex magic, we ignite our desires and birth them into existence with the power of orgasm. But Indulgence does not stop with sex. It is also that extra-large piece of cake, taking time out for yourself, exploring your sexuality without guilt or shame, having the hookup, buying the designer brand, calling off work for a "me" day, and doing what truly makes you happy. This law inspires you to make a conscious effort to treat yourself and indulge in the many pleasures of life.

Note:

This law should not be seen as an act of indulgence in abusive behaviors—i.e., alcohol, drugs, rape, violence, and other forms of abuse. These are not forms of pleasure; rather, they mask a deeper pain. Indulgence in these activities is unethical on many levels and showcases a lack of commitment to the law of owning it, getting to the root of the pain, and healing ourselves. We will explore this more in depth in the Chapters 7 and 9.

Law V: Defend it.

The law of defense inspires you to seek the truth and speak the truth. It encourages you to cultivate equality by allowing balance to ebb and flow in your life. Lilith's tit-for-tat attitude is magnified in this principle. If someone comes for you, you are ready for the fight. Kick up the dust and charge in to cut the head off the devil right then and there. Stand your ground, defend yourself, and never apologize for doing so. That said, this does not give you the ok to go around causing destruction for the sake of doing so. Defense is knowing how and when to use an astral sword strategically to slice away the bullshit. Charging in blindly can result in tripping and falling upon the very sword you brought to protect you. There is a grace that comes with defense—both in picking your battles and in executing them wisely.

At the same time, this law encourages knowing when it is time to humbly bow out. Some battles are not worth the fight. In these instances, we must take flight. This law examines Lilith's retreats into the wilderness in tough times and is a reminder that shelter is sometimes the best means of surviving chaos. Defending it lies in the decision to fly away from situations that do not serve us or to sink our claws into our predators when necessary.

The Witch's Pyramid

Lilith aside, the practice of magic has its own laws, which are shaped through the Witch's Pyramid. This set of principles is based on the four Powers of the Sphinx—to know, to will, to dare, and to be silent. These act as the building blocks for magical manifestation resulting from our spells. When these four combine, they reach a fifth, higher power representing *to go*. Here is a closer look at each corner:

✸ *To know* is to understand. It is the role of the student. In order to practice magic, you must first comprehend the hows and whys of it. You must know the principles and correspondences associated with your spells and rituals. Anyone can find a spell online—or in a book for that matter—and follow the directions, expecting an instantaneous reaction to the working. Unfortunately, it does not really work that way. Knowledge takes time. It takes experience and the precision of knowing when, or when not to, use magic.

✸ *To will* is to want. It is the desire within that motivates action. Do you want it? Are you going to work for it? Some believe that this is the most potent part of the pyramid and that magic manifests by creating change through our will; however, it is also important to be will*ing*. You have to be willing to learn in order to eventually achieve. You have to be willing to show up and do your part. You have to be willing to take the blinders off and embrace the metaphysical elements of the world around you. And you have to be willing to be the best expression of yourself.

⊛ **To dare** is to do. It is the development of your practice. This requires you to challenge yourself and take action. By practicing and challenging yourself with the skills that you learn, you progress in your magical journey. It is through the act of doing that one becomes confident in their abilities and overall practice. To dare encourages you to trust yourself and the actions that you take.

⊛ **To be silent** is stillness. To be silent is often misinterpreted as not speaking of what we do. Some take this to mean that witches have always been mysterious; after all, "occult" comes from the Latin word *occultus*, meaning "secret" or "hidden." Witchcraft is a form of spiritual mystery, but it welcomes the seeker with open arms. From a magical mindset, this silence could be taken as a code not to talk about the workings we do until they have manifested. There is good reason for this because, if we talk about our workings or receive negative feedback on it from others, we are clouding the magic we released with doubt. That said, on a much deeper level, to be silent represents the silence of mind, inspiring us to speak less and listen more to the universe.

⊛ **To go** is mastery and service. This point has been added to the pyramid in recent years. It is the art of grasping the four previous corners and putting them to use in your magical and mundane lives to help yourself and others. It is the point of becoming and being your higher self, aligning with your spirit and inner divinity.

The Lilithian Pentacle

The first recorded five-pointed star was found in Egyptian hiero-glyphs as early as 3000 BCE. Since then, it has come to be known as the pentagram. When encased in a circle, the pentagram be-comes a pentacle, a traditional symbol for witches. Over time, the star, the number five, and the circle have all become significance symbols in magic and witchcraft. Many witches view the five points of a pentagram to represent each of the four elements—earth, air, fire, and water, with the fifth representing spirit. Five also connects to many parts of our lives and the natural world around us. The human body has five primary appendages that sprout from our core—head, arms, and legs. When we extend our arms straight out from our sides and stand with our legs apart, our bodies resemble a five-pointed star.

Sliced in half horizontally, the inside of an apple reveals a five-pointed geometric pattern with its seed pockets. Starfish and sand dollars are aquatic life forms that take the shape of a five-pointed star shape. Various flowers do this with their petal struc-ture as well. We have five fingers and toes on each hand and foot respectively. Biologically, the human experience is lived through five basic senses. Astronomically, Venus' orbit even makes a pen-tagram shape from our view on earth. The number five is constant-ly around us and is embedded in our lives in so many ways.

We are stardust, living on a planet that orbits the star we know as the sun. This orbital shape is a circle, which is also the rudimen-tary basis for a sphere—the shape of the planets, stars, and moons, further emphasizing the constant role this shape plays in our lives. The circle represents unity, infinity, and wholeness and when combined with the star becomes a symbol of life—the magical life led by witches.

Different traditions and magical paths have incorporated these symbols into their practice as a philosophy, a structure, or even a contemplation tool. In Lilithian Witchcraft, the pentagram becomes more than a symbol; it is a spiritual tool that activates empowerment through the Great Lilithian Arcane Mysteries. Each point connects to an element, a Lilithian law, and one of five direct forms of magic—divination, shadow, glamour, sex, and protection. These magics can stand up alone as powerful independent forces, but when all five are used in conjunction the pentagram transforms into a pentacle, connecting each point together as the circle encases the star. Combining the Lilithian laws with the magics make the GLAM Witch "crafts":

⊛ ***Visioncraft*** is mental magic by way of spirit and the essence of our highest self. It connects to the concept of vision and Lilith's elevation to a goddess in modern times. The goal of this point is to strengthen intuition and pay attention to the synchronicities of life through the Lilithian law of *see it*. Spirit

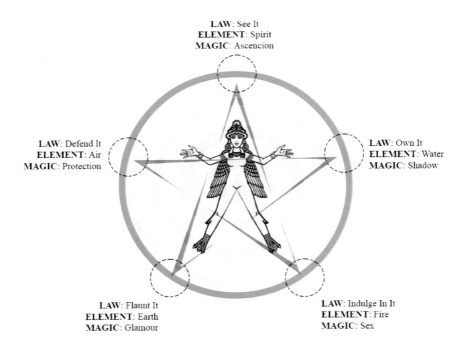

LAW: See It
ELEMENT: Spirit
MAGIC: Ascencion

LAW: Defend It
ELEMENT: Air
MAGIC: Protection

LAW: Own It
ELEMENT: Water
MAGIC: Shadow

LAW: Flaunt It
ELEMENT: Earth
MAGIC: Glamour

LAW: Indulge In It
ELEMENT: Fire
MAGIC: Sex

Photo: The Lilithian Pentacle. Adapted drawing of Lilith by Zvereva Yana.

manifests through ascension magic, an elevation achieved by accessing the realms of our higher self, unlocking our intuitive power, and going forth on the path ahead.

✴ **Shadowcraft** refers to shadow magic by way of water, an emotional element that provided nourishment and healing. It inspires one to dare, to push beyond fear, and symbolizes Lilith's archetype as an outcast. The goal is to know thyself and embrace your truest natures, encompassing the Lilithian law of *own it*. Shadow magic involves the spiritual exploration of the shadow self—the part of us hidden away that we have lost contact with for fear instilled in us by society. Embracing the shadow can be an emotional, healing journey. It is the first step to developing authenticity and is linked to the emotional body of water.

✴ **Glamcraft** is glamour magic by way of earth, the element of formation that takes root in the pyramid point of silence. Physical form needs no words to transcribe a message. It provides a structure for the witch to stand. It connects to the concept of confidence with Lilith's archetype as a femme fatale and enchantress. The goal of this point is to carry yourself with poise, thereby manifesting the Lilithian law of *flaunt it*.

✴ **Lustcraft** is sex magic by way of fire, an element of transformation and manifestation. It aligns with our passions and desires. It connects to the concept of will and Lilith's archetype as a priestess of passion. Our passions and desires fuel the sacred flame burning within us, linking to fire through sex magic and the creative spark of orgasmic power. The goal of this point is to embrace your sexuality, learn to use it as a tool for manifestation, and ignite the Lilithian law of *indulge in it*.

✸ ***Bitchcraft*** is defensive magic by way of air, an element of clarity and thought. It connects to the concept of action and Lilith's archetype as a rebel who has freedom of choice. The goal of this point is to learn the balance of magical fight and flight— when to defend, protect, or flee. Air is the swiftness and power of the astral blade, which slices by means of hexing, establishing impartiality and balancing the scales of justice in our favor. It is about standing up for yourself through the Lilithian law of *defend it* and having the knowledge of metaphysical fight or flight.

Each of these magical forms will be discussed at length, having their own chapters in the next section of the book. As we take the theory and practices of a GLAM Witch, we move onward to the crafts. It is in these that we will learn how to incorporate Lilith into magical practices, furthering the Lilithian Laws.

PART III

The Crafts of

THE GLAM WITCH

6

VIBRANT VISIONCRAFT:

Seeing it with the Mental
Magic of Psychic Power

"A Witch's work is mind work and utilizes powerful metaphors,
allegories, and images that unlock the powers of the mind."
—Laurie Cabot, *Power of the Witch*

It is fairly common today to see our favorite pop culture witches
of Hollywood wield powers such as telekinesis, time control,
flame throwing, premonition, resurrection, and a myriad of others.
It can be a fun fantasy and means of escapism to imagine what
powers develop in our lives as modern witches. Unfortunately, the
real-world powers are by no means as flamboyant and frivolous as
those we see on screen. Nevertheless, we all have precognitive and
intuitive abilities within us just waiting to be unleashed.

Have you ever listened to the radio and thought of a song that played next? Thought of someone you haven't talked to in a while and then—poof!—you get a call, text, or message from them? Or perhaps you have even been able to have a conversation with a close friend with nothing more than a glance. All of these moments are linked together through intuition and represent our innate awareness of knowing. It is the instinctual response of trusting your gut and listening to the voice within.

Reading minds, fortunes, and futures are often seen as acts of witchcraft stemming from psychic ability. What some do not realize is that we are all psychic in our own ways and that these abilities manifest as a result of developed intuition. Our intuition is a primal factor of psychic power—our innate ability to know or sense occult revelations.

Psychic abilities can be developed in a variety of ways, and in some cases, simply through profound spiritual experiences. Many embrace spirituality to awaken and transform. Witchcraft is transformative, and for many it is also spiritual. It is an ascension or inner awakening that raises your vibration and helps tune you into the world around you in a much more vibrant way. Like a video game, ascension is the spiritual process of leveling up. It is an elevation of mind, body, and spirit. And it is from this ascension that one begins to master the art of mental magic.

In the first chapter of this book, I discussed how witchcraft is not an event; rather, it is a process and, for many, a spiritual journey. Rewarding results are not instantaneous. Like witchcraft, this ascension is not an event but a spiritual process that one undergoes. It is important to remain aware of your surroundings, and even more so as a witch because certain messages may be revealing themselves to you! Synchronicities and signs are abundant within the universe; it is just a matter of removing the blinders and walking through life with your third eye open, listening to your intuition, and embracing psychic power.

Synchronicity is one of the major factors of developing your sixth sense and ascending into a place of higher consciousness. By developing your sixth, psychic, sense you not only become more in tune with the universe, others, and your environment, but you also gain better insight into the language of Lilith. Her teachings are based on a series of riddles and often incoherent messages. Lilith is the gatekeeper of occult wisdom. She is the guardian of the huluppu and tree of knowledge. She resides in the "in between," a meeting place between Heaven and Hell, or the higher and lower astral planes. She is the keeper of secrets and mysteries of life, death, and rebirth. Once you lower the wall around you and open your third eye, you begin to see all of her messages much more clearly.

Everyone has their own psychic talents. Some more than others. And still, everyone experiences their ascension differently; however, I have found that there are commonalities and that homing in on your intuitive and psychic powers are building blocks to getting there. In this point of the Lilithian Pentacle, we will examine several ways to tune into higher states of consciousness and develop psychic talents. It is through this that we experience the vibrant visioncraft necessary for our ascension in GLAM.

Journal Entry

Before we move forward, I want you to take out a journal and answer the following questions. This activity will assist in helping you see the connections between your answers and the practices we will touch upon. These will be covered in more depth as we continue.

1. Reflect upon symbolism in your waking life. What imagery stands out to you most? Think about your favorite things, such as colors, animals, smells, tastes, art, etc. Do you see any similarities or connections between these? What and why are you drawn to these things?

2. Do you experience vivid dreams? Think of the most vivid dream you have ever had and detail it. Note the major themes and symbols associated with it. In reflection, do you see how any of these signs mirror your life from the past, present, or future representations of yourself?

3. Which sense do you relate to most? If you could only have one for the rest of your life, which would it be?

The Sixth Sense

Our physical body is comprised of five senses: sight, taste, touch, smell, and sound; however, we all have an innate sixth sense that is aligned to our intuition and psychic power. These are known as the "clairs," which further enhance our existing senses. By identifying which is your most prominent clair, you gain insight into ways that signs may make themselves known to you. It is important to remember that these are not cerebral; they are not logical, so in order to gain the most, you must suspend any cynical and pessimistic thoughts about the subject. If you go in with a negative attitude, you will end up building a higher and thicker wall around your psychic self, trapping it deeper within. Here is a snapshot of the clairs:

✴ *Clairaudience* is the psychic gift of clear hearing. This clair manifests through the ears. You may feel a sensation of hearing voices or little whispers within your head. You may hear something that is not there, or even a deep piercing ringing in your ear.

✴ *Claircognizance* is representative of clear knowing. It is a purely intuitive power that essentially connects to an innate knowing of something to be true without needing the logical proof associated with it.

✴ *Clairgustance* refers to clear tasting, presenting messages through your taste buds. It is connected to the sensation of tasting something when there is nothing in your mouth.

✴ *Clairsalience* is the gift of clear smelling. This clair manifests through the ability to smell things that are not physically in front of you. Because smell is such a personal experience, this is not something that can easily be described, much like clairgustance. The art of clear smelling is essentially the ability to pick up on different scents during divination practices, or while out and about, that do not come from a tangible source. An example of this might be walking down the street and catching a whiff of roses during the middle of winter when there's snow on the ground and no flowering plants in sight. Or perhaps you are doing a psychic reading for a client and smell a peach cobbler, extending from their memories.

✸ *Clairsentience* is representative of clear feeling. This is more than just the hairs on the back of your neck standing up when something is experienced; it is more aligned to aches and pains, or flushes of physical pleasure, when you encounter a person, spirit, or energetic frequency. Those I know with this ability generally link it to stomachaches; it is the literal "gut" feeling of an energetic presence.

✸ *Clairvoyance* is the most common clair discussed in occult practices and is the psychic gift of clear sight. For those with this sixth sense, you have an innate power of visualization. You may possess a photographic memory or receive signs and interpretations through images.

GLAM Hexercise: *Determining Your Clair*

There are many ways to develop your clairs, and many resources available to assist with this process. A quick internet search will provide you with multiple quizzes and photographic tests to help you determine your primary clair. I generally disagree with this method, though. Think back to our understanding of witchcraft as a mystery religion, spirituality, or magical act. It is about personal experience and I have found that the best way to discover yours is through a series of meditation techniques.

In this meditation, we will attempt to unlock the clair(s) most dominant in you. It is possible to have multiple clairs reveal themselves right off the bat. In some instances, others may heighten over time and with practice. Remember, everything is a process and, ultimately, practice makes perfect. So, do not gang up on yourself if you are brand new to this and not instantly experiencing results.

1. Find a quiet space where you will not be disturbed and prepare yourself as you normally would for a meditation. You can use

the outline I provided in Chapter 4 for this. Light any candles or incense that you feel drawn to that help put you in a calm mood. I personally enjoy a mixture of lavender and worm-wood.

2. Ground and center yourself. Align your mental state with the goal of determining which clairs are most developed within you.

3. Close your eyes and declare your intent, asking that which should be made known to you at this time be exposed.

4. Enter a trance state, while remaining cognizant of your surroundings. Are any messages coming to you? Do you have a sense of knowledge on a certain subject that you did not have before? Are you hearing anything—words or other tones in your ears? Are you tasting or smelling something that is not there? Is your body receiving messages through physical touch?

5. When you feel as though your meditation should end, align your focus back to reality. In your journal, make note of any experiences you have had. Note the date, time, and moon phase. As you progress with your studies, you might find that timings are important measures for success; for example, the full and dark moons are particularly potent energy sources for divination.

Signs & Synchronicity

If there is one thing of which I am certain, it is that everything happens for a reason, and if you pay attention, you can start to understand things on a much deeper level through various signs. Signs are not something limited to witchcraft, or Lilith for that matter. Remember that Lilith weaves a web of wonder, though, and communicates best through signs. In order to gain the most from her insight and "level up" through ascension, we must be willing to receive these signs. The key here is that we must also know *when* we are receiving them.

Turning back to the Witch's Pyramid, knowledge is a key component to signs. Signs exist everywhere. At some point, you may have even been at the crossroads of your existence and asked a higher power, or the universe, to show you a sign to give you an indication of what direction to move forward in.

Dreams

Our dreams are gateways to the unconscious mind and are filled with messages that can be utilized to identify signs. Dreams can even be a spiritual journey and are connected with spirit communication and astral projection. I think it is most important to note that dreams are a great place to lock down symbolism and its role in psychic development.

There are several dreams that are very common and, thus, have been recorded in depth in various dream dictionaries and online sources. It is very easy today for anyone to consult the oracle of Google and find an interpretation of their dream. While this can be a convenient solution for some, it can stunt your ability to pick up on signs and symbolism through your intuition. For instance, a dream of a snake can represent repressed sexuality, a trickster in your life, a symbol of the Goddess, fertility, etc. The list goes on and on, and depending on your personal relationship with snakes, it will mean something different. If you have a fear of snakes, the dream will more likely be representative of fear; if you have a kinship with them, however, it will mean something different. Dreams, like signs, are situational and subjective.

Dream dictionaries can be fun and are definitely a starting ground, but my philosophy is that you should cultivate your own understanding of the symbols. While writing this chapter, I have been experiencing very vivid dreams. In one, I dreamt that I was in a garden and found a very plump toad that had gotten caught between a chain-link fence and some dirt. I helped free it, and once it was in my hands, I realized it was a painted slider turtle. But then it hopped out of its shell and was a little black frog, and darted for a nearby pond singing "I'm free!"

I could have easily done a quick internet search or flipped through a book I own on various dream symbols to read someone else's interpretation of what my dream meant. But I didn't. See, dreams are personal experiences and, thus, I don't feel it is quite appropriate to have someone tell you what they mean. Most of these interpretations are dated too. So, I looked at what I knew about toads, turtles, and frogs, in addition to themes that have been playing out in my life. It was clear to me that this dream represented surrealistic transformation. In my waking life, I knew that I had undergone much transformation in the last two years, and this dream mirrored that. But I think that it may also have been a much-needed reminder that it is ok to ask for help and eliminate the possibility of getting bogged down and stuck in the continued process of my transformation.

Dreams can also be a way to communicate directly with a spirit or other entity on the astral planes. Lilith has appeared in many of my dreams, in the same way she has in meditations and pathworkings. In these instances, it is equally important to take note of the symbolism that occurs. When it comes to Lilith, her teachings are often not as straightforward as one would hope. By understanding symbolism and how objects, symbols, animals, etc. relate specifically to you, you strengthen the foundation for identifying signs and their meanings.

The best way to home in on dreams for divination purposes is to write them out. Upon waking, record any symbol or detail of your dreams that you remember. If you struggle with remembering your dreams, a simple and result-driven trick is to wake up several times during the night. Set your alarm to wake up two or three select times. The sound will pull you out of sleep briefly enough for you to recall what was occurring. The more you do this, the more you will be able to recall your dreams and experience them more vividly.

Witchcrafting: *Lilithian Dream Sachet*

Lilith is notorious for having dominion over our dreams. This comes from her legends as the succubus; however, I have found that her rulership of the dream realms is not limited to the erotic. In addition to meditations, one can tap into Lilith's mysticism through dream magic. While she needs no invite to enter your dreams, this acts as a quick oomph to help her manifest.

Materials Needed
- Purple or silver sachet
- Labradorite
- 1 tsp. lavender
- 1 tsp. wormwood
- Mugwort tea
- Journal

As mentioned in the crystals section of Chapter 3, labradorite is a highly magical stone that delivers quite the blow of potency to dream magic. Similarly, lavender, wormwood, and mugwort stimulate psychic sleep. To begin, open your sachet and place the labradorite, lavender, and wormwood inside. Store this in your pillow case. Make a glass of mugwort tea and bring it to your bedroom and enjoy as you relax. Once finished, lay back and begin the following exercise to elicit total body relaxation in preparation for your sleep.

Starting at your feet, tighten up the muscles in your toes as hard as you can then release. Work your way up to your legs and tense those muscles, following with release. Continue to work all the way up to your head, tensing your facial muscles and releasing them. If you are so inclined, play some soft dreamscape sounds in the background, perhaps one known to stimulate the pineal gland. In your relaxed state, call out to Lilith:

Lilith, I welcome thee to my head,
As it rests here in my bed,
Show me what I need to see.
Here and now, come join me!

Allow yourself to drift off into sleep and prepare for messages to be revealed. Upon waking, write down what you can remember from your dreams. As you do this more, your dreams will become more vibrant, allowing you to unlock messages you may receive from Lilith.

Defining Divination

Divination is a common art utilized by witches to better understand the unknown, and is one of the best ways to develop your psychic talents and gifts. Commonly seen as a means of fortune telling, divination helps practitioners understand the past, present, future, and supernatural occurrences. There is a vast variety of divination techniques, from using the elements, to food, to smells. These tools and activities essentially help to further advance our clair abilities and psychic power. Let's take a look at three of my favorites: numerology, scrying, and tarot.

Numerology

When we think of numbers, math may come to mind. Growing up, math was never my forte, and I avoided it like the plague. Numbers were intimidating, and beyond that, I did not see the value in them unless they were tied to money and material means.

As I evolved in my witchery, I started to explore numbers as a magical tool. I started to see that numbers are not only a means of measurement but are found in many things all over the world. And, like most things, numbers can be integrated into witchcraft. It was through this that I started to acquaint myself with the art of numerology.

Numerology is not a divination art that requires any psychic power or gift; rather, it is a way of spotting and identifying signs and synchronicities. Additionally, numerology extends into tarot, which we will take a look at later in this chapter. Having a good understanding of the magic of numbers will only assist in your ability to read the cards as well. The single digits 1 through 9 are the building blocks of numerology. Here is a snapshot of what each number means:

1. **One** is representative of beginnings. It is the first number and is seen as a starting point. It is individualization and ego, connecting to the physical body and overall identity.

2. **Two** relates to partnership. It represents equality, duality, and opposition. It is deeply connected to emotion and intuitive feeling. It also connects to choices and being torn between two ideas, wants, or other decision-oriented experience.

3. **Three** brings another figure into the presence of two, representing teamwork. It also represents cycles, creativity, development, and progression (beginning, middle, and end).

4. **Four** is like the four pillars that make up the foundation of a home. It relates to stability and structure. Being that four is essentially two sets of two, it further represents partnership and successful outcomes. This number is often authoritative and meticulous in nature.

5. **Five** denotes action and change. It is a combination of the four elements and spirit and represents the pentagram. On an energetic note, fives can also represent different perspectives.

6. **Six** ultimately corresponds to harmony. It is free-flowing love, luxury, and pleasure. It is the beauty of life. It also takes the powers of three and magnifies cooperation.

7. **Seven** corresponds to inner wisdom. It is a very mystical number and, as a result, has a secretive vibe to it. Seven is connected to reflection and introspection.

8. **Eight** is connected to power. It is the number of mastery and accomplishment. It is connected to destiny and the strength of ambition.

9. **Nine** is the last single digit and is representative of completion. It is linked to the divine and the highest expression of self.

Adding it All Up

Now that we know a bit about what the numbers mean, let us examine how numerology works. Remember that everything is composed of numbers—addresses, telephone numbers, URL addresses, dates, times, and, yes, people! Not only through our government-issued social security numbers but also through the alphabet. Each letter has a specific number that it is connected to. Numerology is practiced by adding groups of numbers and then reducing them to a single digit. This final digit is then reflected upon with the symbolism we just examined to determine the meaning. There are also various categories and meanings for the numbers. The numerology of your birth name details your destiny number, whereas your birthdate shows your life path number, and so on and so forth. Let's look at some of these.

When it comes to the alphabet, the below chart is used to determine a letter's number. "A" through "I" is the first set of nine numbers, "J" through "R" is the second set, and "S" through "Z" is the final set of eight; therefore, each number has three letters that correspond to it, except for 9, which only has two because the length of the alphabet does not divide evenly into three.

1	2	3	4	5	6	7	8	9
A	B	C	D	E	F	G	H	I
J	K	L	M	N	O	P	Q	R
S	T	U	V	W	X	Y	Z	

A common number utilized in numerology is your destiny number, which reflects your personal destiny and goals of this lifetime. Using my full name, Michael Robert Herkes, here is an example of the numerical equation used to find my destiny number:

Michael: $4 + 9 + 3 + 8 + 1 + 5 + 3 = $ **33**
Robert: $9 + 6 + 2 + 5 + 9 + 2 = $ **33**
Herkes: $8 + 5 + 9 + 2 + 5 + 1 = $ **30**

Now, add the three sums together:

$33 + 33 + 30 = $ **96**

Once you have the final sum, you add the single digits together, until only one single digit is left. In this instance, I would do the following:

$9 + 6 = $ **15**
then
$1 + 5 = $ **6**

From this, my destiny number is 6, which indicates that my destiny is aligned with creating harmony, beauty, and glamour in the world around me.

Now, let's take a peek at the second most common number in numerology, the life path number. This number illustrates the common characteristics that will follow us in life and is calculated using your birthdate. For this, let's say your birthdate was January 1, 1990, or 1/1/1990, which creates the following equation:

$1 + 1 + 1 + 9 + 9 + 0 = $ **21**
then
$2 + 1 = $ **3**

The life path number 3 reveals that this person is going to have themes of progression and cycles within their life, more than the average person. It would signify that teamwork and relationships with others would be very strong.

In addition to these two popular numerology applications, there are so many others you can try—you can literally start doing this with anything. Numerology can become addictive, and it's a great way to observe signs and synchronicities. So get ready to have fun with your numbers!

❀ *Address*—Numerology with your street address will shed light on your home manifestation. When you are relocating, or even changing jobs, take a look at what the address' numerical value is to determine the energetic vibration that will radiate through the location.

❀ *Phone Number*—Using numerology on your phone number can help highlight communication style. This will illustrate how other's view your communication habits. This of course can be further broken down into what type of phone number it is; for example, a home phone number will illustrate your communication style at home, a mobile phone number will shed light on how you communicate socially, and a work number will detail how you communicate in the workplace.

❀ *Personality Number*—Your personality number is determined by adding together the consonants of your full birth name. It details the symbolism associated to your overall personality.

❀ *Preferred Name*—Many of us have a preferred way for how we'd like to be addressed. This can be a nickname, married name, or any other name that we are known by. It is not always our birth name. Your preferred name details how you want the world to see you.

✸ *Social Security Number*—Using your social security number helps dictate your identity in society's eyes.

✸ *Soul Urge Number*—This represents the inner workings of your soul, detailing your likes, dislikes, and primal motivations. It is found by adding the vowels of your full birth name.

Once you've become familiar enough with numerology and have further researched your own numbers, be sure to keep an eye out for them in your daily life. Likewise, pay close attention to any number that is continuously repeating in your calculations. For me these are the numbers four and six. Whenever I see these I look at it as a little sign that I am on the right path.

Predictive Numerology

As you begin to explore numerology more, you can continue to draw upon meanings and messages by looking at times and dates to understand and predict future events. Years, months, and times can all be added and thus incorporated into numerology. When setting goals for yourself, looking at specific dates and times by calculating numerological answers can give you a forecast for success.

Scrying

Mirrors are a common tool discussed throughout this book. Seen as portals to other worlds, mirrors help us access other realms of consciousness. A popular divination device in witchcraft is a black scrying mirror. The shininess of the black mirror is used to still the mind and make out shapes and thoughts that come to you while in a meditative trance. With mirrors being a sacred portal for Lilith, this tool will become one of your most profound in connecting to her energies. In my own scrying efforts, I have used both black mirrors and crystal spheres, each having different results. With black mirrors, I have actually seen objects in the mirror—not like a face staring back at me or anything as clear as something playing out on a television, but instead, it is distortions of color that merge into different shapes. When I have attempted to scry with spheres, however, I have learned to pay attention to thoughts and images that spring into my head. As you gaze at your reflective surface, the signs will reveal themselves to you through one of the clairs. You may notice certain smells, tastes, sounds, physical sensations, or thoughts and images. Be open-minded, go slow, and pace yourself in this practice.

One particular memory of mine involved a divination session, during which I was trying to determine if I should give up on something that was not going quite the way I had hoped. The results were not manifesting in the way I wanted, at least not fast enough. I wanted to know if I should give up and throw it all away. While gazing in and out of focus at the sphere, I suddenly saw a unicorn in my mind. This unicorn started to charge forward and run in the direction of my apartment door. I see unicorns as representing magic, mysticism, and power. The fact that it was charging in my mind in such a courageous way told me that I needed not to give up. That I needed to charge forward and get outside of my current situation. I did and eventually got the results I sought for.

Witchcrafting: *A Black Scrying Mirror*

Scrying is a great way to further develop and understand your clairs. Many occult stores have black mirrors available; however, I prefer witchcrafting my own out of a picture frame!

Materials Needed
- ✸ Empty picture frame
- ✸ Rubbing alcohol
- ✸ 1 tsp. patchouli
- ✸ 1 tsp. wormwood
- ✸ Black paint (nail varnish is a great and cheap alternative)
- ✸ Lancet (to draw a few drops of blood)
- ✸ Silver Sharpie

Your black mirror will be an important vessel in furthering your ritual work and divination practices with Lilith. To begin, find a picture frame that you would like to use. This can be as simple or elaborate as you like; it just needs to have a piece of glass with it. Clean the glass with some rubbing alcohol. Grind the patchouli and wormwood into a fine powder. If you'd like to incorporate any other herbs that aid in divination practices, feel free. Paint the glass on one side in a thick and even coat. Let the paint dry and add a thin layer of the powder. Using a (diabetic) lancet, draw blood and add a drop of blood to each corner of the glass, adding a fifth in the center. Pour a thick layer of paint over the powder and blood, sealing it within. Once dried, take the silver sharpie and draw the GLAM sigil in the center. Write "Lilith" at the top and your name at the bottom. To activate the black mirror, leave it out on your windowsill on a night during the dark/new moon to charge with the energies of darkness.

GLAM Hexercise: *Scrying Template*

1. Prepare your space and ensure that all light sources are off so that you are unable to see reflections in the surface of the mirror. The only exception to this is candlelight. You may position a candle to burn behind the mirror or on either side of it.

2. Gather any other objects that might assist you during your scrying. These could include crystals, incense, or even bells used to align the energies with the goal of the reading and to focus the mind.

3. Close your eyes and ground and center yourself with a light meditation to focus your mind.

4. Open our eyes and direct your focus onto the mirror's surface. Remain focused on the area. Pay attention to the thoughts and ideas that come into your mind (or any other experiences). Often, the images identified through this medium are not actual images that play across the surface of the mirror like a movie. Instead, they are generally a series of images or visions that appear within your mind's eye.

5. Once your scrying has commenced, close your eyes, and re-center yourself from the experience. Once you have exited the trance state, write down the ex-

perience. Once you have exited the trance state, write down the experiences you had. Remember that the more you practice, the more success you will experience. Documenting your experiences not only helps you to record the signs that come to you but also tracks your progress.

Tarot

Tarot cards are among the most popular divination tool and have seen a spike in interest over recent years. Elements have even been featured in runway fashions and haute couture, adding to the glamourous witch aesthetic. Nevertheless, the tarot has a long history in occult practices. It is my recommended tool for anyone new to oracular arts because of its rich symbolism.

The illustrations of the deck connect deeply on an emotional

and spiritual level. They are a prominent way to help understand signs and synchronicities within life. While there are a number of gorgeous decks available, I recommend you begin with, or at least supplement your practice with, the Rider-Waite-Smith deck. It is considered the most common deck utilized in the Western world of occult practices and is saturated in symbolism that is very useful for budding witches.

The Major Arcana

The first twenty-two cards of the tarot are considered the Major Arcana. These tell the story of "The Fool's Journey," and The Fool just so happens to be the very first card of the deck. With so many tarot decks on the market today, each artist has put their own spin on the symbolism of the cards. Because of this, it is impossible to provide a blanket synopsis of the symbols associated with them and important that you, as the reader, pick up on what the symbols mean to you. When I teach tarot or read for clients, I lean heavily on the symbols that appear in the card's illustrations rather than the outline presented within the book. Nevertheless, there are common themes associated with each card in the Major Arcana: Here is a snapshot at their meanings:

Number	Card	Interpretation Keywords
0	The Fool	Beginnings, Vulnerability, Innocence
1	The Magician	Creation, Transformation, Potential
2	The High Priestess	Intuition, Prophecy, Subconscious
3	The Empress	Fertility, Beauty, Creativity
4	The Emperor	Leadership, Power, Structure
5	The Hierophant	Institutions, Teaching, Lessons
6	The Lovers	Love, Partnerships, Choices
7	The Chariot	Victory, Success, Championship

8	Strength	Strength, Power, Courage
9	The Hermit	Isolation, Solitude, Introspection
10	Wheel of Fortune	Destiny, Fate, Wishes
11	Justice	Justice, Equality, Karma
12	The Hanged Man	Sacrifice, Detachment, Letting Go
13	Death	Endings, Transformation, Cycles
14	Temperance	Balance, Moderation, Flexibility
15	The Devil	Manipulation, Temptation, Fear
16	The Tower	Change, Starting Over, Collapse
17	The Star	Wishes, Inspiration, Favor
18	The Moon	Intuition, Cycles, Illusion
19	The Sun	Positivity, Vitality, Optimism
20	Judgement	Ascension, Awakening, Rebirth
21	The World	Success, Completion, Fulfillment

Minor Arcana

The remaining cards in the deck are considered the Minor Arcana, which is divided into four suits: wands, swords, cups, and pentacles (or coins). These are then further divided into an ace, the numbers 2 through 10, and a set of court cards. Each suit has its own overarching energetic representation, and once these are learned, numerology can be applied to them for interpretation.

Where the Major Arcana represents chief events in a reading, the Minor Arcana is representative of more routine, everyday actions.

Suit	Element	Energies
Wands	Fire	Ambition, Creativity, Will, Passion
Swords	Air	Inspiration, Thought, Action, Power
Cups	Water	Emotions, Spirituality, Partnership, Relationships
Pentacles/ Coins	Earth	Abundance, Career, Materialism, Prosperity, Property

The aces of the deck are representative of the numerological essence of the number 1. They are the pure elemental power of the suit. Likewise, tens are overall completion and success achieved through the overall suit. Going back to what we know of numerology, the Ace of Wands will represent the birth of a new creative endeavor or a period of high drive and ambition. Likewise, the Five of Cups can represent emotional changes or actions that lead to change, thus causing grief.

Court Cards

The court cards are archetypes of a royal family—page, knight, queen, and king. These cards are representative of specific individuals. These may be people who influence the person receiving the reading or aspects of the person. Often, readers will place emphasis on physical gender to the card representations. I look at these on a more energetic level of anima and animus rather than a hard and fast male- or female-born individual.

Position	Rulership	Representation
Page	Youth	Beginnings, Eagerness, Future Ruler
Knight	Messenger	Change, Defense, Movement
Queen	Heart	Composure, Elegance, Emotional Maturity
King	Master	Authority, Elder, Skill

While queens represent elegance and maturity, it is important to also look at the elemental representation of the suit they fall in as well. The energies of the Queen of Swords are going to be very different than those of the Queen of Wands. Swords have a sharpness and swiftness to them, and it is here that the Queen's sword becomes her tongue, as the energies of swords are ruled by thought and communication. The appearance of the Queen of Swords in a spread might represent a manipulative feminine energy with a harsh communication style. Likewise, a Queen of Wands will combine elegance with fiery passion, marking a seductive queen.

Reading the Cards

Again, there are many ways to read tarot cards. Different readers have different ideas on spreads, shuffling techniques, rules on fallen cards, and other ways of going about reading. The biggest rule of all, at least that I follow, is that there are no rules to this! Do not feel that you have to do your readings in one set way. Deviate as you feel fit and create your own rules along the way. This flexes your intuitive muscles and also helps you to further establish a relationship with your deck. There is no one right, true way to work with the tarot. That said, for introductory purposes, here is a template I use for successful readings:

1. Gather your cards and any other objects that might assist you during your reading. These could include crystals, incense, or even bells used to align the energies with the goal of the reading and to focus the mind.

2. Ground and center yourself with a light meditation to focus your mind.

3. Pick up your cards and shuffle them for as long as you feel is necessary. There is no right or wrong way to shuffle your cards. While doing this, focus on the area for which you seek insight. Sometimes, I simply focus on what I need to know at this stage to further my path. I think this is often the best approach because, as the cards are laid out, you will have a good sense of the reading's theme.

4. Once ready, hold your cards to your chest and focus on your question. Hold the cards to your lips and gently blow on them. This is a technique I picked up through experience with my cards. I feel that, by doing this, you push your life energy into the cards with your breath, aligning them directly to you. When reading for someone else, I will have them shuffle and blow directly on the cards instead of me.

5. Now, you will lay out the cards into three separate piles and restack them in whatever order you feel drawn to. Now, lay them into your desired spread. Here is a look at some of my favorite spreads.

Daily Card

For anyone just beginning tarot, or perhaps picking it up again, I strongly suggest the method of pulling a daily card upon waking. Simply ground yourself, shuffle, and ask the universe to show you what you need to know for the day. Split the cards into three piles and restack them together. Flip over the top card and take note of what it is and the symbolism associated with it. Write this down and pay attention to the events throughout the day. Before bed, take a moment to return to the card you pulled and try to correlate the events of the day with the images in the card. See how these events manifested. By doing this, you learn to build a relationship with your cards by using your intuition and practical nature to interpret messages and symbols through natural events. This will take a little bit of time to develop, but once you do, you can start to draw on these experiences for future readings.

Three-Card Spread

Three-card spreads are great beginner spreads or for when you want to understand a well-rounded approach to a specific situation. In my experience, this spread works well with a specific question rather than as a general reading.

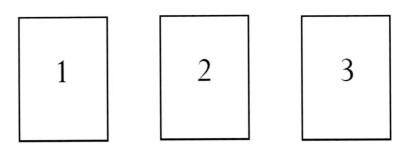

1. **Past**—The first card of the spread indicates past influences. This can show events that have happened in the past or the initial blockages that have led to the present. This card shows the reader what lessons have been—or need to be—learned from.

2. **Present**—The second card of the spread shows the energies that are abundant at this time. It is important to note that, in some instances, this card may not initially represent your current moment, but the overarching themes you are currently experiencing in your life.

3. **Future**—The last card showcases what the overall outcome of the situation is. It dictates what the future holds if the person continues on their current path.

Celtic Cross Spread

The Celtic Cross spread is one of the most common used by readers and is believed to have been invented by Arthur Edward Waite. This is a great spread to use when doing a generic reading to see what the universe wants to know and understand on your path at this time. Depending on the reader or personal preference, there may be some variation on what each position means. Most notably, I have found that many readers will reverse cards five and six. Here is the outline of the spread, as I use it:

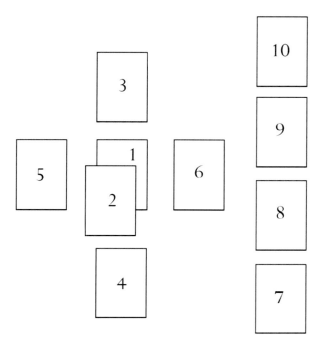

1. **Querent**—The first card represents whoever the reading is for.

2. **Cross Card**—The second card illustrates the reason for the current situation. This may be seen as an obstacle that crosses the querent at the time of the reading.

3. **Known Influences**—The third card shows the conscious influences that surround the situation.

4. **Unknown Influences**—The fourth card details the subconscious elements of the situation, often representing an element that is unknown to the person being read.

5. **Past Influences**—The fifth card showcases the past influences or events that influence the current situation.

6. **Near Future**—The sixth card illustrates the near-future outcome of the situation at hand.

7. **Your Thoughts**—The seventh card represents the person's feelings surrounding the situation or events in their life.

8. **Others' Thoughts**—The eighth card details how others are influencing or view the person having the reading at this time.

9. **Hopes or Fears**—Depending on the energy of the card drawn, the ninth position shows the person's hopes or fears that relate to their situation.

10. **Overall Outcome**—The last card reveals the overall outcome or message that the individual should reflect upon. Sometimes, there may be a stark difference between six and ten—where the sixth card shows one particular theme from the future—and that is ok.

The Lilithian Pentacle Spread

In this spread, you will arrange the cards in the shape of a pentagram, with the first card representing your current state in the center. Use the corresponding diagram to arrange the cards. Here is what each position means:

1. **You**—The first card you draw will represent you in your current state. This is the root cause and situation that must be tended to.

2. **Own**—The second card is connected to your shadow self and what you need to own. What elements are you running from or trying to suppress in the matter?

3. **Flaunt**—This third card signifies what you need to showcase to others. It can indicate the strengths that you bring to the table and need to call upon.

4. **Indulge**—The fourth card illustrates what you need to take pleasure in.

5. **Defend**—This fifth card shows what line of defense needs to be taken. Should you fight or fly? How should you handle the obstacles presented to you at this time?

6. **See**—This final card shows you the sign(s) you need to pay attention to now. Pay very close attention to any of the symbolism portrayed by this card and watch for these signs in your practical life.

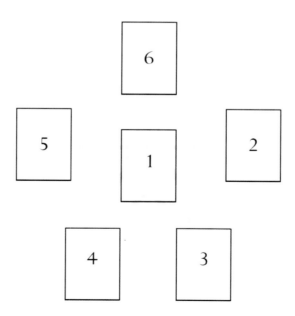

Reversals

When you lay out your cards, some of them may appear upside down and considered reversals. Reading reversals can come off as daunting to many new readers who get freaked out that, on top of learning the meanings of seventy-eight cards, they must learn double that. Many readers, amateurs and experts alike, do not work with reversals. Again, this is personal preference. In some instances, if you are doing multiple readings for a person, reversals can be beneficial in exploring themes in a more specific way. As you gain exposure and experience with your cards, you will be able to gauge whether you want, or should read, the reversed cards this way.

A Reflection on Signs from Lilith

In my introduction, I provided a snapshot of the synchronicities through which Lilith called out to me. While ignoring the signs and holding her at bay, I would routinely find myself coming across a variation of her name. This aside, there was one other time that Lilith practically screamed at me and I ignored the signs. In my mid-20s, I was in a toxic two-and-a-half year relationship with someone 25 years older than me. There was a lot of mental manipulation and shady behavior, which I endured and ignored while putting up with my own unique, dominating Adam.

During the course of the relationship, I had completely suspended my practices as a witch while I tried to be a domestic houseboy, subordinate and quiet. I kept it hidden, in the beginning, out of fear. My devotions to Lilith died out too. Near the end of the relationship, it was clear to me that Lilith was fed up. One day I came home to find my first terracotta Lilith statue, which I had had since I was a teen, in a pile of crumbs on the floor. I had put her out on a shelf, and it was as if she leapt off of it herself. No fur babies could have tampered with it, and no one was in my home. The shelf was still completely intact as well, but she was on the floor.

Several weeks later, my other Lilith statue, a gold-gilded replica of John Collier's painting of her, made its way to the floor as well. Once, perhaps a coincidence; twice, in that short span? Well, I call that a sign. It was shortly after the second fallen piece that I had realized it was time to go and courageously ended the relationship. And in an instant, after I pulled the plug, I had felt a sense of empowerment and freedom.

I share this story to illustrate the importance of intuition and signs. The entire course of my relation-ship featured me having a nagging pit inside that things were not as they seemed. I had many intuitive feelings to head for the hills, but I ignored them; I ignored them so much that Lilith had to literally throw herself in front of me—twice—for me to really get the picture. So, trust your instincts and the signs that you see around you.

Visioncrafting: *A Lilithian Psychic Sight Ritual*

After exploring several divination techniques and finding your preferred method, you can create ritual practices around them. In most cases, a simple cleansing of the space is all that is needed for divination activities. Though, a full blown ritual can be extraordinarily rewarding. The following ceremony involves the use of divination in a Lilithian ritual setting, calling on her great wisdom for assistance in your divine dealings. This ritual should be performed on the night of the full or dark moon, as these phases magnify the lunar energies connecting to our intuition.

Materials Needed
- ✸ Your preferred divination tool(s)
- ✸ 6 silver candles
- ✸ Knife for carving
- ✸ 1 tsp. wormwood
- ✸ Oracle oil (See page 274)

Optional: Lavender tea or absinthe

When working this ritual, I will often utilize my tarot cards and ask for guidance in whatever situation I am involved in. If using cards, you may also decide to use the Lilithian Pentacle spread, as it is designed to align with GLAM. Scrying is another great practice to use for these rituals.

Create a circle around your altar space with five silver candles. Create a sacred space in whatever manner you wish. Call upon Lilith and invoke her into your space. With your remaining candle, carve the word "vision" on the candle and seal it with your essence. In a mortar, grind your wormwood into a fine powder. Anoint the candle with the five drops of your oracle oil and roll in the crushed wormwood. Light the candle and recite the following:

Lilith, great guardian of the tree,
I seek your knowledge and divinity,
Queen of Heaven, Mistress of Hell.
Show me meaning and how to tell.
I call upon your essence and power,
To illuminate my mind upon this dark hour.
In between time, in between space,
I welcome your knowledge, dark beauty, and grace.

Take several deep breaths. Have a sip of your libation and relax further into the space. Focus your attention to your third eye and begin to engage in your divination practice. While you do this, pay attention to your clair(s) and how messages come to you. Do you see things within the gazing surface or cards? Do you hear a whisper in your ear? Do you feel any changes in your physical body that help point you in the right direction? Do you smell an odor or experience a taste? I have found that in rituals for Lilith, I can gauge her presence with a sweet but pungent aroma that smells like rotten earth and florals—the essence of life and death, ancient and beautiful. Observe your results and make note of them—anything that you experience or that comes up during the ritual. If you are reading tarot, make note of which cards and positions they appear.

Once your ritual is complete, extinguish your divination candle. You may use this for any additional divination rituals that you use in the future. Head to bed and top the evening off with the Lilithian dream sachet from earlier in the chapter, to further draw upon Lilith's psychic sight in your sleep.

Signs are Everywhere

While continuing your magical journey, it is important to remain in tune with the signs and synchronicities that expose themselves to you. Often, these are not solely seen in ritual settings or even divination practices. Instead, they are found around us at all times. The following are universal signs to pay attention to:

1. **11:11**—If you happen to notice the time on a digit clock aligning so that all numbers duplicate, it is considered one of many "signs" associated with spiritual ascension. 11:11 in particular is a magical sign from the universe to pay attention to your surroundings.

2. **Empathy**—Empathy can sometimes be considered an additional clair, the art of clear emotional feeling. This is not the same as everyday situational empathy. It is the ability to pick up on and read other's emotions by experiencing them yourself. This specific ability is generally easier to establish with those who you have a close bond to, such as friends, family members, or romantic partners; however, it is not uncommon for these feelings to grow as your abilities enhance. You may be in a very jolly mood, but when you connect with someone's vibration, you intuitively pick up that something is wrong.

Like the other clairs, this is an ability that we all have within us. As you grow in your magical practices, it will strengthen. Pay attention to this as a sign of further awakening.

3. **Déjà vu**—Déjà vu is the sensation that you have already experienced a situation that is currently occurring. This can be peculiar and uncomfortable, and even frustrating, as you try to determine what prompted the feeling. These can be extraordinary moments of past-life recall, or also a trigger from the universe or your spirit guides that you are on the right path. Regardless, experiencing frequent bouts of déjà vu can be seen as a sign that you are awakening on a level of higher consciousness.

7

SECRETIVE SHADOWCRAFT:

Owning it with Shadow Magic & the Astrological Application of Lilith

"How can I be substantial if I fail to cast a shadow?
I must have a dark side also if I am to be whole."
—Carl Jung, *Modern Man in Search of a Soul*

Darkness is a natural part of life. Not only is it an essential part of our day, but when we close our eyes, it envelopes us in a black abyss. Though it is natural, darkness can be scary. As a survival instinct, we are naturally afraid of the dangers that lurk from the unseen. Personally, I was petrified of the dark growing up! I was reliant upon the protection of a night light to feel safe and fall asleep. As I grew older, my fear of visible darkness decreased while fear of emotional darkness crept in. Fear, depression, sadness, and insecurities that were caused by emotional wounds perpetuated rage, anger, and resentment within me. And from this, my shadow was born.

Just as the physical world produces darkness, our emotional world does too. This is represented as our shadow self, a psychological theme popularized by the work of Carl Jung. In *The Portable Jung,* he explains, "The shadow is a moral problem that challenges the whole ego-personality, for no one can become conscious of the shadow without considerable moral effort. To become conscious of it involves recognizing the dark aspects of the personality as present and real. This act is the essential condition for any kind of self-knowledge, and it therefore, as a rule, meets with the considerable resistance."

Essentially, this shadow is composed of parts of our unconscious mind that our conscious ego rejects. In our development into adulthood, we have learned that many actions are considered acceptable. Meanwhile, those we learned as unacceptable gave birth to our shadow. As a result, the shadow becomes the embodiment of our negative personality traits accumulated throughout our lives, magnifying the qualities that society deems undesirable. In some instances, these traits are instinctual behaviors that we have come to identify with negative consequences.

The shadow self is psychological in nature but is utilized in magical practices to establish harmony between inner light and the dark half of our personal gnosis. The goal of shadow work is not to release or let go of the reasons that have rooted themselves in our unconscious mind. Shadow work for the GLAM Witch is utilized by demystifying our inner wounds, rage, and the reintegration of their released energy into society with a Lilithian-based approach.

We all have inner wounds that we have collected over time. Sometimes, in an attempt to heal these, we just suppress them. We live in an age in which we are told to let go and be happy with the positive allocations of life. So many individuals believe the key to spiritual enlightenment rests on the establishment of a "love and light" philosophy. But light can be extremely damaging. Unconditional positivity may promote happy and carefree feelings, but it can also be delusional and unhelpful to problem solving and growth. Metaphysically, this excess light can become the equivalent of a spiritual cancer. It can blind us from the lessons, truths, and experiences that are needed for elevation and growth. It can stunt us from becoming our most authentic selves.

If we look at spiritual darkness in a more positive way, we see that it is a catalyst for healing, thus evoking the soothing elemental energies of water. Water is the flowing current that makes up sixty percent of our bodies, and it is the representation of our emotional unconsciousness, which brings us back to Lilith. In *Mysteries of the Dark Moon*, Demetra George suggests that in the wake of Lilith's sadness from exiting Eden "she made love with the water elementals, and many beings arose from this union—namely the sea of the unconscious, from which the feminine aspect of our wisdom arises from the depths of our psyche."

As an element, water is responsible for washing away what no longer serves. It washes and cleanses. It heals. The power of water can be violent and can also cause much destruction. Water can move earth. It can move mountains. The power of water is vastly underestimated. But, just like rainstorms falling from the sky, a tsunami will subside and roll back to its home with the tide, eventually flowing in peace once more. It is this connection to the water that we will strive to achieve with the practices of this chapter.

Before continuing the path of the GLAM Witch, it is important to come face to face with your shadow self. This cannot simply be a look in the mirror and an admission to having some unpleasant qualities; you have to truly know and embrace your shadow in order to achieve balance and harmony. In this GLAM Witch "craft" we will experience this darkness and attempt to heal our shadows by acknowledging them. We will not suppress our fears, hurts, or angers here. We will let our shadowy souls scream like banshees in the dark of night. We will not ask the universe to stop the emotional hurricane from plowing our light lit lands of false bliss. We will recognize and reintegrate the shadow into our lives so that we can be our own star and rely on our inner light to shine bright. But first, we must welcome the dark nights of our soul.

Journal Entry

Before moving forward with shadow work, I want you to make a journal entry to help identify parts of your shadow self. This will serve as a pseudo pre-test for the coming material. In it, answer the following questions.

1. What do you consider to be negative qualities? What qualities do you detest most in others? Which can you associate back to yourself? What aspects of your personal darkness can you own right now?

2. Where are you in your journey? What are the goals you are trying to achieve? Is there anything that you feel is holding you back? If so, what, and how, can this be fueled into productivity?

3. What parts of you need healing? What are you struggling with at the moment, and how are you actively trying to better the situation?

4. Who, or what, are you afraid of and why? Why do you think this fear exists? What caused the initial traumatization?

5. What are your attitudes toward your sexuality? Do you explore your sexuality in healthy ways? Do you use sex as a manipulation mechanism?

6. Do you get mad? How do you experience anger? How do you express your rage? If you don't, why not? What are the consequences of both?

7. What is your relationship to material objects? Do you prefer quality or quantity? In what ways are you possessive of people or other items?

8. How do you view success? Do you require validation? How do you react to losing or to rejection?

9. What are your addictions? What do you enjoy about them? What positives have they brought to your life? What negatives? Do they bring release, or are you attempting to escape from a situation?

10. In what ways are you critical? Are you close-minded in any way? What could you be more open with?

While answering these questions, it is really important to be honest with yourself. This is not something that you will be sharing with others or plastering on your social media pages. This exercise is meant to be a deeply personal one. It is designed to help you begin to recognize the parts of your shadow self on a conscious level. Try to make your responses well thought out and specific. A general "yes" or "no" is not the goal. This is a reflection on your self—your dark self. Be true to yourself and tap into the corresponding Lilithian law of *own it*!

The Astrological Dark Side

Some say that our lives are written in the stars and that the interlacing cosmology of astrology dictates our destiny. For this reason, many of us engage in, and have fun with, astrology. Whether this involves long coffee chats with friends, is used as an outdated pick-up line, showcased on your body as a tattoo, or simply through reading your weekly horoscope from your favorite #insta-witches, the vast majority of us partake in some form of astrological curiosity. Witches will often utilize astrological phenomena as energetic sources to tap into for spells and rituals.

Astrology relates to the influence of various constellations, planets, asteroids, and other space forces on our lives. The zodiac sign is the most common form of astrology that people are familiar with and is also called a sun sign. While much influence is placed on this particular sign, there are many more astrological influences aside from this one. Your sun sign just happens to be the position of the sun, in accordance to a specific constellation of the zodiac, at the time of your birth. The characteristics of your sun sign are known to showcase traits in accordance to your identity in this life, understandably making it the most popular one used in pop culture. But, at the same moment of your birth, different planets and astrological objects were also positioned in other realms of the zodiac wheel, further shaping your identity in more detail. For instance, we also have a moon sign that rules our emotions, a Mercury sign that governs our communication skills, a Mars sign that denotes our aggression and passion, and a Venus sign that dictates our style of love. But this only begins to scratch the surface of our star signs!

All of your positions can be determined through a graph known as your natal chart. This chart acts as a snapshot of all the placements that occurred at the moment of your birth. Your natal chart is a spiritual blueprint that has been handed to us by the stars. In looking at astrological influences, one can achieve growth and development. It can illustrate our strengths and weaknesses and provide insight into the shifting energies that relate to the makeup of our cosmic connection. But what does this have to do with our shadow, and with Lilith for that matter? Well, the lovely Ms. Lilith happens to govern three (yes, three!) astrological bodies that all correspond to our shadow self.

The Lilithian Shadow Trinity

In Lilith's role as the outcast and rejected feminine, she is often portrayed as the shadowy personification of our dark unconsciousness. She represents the wild part of us that wants to be free but that has retreated into a phantom wilderness. As a result, Lilith has been named as the shadow side of astrology. It is here that she represents the darker manifestations of whatever sign and house she occupies in your natal chart. Because of this, and because witches will use astrological energy in their magical workings, Lilith lends herself perfectly to the practice of shadowcraft.

Within astrology, Lilith governs three astrological entities—Asteroid Lilith, Dark Moon Lilith, and Black Moon Lilith—each of which has different associations to our shadow selves. Based on the astrological positions in which the Lilith signs take root, we can begin to understand our shadowy natures that may not be known to us; therefore, understanding and working with her astrological influence is a major attribute of GLAM.

With Lilithian shadowcraft, we work to bring Lilith out from the shadows to which she has fled. This is done by examining our personal shadow selves in relation to our Lilith(s) and embracing our inner shadow Lilith(s). The shadow wreaks havoc when suppressed, ignored, and denied. It causes insecurities, addictions, and resentment. This becomes rage and signifies Lilith's vengeance. Through providing it the appropriate recognition, we can integrate it with our light halves to create compassion, authenticity, and equilibrium.

Many astrologers suggest that her representation in these positions illustrates our dark sexual natures and places significant emphasis on this; however, there is much more to the meaning of these signs than sex. Sexuality has its place in the shadow but is not the major influence here. Additionally, it is routinely thought that the purpose of working with Lilith's astrological influences is to tame that wildness in yourself. But I disagree. Taming Lilith goes against her very nature. It will never happen. Instead, I have used Lilith's positions in my natal chart to help me better understand my shadow qualities and push them into the light, to find productive ways of working with my own darkness in constructive and witchy ways.

The Triple Goddess

A popular image in modern goddess worship is the Triple Goddess. This application divides the Goddess into three parts that associate with the feminine lifecycle of maiden, mother, and crone. The maiden represents the young feminine force. The mother signifies the fertile and ripe creatrix at peak power. The crone is the bold and upfront grandmother who has lived her life and, in its wane, has no tolerance or patience. She can be kind and soothing, or harsh and tyrannical.

While Lilith often gets cast in the light of the crone for her harsh, unpredictable nature, she is prominent in all symbolism of the Triple Goddess, and each association can become a correspondent in her astrological roles.

⊛ *Asteroid Lilith*—Asteroid 1181 is the first astrological position that was named Lilith. This form represents a physical piece of rock that floats among other asteroids in a space between Mars and Jupiter. An interesting theory is that these asteroids were all once part of a larger planet that existed in this space. This has been theorized based on the distance between the sun and Mercury, Mercury and Venus, Venus and Earth, and Earth and Mars.

The image used for the Asteroid Lilith glyph makes the shape of your left hand or right palm when turned toward you. This echoes the connection of Lilith being the "hand" of Inanna in Sumerian legend. Being that Asteroid Lilith is the first of the positions named after her, she takes on this representation as the maiden aspect of the Triple Goddess. Asteroid Lilith manifests as the original source of pain in our lives. It is here that Lilith represents our wound. She is rejection and how we deal with this rejected element of ourselves. This will represent how you feel suppressed in your life, or perhaps even how you suppress others.

⊛ *Dark Moon Lilith*—Dark Moon Lilith is represented by an elusive second moon that is said to orbit Earth. This body does not reflect light, and thus cannot be seen by the naked eye. Its glyph is drawn as a circle with a forward slash going through it to illustrate the absence of light from this moon. It is a highly controversial subject, just like Lilith, and many question its existence; however, there have been records of this phantom moon since the 1600s, later recorded by astronomer Georg Waltemath (also known as Waldemath by astrologers) in 1898.

This was later confirmed by 19th century astrologer Dr. Walter Gorn Old, who went by the pen name Sepharial and used Waltemath's initial calculations to pinpoint the moon's location. In this moon, Lilith is rage and the mother aspect of the Triple Goddess. It is this that shows how we deal with the wound from the asteroid.

✸ *Black Moon Lilith*—Black Moon Lilith, often referred to as BML, is the most common of the Liliths used in astrological readings and represents a lunar apogee of the moon's orbit. Its glyph is represented by a waning crescent moon atop an equal-armed cross it is the symbol I incorporate into my Lilithian sigil from Chapter 4. Many people use this position to represent the main detail of their shadow persona; however, one gains further insight into their dark habits when used in connection with the other Lilith signs. In doing this, Black Moon Lilith represents the dark part of our authentic self after it has gone through the motions of Lilith's wound and rage. This point reflects on the re-entry of Lilith's shadow into the world and how it evolves over time and is representative of the crone.

GLAM Hexercise: *Finding Your Liliths*

In this *hexercise,* I want you to locate your Lilith signs by obtaining your natal chart. For this, you will need an internet connection, your birthdate, time, and location. Understandably, there are some instances in which you may not have access to your birth time or record. For this, you can get away without knowing your time; and if you are unable to locate your birth place, use the town you grew up in. The calculations might differ slightly but should not have a huge impact, at least in regard to the Lilith signs.

True vs. Mean BML

Like her stories denote, the oscillating void of Lilith
is unpredictable and always moving like the wild
force she is! As a result, two mathematical equa-
tions are used to determine her position, resulting in
true vs. mean Lilith. Mean, not in a terrifying way,
though some do and will consider Lilith terrifying;
rather, mean Lilith refers to an average calculation
of where she may have been located at the time of
your birth. The true Lilith is an extended calculation
that pinpoints her exact location. The problem with
reading a mean Lilith is that she may have really
been in a completely different sign and house,
making your interpretation of her false. Most sites
providing Lilith signs will use the mean, but we will
not do so here due to its inaccuracy and attempt to
confine her!

1. Go to www.astro.com.

2. Scroll down to find the section on the homepage for "Extended
Chart Selection."

3. The next page will ask if you want to continue as a guest or
registered user. You can select guest user if you'd prefer not to
create a user profile.

4. Fill out the birth data entry page. If your birthtime is unknown, you must select "Unknown" instead of the preselected group of question marks.

5. On the next screen, select "Additional Objects" and find Lilith in the dropdown menu. In the Manual Entry box, type in "1181" for the Asteroid Lilith, "H58" for Dark Moon Lilith, and "H13" to calculate True Lilith's position. Make sure to separate these with commas. Continue to the next page.

6. Your natal chart will then be displayed. You will notice that, at the bottom of the chart, there is a key. The key will contain three "Liliths" and "Waldemath." You will be paying attention to the "1181 Lilith," "Waldemath," and "Lilith (O)." The very top Lilith that is represented with her crescent moon and cross glyph represents the "mean" Black Moon Lilith sign, which we will not be paying attention to. You can use this to see the difference between it and the "Lilith (O)" for Oscillating Lilith, also known as "true" Lilith. Sadly, the key does not match up correctly to the actual chart. Your "1181 Lilith" is representative of Asteroid Lilith and shows on the chart as "Lilit." "Waldemath" represents your Dark Moon Lilith and has been abbreviated as "Walde" on the chart.

Lilith through the Signs

After determining what your Lilith signs are, you can use this next section to gain further insight into their meaning and in what ways Lilith influences your unconscious shadow. Astrology can be as simple or as complex as you wish to make it. The more you study and expose yourself to it and the various nodes, points, planets, stars, constellations, etc., the more you can better gauge your spiritual blueprint. Likewise, the amount of exploration one can do with the Lilith signs is just as vast.

Much analysis has been done on each of these signs, and this section will serve as a small overview on how I connect Lilith's shadow to each of them. It is through this that I will provide you with an introduction to working with these signs. Further recommended reading will be listed at the end of this part for those who become caught in the web of darkness weaved by Lilithian astrology. Remember what role each of the Lilith signs play (wound, rage, release) and try to apply their individual affiliations to the overview of their corresponding sign; for example, if your Asteroid Lilith is in Aries, the overview on Lilith in Aries will represent your shadow wound. Then, if your Dark Moon Lilith is in Cancer, read the overview on Cancer to determine how the Asteroid Lilith in Aries wound manifests into the rage from this next Lilith sign. And so on and so forth.

Some may feel a connection to the information right away, while others may struggle. If what you are reading resonates with you, it indicates that you have a fairly decent relationship with your unconscious shadow already. If you do not connect, try to remain objective and be honest with yourself. Remember that no one is looking over your shoulder or judging you on this. Ask yourself what aspects of this information correlate with you and write them down in your journal.

I also want to stress that, although our shadow is traditionally seen as negative, there is a positive side to each of these representations as well. There is a unique gift from Lilith in each, and through identifying this gift and using it wisely, one can successfully assimilate the shadow in productive ways, such as by channeling it into acts of service.

✪ **Sign:** Aries
Shadow Persona: The Violent Child
Keywords: Aggression, Competition, Immaturity, Temper, Violence

Overview: Aries are headstrong and fiery. They are the representation of the spark of fire. When Lilith manifests in Aries, she brings out feelings of unpredictability, stubbornness, destructive rampages, and childishness. The ambition and drive of Aries magnifies in this Lilith placement, as she kicks the ruling planet of Mars into overdrive and runs wild with dominating masculine energy.

In this position, Lilith rules on top, and those who challenge her ability to be there meet a blistering fit of rage. Aries is the youngest zodiac sign, and those who have Lilith in this position will resort to childish temper tantrums when they do not get their way. With this placement, there is a surge of ambition and drive. These individuals want to be the conqueror, and they become addicted to personal success, leading to arrogance and anger when challenged. Also, they will habitually engage in internal competitive battles with others.

Cause: The shadow tendencies of this sign manifest through lack of self-esteem. In attempting to define themselves by the merit of others, they lose a sense of who they are and struggle with personal power. As a result, there is an anger in them for others and for the world. This often results in them relishing in their independence; however, this independence is toxic because it is self-destructive and confining. True independence comes from freedom and emotional liberation.

Strength: Like a child, Aries has an abundance of personal energy. It is here that Lilith can run free and express herself through Aries' exuberance.

Integration/Lesson: If one of your Lilith signs is in Aries, look into your need to win. You need to be cognizant of your actions with others. Ask yourself why this is important to you and what you can learn from letting it go. Instead of comparing what you do not have with others, focus more on what you have in common and build that compassion. Instead of trying to win by impressing others with your achievements, try to win them over with your personality. Let your authenticity be the fuel to your inner fire and challenge yourself to balance competition with compassion.

Additionally, physical activity is a wonderful way to engage the competitive and aggressive traits of the Lilith in Aries shadow. This does not mean you have to join your local soccer or volleyball team, but perhaps consider getting involved in group fitness classes or even taking up hiking, running, or another form of physical activity. These are all excellent ways to acknowledge and feed the dark aspect of the shadow Lilith in Aries.

✵ **Sign:** Taurus
Shadow Persona: The Materialistic One
Keywords: Greedy, Jealous, Lazy, Possessive, Stubborn
Overview: When Lilith falls into the zodiac sign of Taurus, the person will often carry a materialistic and possessive attitude. It is through their possessions that they feel a sense of security; however, it is a false security that they cling to. Quantity is appreciated over quality in Lilith in Taurus. There is an overwhelming greed that manifests in the shadow of this person. Anything from people to food and ideas become considered "yours," and you do not dare to share. This also makes those in this sign prone to jealousy.

Due to their materialistic nature, those in this sign may also fall victim to gambling or other methods to gain more. The greed that manifests here is not rooted in wealth and money, but these are seen as catalysts to the gluttonous habits of the Taurean Lilith. Taurus is also known for being lazy, as a result of their ruling planet Venus, which dominates pleasure and luxury. Lilith gets comfy here and only aids in Taurus' stubbornness.

Strength: The flipside to the Lilith in Taurus' resistance to change is loyalty. Those with this placement have an innate faithfulness, making them reliable sources who thrive in routine. This refusal to change can stand true to Lilith's inability to conform to the patriarchy.

Cause: The root cause of the Lilith in Taurus' shadow is insecurity. The fixation to "things" acts as a security blanket to those with this Lilith sign, making way for their comfort zone. Anything that deviates from what they have become used to is scary, and it is this fear of the unknown that spirals into their possessive tendencies.

Integration/Lesson: To help integrate the shadow into your life, you must start to assess your fears of change. You must understand your relationship to your possessions. Ask yourself, "how much do I really need?"

Though it will be uncomfortable, you must cut back on that which you are indulging in for comfort and channel that energy into something else. One simple approach to this is to focus more on gratitude. This will assist in shifting the materialism into more healthy indulgences. Being thankful for the "things" in your life is a great way to counter the greed associated with them. It is here that you also learn to balance selfishness with selflessness and giving rather than taking. Instead of looking for more, give back. Perhaps offer up some of the "things" in your life to others in need as an act of service.

✵ **Sign:** Gemini
Shadow Persona: The Chatty Con-Artist
Keywords: Gossip, Lies, Manipulation, Rejection, Superficial
Overview: As the zodiac ruler of communication and thought, a Gemini Lilith makes for mental manipulation. A person with Lilith in this placement is going to have a knack for seducing through communication. They are going to know how to manipulate a situation with their communication style. Like the twins that represent Gemini, Lilith will try to mirror other's wants and desires. Their words are very powerful as a reflection of the other's communication style. They watch and study

their prey and use their intellect to give others the perception of what they are after. In this position, Lilith becomes the expert salesperson of a used car dealership. These individuals are also prone to spreading gossip and lies in an attempt to make them more interesting and liked by others. They can also stretch the truth and exaggerate things to make them seem more interesting.

Strength: The greatest strength of Gemini lies in their communication abilities. This sign provides Lilith with the voice she lost with the rising patriarchy.

Cause: The shadow of the Gemini Liliths lies in an overwhelming fear of rejection. The lies and manipulation spread by them come from an attempt to control how others perceive them. They offer half-truths and fabrications in the hope of acceptance. They want to be liked, adored, approached; they want to feel validated, and so they use a con-artist approach to tell people what they want to hear.

Integration/Lesson: People in these signs must evaluate the reasons for their actions and become self-sufficient. The driving force behind your actions needs to be for you, not others or their approval. It is important that individuals with this position learn to charm with authenticity rather than a phony form of illusion. When interacting with others, try offsetting speaking for listening. By doing this, you will stop saying what you think others want to hear and pay more attention to what they are telling you.

⊛ **Sign:** Cancer

Shadow Persona: The Abandoned Soul

Keywords: Clingy, Cold, Dependent, Detached, Hypersensitive

Overview: A Lilithian Cancer is one that is sensitive, cold, emotionally withdrawn, and sometimes clingy. Cancer governs relationships with family and when Lilith falls here, the individuals are likely to experience toxic family relationships. There is often an underlying struggle of affection and attention within family dynamics, either as a child or later in life as a parent. In relationships, a Lilith in Cancer is likely to be starved for love from friends, family, and lovers. As a result, they build up walls, hiding in their cold crab shells and withholding affection from themselves. The struggles from early home life are so intense that this sign tends to fall into the trap of becoming what they have loathed the most, mirroring back the lack of love and affection they received, thereby becoming a self-fulfilling prophecy.

Cause: The shadow manifested through Lilith in Cancer stems from early feelings of abandonment as a child. This subsequently leads to them having a very dependent outlook on life. They constantly need the help of others and emit a helpless demeanor toward them. In the event they are not able to get the aid in which they need, they yield a reclusive and cold emotional persona that further drives others away.

Strength: The detached personality of Lilith in Cancer individuals works to their favor when it comes to creating boundaries. When harnessed appropriately, the shadow persona of these individuals can be used to create independence that can help ensure relationships are built through mutual support and care.

Integration/Lesson: The lesson of the Lilith in Cancer shadow is to forge independence. Instead of relying on someone else to do something for you, make better attempts at doing it yourself. Learn to be your own rock and reliant upon your will and determination rather than others. Become your own support system and challenge yourself.

⊛ **Sign:** Leo
Shadow Persona: The Narcissist
Keywords: Arrogant, Conceited, Egocentric, Pretentious, Self-Centered
Overview: Leo likes to be the ruler of the jungle, and a Lilith in Leo is going to magnify the sign's dominating arrogant qualities. Lilith in Leo is extremely narcissistic. It is here that Lilith

faces a challenging role of playing the sun while being a moon
entity. She is aggressive in her desire to take hold of the stage.
As a moon entity, Lilith is comfortable in the shadows of night,
but when Lilith enters the sign ruled by the sun, she wants to be
seen! She becomes addicted to attention. As a result, these
people are known to have extreme mental breakdowns when
they do not receive stardom. Sadly, to help mitigate the situation, those in this sign often enter into taboo situations where
their scandalous lifestyles help gain an audience.

Cause: The birth of the shadow in Lilith in Leo comes from
their relationship to validation. Their definition of self-worth is
tied with an award-winning mentality. These individuals have
serious struggles with the ego and self-esteem. They are prone
to depression from their narcissistic tendencies.

Strength: Lilith in Leo is egocentric but, when harnessed
properly, manifests a strength of passion. The exuberance of
enthusiasm and zest within not only charm them but give them
an elasticity of determination.

Integration/Lesson: Leo Liliths need to determine the root
cause of their need for attention and find a creative outlet to let
it shine. A major lesson for those in this sign is to focus less on
themselves and more on others. To assist in helping to use the
energy of this shadow force in a constructive fashion, I would
recommend that they seek out positions in which they can
teach and mentor others as a selfless act of service. If one of
your Liliths manifests here, try turning one of your hobbies or
other interests into something that you can engage in with others to the point where attention is created through authority.

✪ **Sign:** Virgo
Shadow Persona: The Masochist
Keywords: Critical, Judgmental, Overanalytical, Obsessive,
Perfection
Overview: A Lilith in Virgo is a tough combination to have.
Virgos in general are very analytical, and when Lilith shows up
in this placement, she pushes this perfectionist nature into ex-

treme judgment and often self-sabotage. The Lilith and Virgo relationship is one of the masochist. It takes Virgo's prudent nature with Lilith's "I don't give a fuck" attitude and creates an internal battle within the person's life. A Virgo Lilith is someone who will notoriously be putting themselves down, obsessively caring about what others think of them, resulting in acts of self-punishment.

Cause: The root of the shadow personification in Virgo Liliths is perfection. A Virgo Lilith has an overwhelming fear of failure. This is not the kind of failure that is associated with winning but rather an unhealthy obsession with how to be perfect. Their judgmental qualities are a reflection of their own fears and may result in them spiraling into self-loathing.

Strength: Virgo's perfectionist qualities help Lilith excel in detail. Knowledge is power, and it is within these details that Lilith gains her wisdom.

Integration/Lesson: Lilith in Virgo benefits from looking at failures as life lessons. They need to look at them as constructive instead of taking them to a destructive place. It is through failure that we grow and learn; it is through failure that we evolve. There is beauty in imperfection, and it is here that genuineness shines. Often those with this placement do well at finding employment opportunities as analysts, consultants, or editors whose job it is to fix things. By doing this, you utilize the judgmental perfectionist nature of your shadow in a way that does not promote affliction to self.

⊛ **Sign:** Libra
Shadow Persona: An Unbalanced Beauty
Keywords: Contradiction, Equality, Justice, Petty, Vain
Overview: With Venus as the ruling Libra planet, there is an emphasis on beauty, harmony, and partnership in this sign. Since Libra is the sign of balance, Lilithian Libras are likely to experience inequality in their lives. This could be through partnerships (romantic and platonic), work-life balance, health, and any other areas that weigh polarity. An internal dichotomy is

often created within these people that expresses itself with two-faced tendencies. With Libra trying to cling to the harmonious quality of Venus, Lilith in this position infects the sign with passive-aggressive tendencies, creating a petty mess express. She also manifests through superficial glamour and a deep-rooted fascination with beauty. Where Lilith in Leo is narcissistic, being obsessed with their personality and role, Lilith in Libra is vain, homing in on their fixation for their physical beauty. Those with this placement will often use their charm to their advantage. Additionally, if the Libra symbol is the scales, the Libra in Lilith's symbol is the drama masks, as they have an innate ability to find drama in any situation and thrive in it.

Cause: The underlying cause of the shadow manifestation of Libra Liliths is related to equality. Libra represents the scales of justice, and in a perfect world, these will be set at equal weights; however, it is when one scale begins to weigh more that the shadow takes over and unleashes itself within these people.

Strength: Lilith in Libra's greatest strength is their flexibility and understanding of duality. These individuals are able to take on many tasks and assume many positions, much like Lilith does in her many roles.

Integration/Lesson: The best approach for integrating the Libra Lilith shadow is to establish boundaries with yourself, your ideas, and your situations. These boundaries also represent proper time management that allows you to spread yourself evenly without going too thin. Self-care is an important element for everyone but even more so in this pairing. Instead of looking for outside partnership, find partnership within yourself and by exuding Lilith's self-love. Additionally, those with this Lilith placement in Libra do well in creating a partnership with their artistic expression, exploiting their Venusian love of beauty and arts, converting them into creative undertakings.

✪ **Sign:** Scorpio
Shadow Persona: The Grieving Villain

Keywords: Dominant, Jealous, Malicious, Secretive, Vengeful
Overview: A Lilith in Scorpio shadow is a very powerful and potent source of Lilithian energy. Due to this sign's natural dark and seductive nature, Lilith does not have to influence much here; however, she does so anyway, making those with this Lilith placement extremely dominating. In this position, Lilith perpetuates mystery, giving Scorpio a secretive residence to occupy. It is from this, though, that the ambush predator nature of the Scorpio is magnified with malicious venom. People in this position prey on others' weakness and enjoy torturing them through psychological warfare. This is the position in which Lilith becomes a chaotic storm of vengeance.

Cause: The Scorpio Lilith shadow manifests through death. This death is not necessarily literal but can be figurative. Death, loss, and any thought of losing something creates vindictive tendencies in this position. Due to fear of loss, these individuals will routinely build a wall to protect themselves from it, creating an air of mystery to them. Similar to the Lilith in Taurus shadow, the fixation on the idea of loss can also create a possessive nature that makes these individuals jealous as well.

Strength: Lilith in Scorpio's greatest strength is truth. This may be surprising, as they spend their lives cloaked in mystery. As secretive as they are, Scorpio understands truth and can see through a façade much easier than most. It is here that Lilith has a very distinct radar for smelling bullshit.

Integration/Lesson: Engulfing yourself in detective-like abilities is always a plus that provides a healthy expression of the shadow qualities. Instead of looking at weakness and using it against others, use it to help, heal, and inspire. Use this sign's elemental association of water not to crush but to heal.

✪ **Sign:** Sagittarius
Shadow Persona: The Dogmatic Soul
Keywords: Bigoted, Dogmatic, Experience, Lies, Tactless

Overview: Sagittarius is a fiery sign with a passion for philosophy, logic, and travel. They are rootless individuals, and it is here that a Lilith in Sagittarius becomes a rolling tumbleweed of fire. Governing philosophy, the shadow of the Sagittarius can become one who is bigoted and uninterested in other's views. Like the arrow associated with this sign, it's path is straight and narrow, leaving little wiggle room. It is here that one becomes so set in their ways that they believe they are the one true and only way to be, thus fighting anything that challenges their beliefs.

Cause: The root cause of this shadow aspect of the Lilith in Sagittarius individual comes from their perception of truth. In general, Sagittarians are always in search of the truth, the answers of life. But with this shadow, they lose focus on their search and focus only on what they know.

Strength: Ruled by the power of philosophy, Sagittarius' keen intellect is their greatest strength. When applied to Lilith's mentality, it opens the doors to deeper and faster understanding of esoteric philosophy.

Integration/Lesson: Discover your own personal truths and the meaning behind them. Seek and speak the meaning behind your joys and happiness. Instead of flaunting your own personal agenda, try to determine why they are meaningful and how your way can resonate with others. By understanding this, you have a better opportunity to spread your ideas with others without coming across as pushy. This sign benefits from exploring other ideas and philosophies to expand on their truths.

⊛ **Sign:** Capricorn
Shadow Persona: The Tyrant
Keywords: Authoritative, Cut-throat, Controlling, Dictatorial, Ruthless
Overview: Capricorns rule legacy and career, and when Lilith enters this sign, she is ruthless in her pursuits of authority. People with this placement are laser focused on their careers and have a cut-throat drive. Nothing—and no one—is im-

portant to them except their success. They will lie, cheat, and steal to get their way. They have no moral compass when it comes to achieving their dreams. Due to Lilith's sexual nature, it is not unlikely for them to have used their sexuality to climb their way to a place of power. Because Capricorn represents legacy as well, these individuals may find themselves having trouble with public image. As with Leo, Lilith Capricorns have a tendency to showcase the skeletons of their closets publicly, often losing credibility in their ambition.

Cause: The root cause of a Capricorn Lilith shadow comes from a want and need to control. This control is seen as a way to dominate and have power over others. The thirst for power becomes unreal here, as their perception of reality is skewed.

Strength: Capricorns are persistent, and the greatest strength to Lilith in this placement is that these individuals never give up. "Obstacle" is not a word in their vocabulary and any challenge that is presented in front of them is just another adventure.

Integration/Lesson: Your need for control needs to be balanced with grounding yourself. Take extra time to practice your meditations and breathing exercises to help navigate the dark parts of yourself.

✪ **Sign:** Aquarius

Shadow Persona: The Rebel without a Cause

Keywords: Aloof, Erratic, Impulsive, Rebellious, Uncaring

Overview: Aquarians in general are known for their eccentric personalities, and it is here that Lilith kicks up the dust and powers at full speed against the grain. Lilith is a rebel, but in the position of a shadowy Aquarius, she becomes the rebel without a cause. There is flightiness to this position, and those in this position tend to join a fight of righteousness without knowing what they are even fighting for. Aquarians are also known to have a good concept of technology, as they are known to be experimental. It is possible for those in this position to develop unhealthy fixations to technology, including but not limited to games, pornography, chat rooms, and social media wars. They take on the personification of an alien agent of technology versus nature.

Cause: The cause of this is an unhealthy desire to leave their stamp on the world. They crave to be remembered and struggle in their search for what it will be. In bouncing around from place to place, idea to idea, and cause to cause, they are not able to become fully substantial. They are always looking for the next new, bright and shiny, glowing disco ball as if it will lead them to their place of power.

Strength: The quirkiness of the Aquarius nature helps them to attract attention. They are moths to a flame. This shadow's greatest strength is their ability to assemble people for their cause.

Integration/Lesson: Lilith in Aquarius needs to slow down and establish roots in something. They need to learn decisiveness.

Sign: Pisces
Shadow Persona: The Addict
Keywords: Afraid, Dreamy, Escape, Fantasy, Illusions
Overview: Pisces are known for being a very spiritual sign that are deeply in touch with their subconsciousness. They are known for exhibiting dreamy, emotional water energies. Consequently, when Lilith falls in the placement of Pisces, it becomes a challenging and dark realm of escapism. As a result, those with a Lilith in Pisces sign can become reliant upon alcoholism, drug, and sex to mask the pressures and challenges of the world. Trapped in the dependence of illusions, they gravitate toward anything that is euphoric and provides an outlet for fantasy.

Cause: Pisces are prone to victim mentality, and here Lilith challenges that and wants to escape.

Strength: The biggest strength within a Lilith in Pisces is their overflowing imagination.

Integration/Lesson: More than with any of the other shadow positions, Lilith in Pisces benefits most from expressing and developing their artistic abilities. This helps integrate the surrealistic worlds these people want to cling to. Additionally, if you regularly feel you are the victim of situations in your life and put yourself down because of it, channel this energy into something productive, such as helping those who suffer from physical violence. Becoming a mentor or involving yourself in organizations that assist with abuse, you will provide a sense of empowerment within.

Lilith through the Houses

The zodiac wheel is split into twelve equal parts, known as houses. Each house has a corresponding sign that lives in it. For example, Aries is the first sign of the zodiac and lives in the first house. Taurus corresponds with the second, and so on and so forth. Each of the houses contains an energy that is similar to the zodiac sign attributes; however, when it comes to Lilith's house placements, these are the stages in which our Lilith signs sing. They are the platform for her performance and the underlining reason behind their manifestation.

Combine your Lilith houses with the signs we just examined to gain further understanding of your shadow destiny. Review your natal chart and determine what house your Lilith signs are in. From there, review the characteristics of the house below as it represents how the corresponding Lilith sign manifests. For example, if you have an Asteroid Lilith in Capricorn, in the second house, the house will show you in what way that Lilith in Capricorn shadow came to be. Like the Lilith signs, there are many resources available that provide extensive analysis of the Lilith houses. Let's look at what each house represents and further apply this to our signs.

✸ *First House*—The first house is the personification of self. It corresponds to our physical appearance, body, attitudes, and identity. Lilith's position in the first house will represent dangerous beauty and charm.

✸ *Second House*—The second house represents habits, priorities, and work ethics. Lilith in this capacity can be overwhelmingly materialistic with a stubbornness to change.

✸ *Third House*—Lilith in the third house denotes overthinking and struggles with communication and social situations. In this position, Lilith becomes the gossip and had the need to spread other's business in a malicious capacity.

✸ *Fourth House*—The fourth house rules family and home. This house of Lilith is very difficult and traditionally denotes a very unhappy childhood. Lilith in this position will magnify abandonment issues.

✸ *Fifth House*—The fifth house needs to be the center of attention. When it comes to Lilith in this position, she becomes a chaotic seductress, doing anything she can to gain attention.

✸ *Sixth House*—The sixth house represents routines and is often associated with health and daily environments. In this position, Lilith can be lazy and unwilling to get the job done. Individuals in this position may feel as if hierarchy and structure are against them and may rebel against it, making for potential legal altercations.

✸ *Seventh House*—The seventh house represents partnerships and equality. In this position, Lilith struggles with long-term relationships and will often find herself in toxic ones. There is a masochistic enjoyment that comes from this.

✴ *Eighth House*—The eighth house is ruled by sexuality and death. In this position, someone may have extreme fetishes that involve bondage and other masochistic or dominating characteristics. Their darkness lies in pain and enjoying the pain, physically and emotionally, in life.

✴ *Ninth House*—The ninth house embodies travel, philosophy, and culture. A person with this position may take on the archetype of a tyrannical ruler. They force their opinions down the throats of others and are closed off to other points of view. Their focus is solely on what they know and believe to be the one true way.

✴ *Tenth House*—The tenth house is related to legacy, career, and long-term goals. In this capacity, an individual may struggle with public relations and put themselves in positions that will hurt their reputation.

✴ *Eleventh House*—The eleventh house represents friendships and social interactions. This person will experience an abundance of jealousy and may not be able to play nicely with others in the sandbox.

✴ *Twelfth House*—The twelfth house represents our subconscious and our spirituality. This is a rough position to be in, as it is the combination of dark subconscious and unconscious. It is a realm of fears and doubts.

As a whole, astrology can be daunting and quite dense. The more you exposure yourself to it, the more understanding you will have. For further exploration of Lilith through the signs, I highly recommend the book *Lilith: Healing the Wild*, by Tom Jacobs. He does an impeccable job of breaking down each position, house, and conjunction of Lilith and how to further work with your position to heal the wild shadow within.

Journal Entry

Once you have examined and researched the different manifestations of your Lilith signs, return to your original notes. In a new entry, list your three Lilith signs, corresponding houses, and in what ways you feel you relate to them. Dig deep into your personal experiences and write out the ways in which you can associate them to your life thus far.

Shadowcrafting: *A Lilithian Ritual for Shadow Work*

In the beginning of this chapter, I suggested you write your shadow out. This was the first stage of giving it acknowledgment. As we have learned more about it, and the shadowy aspects of our astrological Lilith qualities, we will turn our shadow writing into a shadow rite.

The following is an intense healing ritual that will encompass twelve hours of witchin' and bitchin'! The ritual itself will not take the full twelve hours. You will be doing a variety of other magical activities that build on the ideas from this chapter throughout the time. The ritual should be performed on the night of the dark moon (the night prior to the new moon). Due to the length of time, I recommend starting the spell between 6 and 7 p.m. It is important that you remain undistracted for this spell. Turn off your phone and disconnect from the world around you. If you live with others, try to find a private space where you will encounter minimal disruption for the evening.

Materials Needed

Bath
- ✪ Black bath bomb
- ✪ Sprinkle of lotus petals
- ✪ 1 tumbled rhodochrosite for healing emotional wounds
- ✪ 1 tumbled labradorite for healing transformation
- ✪ 1 tumbled indigo gabbro to integrate dark with light

Optional: black candles; 5 drops lotus and sandalwood oil; lotus incense

Ritual
- ✪ Black mirror
- ✪ 2 black candlesticks
- ✪ Image of Lilith
- ✪ Cauldron or large fireproof pot
- ✪ 5 black votive candles
- ✪ Black biodegradable paper
- ✪ Black pen with non-toxic ink
- ✪ Personal effects (e.g., a strand of hair, nail clippings, or bodily fluids)
- ✪ Journal

Tea
- ✪ 1 tsp. lotus root
- ✪ 1 tsp. lotus petals
- ✪ Tea sachet bag
- ✪ Teapot
- ✪ Filtered water

Begin your dark night of the soul with a meditation. This will help initiate the energetic theme of the evening and center you for the night ahead. Once finished, set up your ritual space. Be creative with it and have fun.

Once darkness falls and night begins, draw yourself a hot bath.

For extra energy and aesthetic, you may light some black candles around you in the bathroom. Toss your bath bomb into the water and let it bubble and fizz as it transforms the water into a black bath of magic. While this happens, add drops of oil to the water and light the incense sticks if you feel so inclined. Sprinkle in the lotus petals. Place the crystals nearby. Disrobe and slip into your shadow pool.

Relax into the water until you reach a place of peace. Once settled, take hold of the tumbled stones in your left hand. Make a tight fist around them and hold to your heart. Repeat these words:

Rhodochrosite, heal my wounds!
Labradorite, transform my rage!
Indigo Gabbro, integrate my dark with light!

Visualize the soothing and transformative energies of the crystals pouring into your heart and filling your body. Place the crystals into the bath with you and continue to relax, reflecting on your shadow identity. Once you have allowed the water to cleanse and relax you into a spiritual state of mind, you may get out of the bath and dry off. Slip into something comfortable and black, or perhaps remain naked for the remaining ritual, furthering the exposure of your identity.

Your ritual space should be set up in a private, distraction-free space. You will also need to make sure that your space is in complete darkness without any reflections of light, aside from the candles you will have. On your altar space, position the black mirror between the two candle sticks. Place the representation of Lilith behind the mirror and your cauldron in front if it. Create a circle around your altar with the five black votive candles. Make sure you have enough room to comfortably stand or move around the space as necessary.

This shadow ritual will involve drinking lotus tea. Blue lotus petals and pollen can be easily obtained online inexpensively. Lotus is one of Lilith's sacred flowers and has profoundly spiritual metaphysical properties. As a water flower, it grows from dark depths, rooted in the dank sludgy soil underwater. From this darkness they emerge, blooming into a gorgeous flower that floats in tranquility above the darkness. This association makes them perfect for shadow work, as the flower will help us to work through our darkness, ultimately allowing us to bloom in our own tranquil mindscapes. I recommend that once you have obtained the petals and pollen, place a scoop or two into a disposable tea sachet bag. Bring a teapot of hot water into your ritual space and let your teabag steep in a glass of hot water for about ten minutes while you prepare the rest of your space.

Once everything is set up, follow the ritual template from Chapter 4, including the in/evocation of Lilith. Acknowledge your shadow and state the ritual's intent by reciting:

Dark above and dark below,
Black shadows ebb and flow.
Dark within and dark without,
I acknowledge my fears and doubts.
They make up all of me,
And in the shadow of night,
My shadow I can clearly see.

Holding your cup of lotus tea, recite the following:

Sacred lotus, gorgeous bloom,
Growing from the dark and murky wound,
My pain and rage transform into a gate,
From which you will sprout and cultivate.
Rise to the surface, and there will rest,
From the dark, I become my best.
Bloomed into tranquility.

As I will it, so it shall be.

Sip on your tea and reflect upon your shadow. From here, you will begin to work with your mirror. Say:

> *Black as night,*
> *Enhance my sight,*
> *As I call my shadow to candlelight.*
> *Merge now here with me,*
> *From the wilderness, I call on thee.*
> *Lilith, Queen of the Shadows, I set you free.*
> *I own my shadow; I own the part of you in me.*

Gaze into the mirror at your reflection. Focus your sight in and out. Reflect upon all of the shadow qualities that you have uncovered while you gaze at your dark shadow reflection. It is here that you will take out your paper and begin to write out the qualities that you have claimed and understand to be your shadow. As you do this, you may feel overwhelmed with emotion. Let it out—let your rage boil or your sadness seep. You are letting go. Place the paper into your cauldron of water along with your personal effect(s) of choice and say:

> *Here and now, at this time,*
> *I merge with my shadow.*
> *May my unconscious shadow dissolve*
> *And integrate with my consciousness.*

Once your ritual is done, head straight to bed. Be sure to keep your journal nearby to record any dreams you may experience due to the ritual. Set your alarm for no later than 5 a.m. This allows you an hour to do the concluding part of the ritual. Upon waking, record any dreams you might have experienced and reflect upon them. Note how you feel and if you have a sense of lightness and ease.

Return to your cauldron of water with the paper. Overnight, the water should have dissolved the paper. If not, give it a little stir to help break it apart. This act is to symbolize your unconscious shadow dissolving into your conscious emotional current.

Take your vessel of shadow water outside. In the morning dawn, dump it onto a patch of earth or, even better, into a body of water if you have one nearby. As you do this, envision the subconscious wall that acts as a subconscious barrier falling away. Move forward knowing that in the dawn of light, your shadow is with you. Repeat this ritual whenever you feel your shadow clawing for escape from within.

The Practical Shadow

Shadow work is an ongoing process, just as are all of the magical crafts outlined here. With any kind of magic, it is important to also act practically, as this aids the universal law of attraction. If we are aiming for the results we want in the real world, our spell has a greater chance at rooting itself in our universe and growing abundantly. In the closing of this chapter, here are some simple tips to help embrace your shadow:

1. **Be honest with yourself.** Honesty is harsh, and this is why many of us do not enjoy it. Nevertheless it is important to remain observant of your habits and check in with yourself frequently.

2. **Seek constructive feedback.** Sometimes we can remain ignorant of our shadow because we do not want to admit to what is really going on. Some-times our own personality becomes biased. So, asking a close friend or even a neutral party, such as a thera-pist, can be fulfilling. I started seeing a therapist a little over a year ago. Before doing so, I never felt like I needed to—I never thought it would be benefi-cial to me—however, our biweekly sessions have proven to be a very healing process for me to give my personal shadow validation and receive construc-tive feedback.

3. **Journal about your shadow.** Creative writing is one of the best ways to work with your shadow. This can even be done through writing a letter. This prac-tice is often cathartic and lends to healthy channels of release. To add a bit of a witchy element to it, burn the paper afterward.

4. **Art, art, art!** Artistic endeavors are such an im-portant element of our mental and spiritual health. Enroll yourself in a pottery class, or maybe even an improv or acting course in which you can channel the essence of your shadow into characters for re-lease.

8

GLITTERING GLAMCRAFT:

Flaunting it with the Confidence &
Style of Glamour Magic

"Bewitching is not a fashion statement—it's more of a spiritual
statement—but that doesn't mean you can't be fashionable."
—Fiona Horne, *Bewitch a Man*

The cosmetic world teaches us today that we can contour our
faces to create illusionary shadows and highlights that accentuate our beauty. This can be an effective way of creating subtle
changes in our appearance to reap the rewards of attraction. Beauty
regimes and the tools behind them can be incorporated into magical practices, however these tools can only go so far. Someone can
be drenched in the physical aesthetics of glamour from head to toe
but still appear invisible, unable to attract more than superficial
advances. In glamour magic, the most effective form of contouring

is the contouring of energy that surrounds you and then shaping it into your desired likeness.

Unlike what the movies have taught us about glamour magic, it is not about creating an *illusion*. Instead, a witch utilizes glamour magic to obtain their goals through *allusion*. The difference between the two is subtle and very important to understand. An illusion is a form of trickery; it casts a camouflage of deceit. An allusion, on the other hand, is a concealed reference to someone or something. It is the projection of recognition, an artform by means of fantasy and escapism. Think of the modernized traditions associated with costumes on Halloween. We dress up and become a different person or thing when we head out for a night of tricks and treats. We take on the personification of our costume and, in doing so, we create an allusion. In many ways, glamour magic calls upon this same principle. It is important to remember, though, that glamour is not solely physical or even material for that matter. While they are components, glamour magic first starts from within and flows outward into our visual physique. Nevertheless, glamour is also a form of manipulation in that it calls on us to shape others' perceptions of us by tapping into the qualities that make us the most unique version of ourselves.

On an elemental level, glamour magic takes shape and form through earth. It also aligns Lilith through earth energy as she was said to be created from earth in the same fashion as Adam. In this regard, Lilith is the earth mother. She is the voluptuous peeks and deep valleys, the naked desert, open prairies, and dense forests. If we consider her stance on not "lying below a man" in a more symbolic way, perhaps it means that she as earth does not wish to fall victim to the erect towers of architecture and technology brought by mankind.

Earthly energy mirrors glamour as both a physical form and a grounding force. The earth can be decorated with fashionable foliage and glittering minerals like the adornments we wear. On the flipside, it can also be exposed, naked and bare like a vast desert. It provides substance and foundation. If we examine a tree, for example, its roots burrow deep in the ground. The earth provides nutrients to the tree and allows it to stand firm. The deeper the roots, the more anchored the tree is, the more able it is to withstand disturbance. The earth is its home, its place of refuge.

Similarly, glamour roots itself in our physical projection, both through our bodily appearance and our energetic vibration. We are the tree, and glamour magic is the earth in which we take root as witches. The energetic nutrients of confidence and good vibes provide nourishment for our well-being; they help us to radiate and dazzle. As we are nourished by the energies of glamour, it flows out into our physical by way of material objects.

Like a magnet, glamour is an attraction tool. Use it correctly and you will attract abundance into your life. Glamour is a combination of internal confidence and exterior allure. Glamour magic is taking this confidence and allure and thrusting them into your energetic magnetism, along with everyday objects, to attract your goals. Glamcraft represents the Lilithian mystery of attraction and the ultimate witch power of enchantment. This chapter will cover several techniques used to manifest glamour magic, the third point of the Lilithian Pentacle, which a GLAM Witch uses to empower their life. Being that the root term of glamour is "glam," it would make sense that this be one of the most potent magics manifested by GLAM Witches.

The Power of Persona

In looking at Lilith's legacy, we see that she captivated the minds of men and women alike. Whether through fear or fascination, she spawned an obsession that would in turn elevate her to her position today, a small reclamation of the divine force she once was. Lilith was on her own in the desert, but she survived through her confidence. Society had cast her out in the cold for standing up to mas-

Journal Entry

In the last chapter, we focused on our darkness, and in this chapter, we parallel it with our light. Our shadows give us authenticity, and our shine gives us confidence. Think about how you want glamour to manifest in your life, and what steps you can do to achieve it with the following questions:

1. What does glamour mean to you?

2. How do you define confidence? Describe a time when you were at your most confident. How did this make you feel? How can you tap into this more frequently?

3. What are your favorite personality traits in yourself? What do you consider your best physical features? Have you ever tried combining the two and accentuating them?

4. What is your favorite color? Why is it your favorite? How do you incorporate it into your life?

5. Who is the person you admire most? The ultimate representation of physical glamour and beauty? What is alluring about them?

Write down your thoughts in your journal and meditate on them. We will be coming back to these periodically throughout the chapter.

culine dominance. She knew that, to stay in the game, she had to play it. So, she took whatever label society wanted to slap on her and owned it. Her spiritual sexuality, once praised and worshipped in ancient times, was now deemed the personification of the femme fatale. Her defiance made her evil. Her allure made her sinful. Her sexual appetite and liberation made her demonic. But she persevered in her authenticity. It is through this that she displays confidence, drawing a rich and gripping glamour.

In addition to her confidence and enchanting attraction, another key connection between Lilith and glamour is that her myths reveal her to be a shapeshifter. If you recall from Chapter 2, myths exist suggesting Lilith's return to the Garden of Eden as the serpent who tempted Eve. In the same vein, her ability to take on many different "forms" in the eyes of society over the years exemplifies her versatility. To some, she is an owl or a snake; to others, she is a wild, terrifying beast. Some see her as the bewitching beauty, and some see her as a shadowy black figure. Her persistent presence drips with sensuality. She was the untamed beauty. She creates a presence unlike any other, and from this she is personified.

Projecting Persona

True shapeshifting is impossible but we can metaphysically shapeshift into other people by using our magical minds to project a persona, like Lilith. In the marketing world, businesses will create a persona based on their brand, and we do the same with glamour. It is the GLAM Witch's magical self-marketing platform. It is carrying yourself in the way you want to be seen by others. This can work by using the persona of another or by creating your very own. Either way, this practice requires dedication and constant visualization skills to ensure potency.

Projecting a persona is a wonderful ability to develop and can be used on a broad spectrum of instances to assist you in your life.

A persona is the energetic core of glamour. Think of your persona like it is an outfit. It is the aura of attraction and magnetism that you project from your mind's eye. Adopting a persona may feel like role-playing in the beginning, but as you develop in your practice, it will become your second skin.

If you are heading to a job interview and want to embody the likeness of someone who is confident, knowledgeable, and successful, you can shape your personification with this style of glamour magic. If you are heading out on a first date and want to attract your mate, channel the image of someone you feel is sexy and confident, someone who others find irresistible and charming.

As a child, I had an acute sense of visualization and would often cloak myself in the embodiment of a variety of characters. From witches to warriors and other creatures, I would envision myself taking the shape and form of roles from my favorite media outlets. I would channel their persona and archetypes of the characters they represented as I played in the backyard—conjuring fantasy into magical worlds. As I got older, this approach evolved from child's play to an application of persona for confidence. Like role-playing, it allowed me to draw energies from their identities and exploit them through myself.

When it comes to the personification of others, your selection is as broad as you wish. Your persona can essentially be anyone. They can be celebrities like Beyoncé, Marilyn Monroe, Tom Cruise, or characters like Olivia Pope, Buffy Summers, or James Bond. Even the personification of Barbie or G.I. Joe is possible! The individuals do not even have to be cookie-cutter objects of attraction, either. Perhaps you want to be left alone and unbothered and channel the mean old man that lived down the street from you growing up! You can attract or repel as you see fit.

The next time you are in a public setting, think of the person that you admire most when it comes to glamour and try them on. This could be on your commute to work, in a park, at the gym, coffee house, diner, anywhere! Reflect their image from you. Study them ahead of time and really take note of their glamour. Select an outfit they would wear, style your hair similarly, etc. As you do this, visualize that you are them. Think of yourself in their role. How would they walk? What would they order? Where would they sit? Would they like to be front and center, making a grand entrance? Or would they like to slip by unnoticed? Remain in the role. Keep your mind permanently fixated on them.

As you do this, pay attention to how people act around you. Test other's reactions to your presence to gauge how you are doing. A great cover-up trick, if your character is inclined to wear them, is to wear some dark sunglasses, so as you measure your audience's reaction, you don't come off looking like a creeper! Try this process a few times and switch it up too. Then try another character, and as you do so, notice which take hold and which do not. Which personas come more naturally to you than others? Keep track of your progress and findings in your journal.

The only problem with wearing others' personas is that you can lose sense of yourself in the process; therefore, it is best not to lean too heavily on this type of application. Using others' personas is a great building block for creating your very own persona. This is achieved by picking a variety of qualities that you associate with your idols and merging them with your best qualities. In doing so, you can start to channel an archetype instead of a specific person.

Personal Persona

It is one thing to take on the personification of someone or something else, but one of the biggest tools any witch has to their advantage is to create their own persona by investigating themselves. Remember, shadowcraft assisted in helping us understand aspects of ourselves that society claims to be negative. Here, let's reflect upon your best traits to determine how to create a persona that mirrors your most magical self.

Your persona works because it is your projection of confidence. It is combining the traits you love about yourself with those you wish you had. Confidence is sexier than anything. Think of the one that walks into the room and turns everyone's head without being the cookie-cutter equivalent to society's definition of beauty. It's not always a swimsuit model or Hollywood heartthrob—it is the one with a commanding presence.

Return to your journal and review your answers to the questions presented at the beginning of this chapter. What are your favorite qualities of yourself, both emotional and physical?

Witchcrafting: *Your Glamour Persona*

1. First and foremost, we must determine the goal of your persona. What are you doing this for? Attention? Seduction? Job interview? By determining what your glamour goal is, you can determine the characteristics that your persona needs to reflect.

2. Next, determine what qualities are needed to achieve maximum efficiency for your glamour goal. Which of these do you possess? If you do not have them, determine ways in which you can push yourself out of your comfort zone to attain them.

3. Research, Research, Research! Whether you love it or hate it, we have to apply some research to this too. Look for examples of individuals that exude the traits needed for your glamour goal and study them. This can either be done in natural observation through

"people watching" or even through watching your favorite movies and television shows. Pick up on these traits and see how you can draw upon them.

4. Research, Research, Research! Whether you love it or hate it, we have to apply some research to this too. Look for examples of individuals that exude the traits needed for your glamour goal and study them. This can either be done in natural observation through "people watching" or even through watching your favorite movies and television shows. Pick up on these traits and see how you can draw upon them.

5. The key to this glamour is to be committed to it. When an actor falls out of character, it can kill a performance. Glamour is just that—a performance. But this performance can become your life. The important part of this type of personification is not to let the persona own you—you own the persona, and you have the ability to pull its reigns and change the direction.

While it is important to test your persona in the natural world around you, it is also a good idea to prepare this first by observing yourself in a mirror.

Silver Mirror Magic

In Chapter 6, we talked a bit about the divination vessel known as a black mirror and incorporated it into our closing ritual. There is much, much more to mirrors when it comes to magic—and to Lilith for that matter. In the book *Lilith's Cave*, by folklorist Howard Schwartz, we are provided a selection of stories from Jewish folklore on the supernatural. One of the stories discusses how the wife of a man became "drawn into Lilith's web" via a mirror from a house in Tunis. It reads:

> For every mirror is a gateway to the Other World and leads directly to Lilith's cave. That is the cave Lilith went to when she abandoned Adam and the Garden of Eden for all time, the cave where she sported with her demon lovers. From these unions multitudes of demons were born, who flocked from that cave and infiltrated the world. And when they want to return, they simply enter the nearest mirror. That it is why it is said that Lilith makes her home in every mirror.

Sadly, this folktale was used to further demonize Lilith and teach women to avoid mirrors. Any sense of self-appreciation in the form of beauty and sexual empowerment that mirrors could bring were feared. As a result, confidence was aligned with vanity. Nevertheless, mirrors certainly can be used as portals for occult practices and supernatural occurrences.

The vast majority of us engage with our reflection multiple times a day, whether through styling our hair, putting on makeup, adjusting our garments, or simply passing a reflective window. We look in the mirror and strive to achieve perfection in our appearance. But do we ever *really* look into the mirror and see ourselves? Being that mirrors are associated with vanity, glamour, and beauty, and that they have been considered gateways to Lilith's land, we utilize them even more with this point of the Lilithian Pentacle. Here is where we look deep into our eyes. Eyes are the windows to the soul, and mirrors are the windows to glamour. It is here that we

Photo: Lady Lilith (1880) by Dante Gabriel Rossetti – Public Domain

must learn how to not only see ourselves, and the rich landscape of beauty we possess as divine expressions of Lilith, but to see what we want others to see.

GLAM Hexercise: *Aura of Attraction Mirror Wash*

Building off your energetic persona that you are cultivating, it's time to use a mirror to your advantage. This simple charm can be used anywhere at any time. All you need is a mirror and mirror wash—a liquid potion infused with a variety of herbs that are used to cleanse and empower a reflective surface.

Materials Needed
- 1 fresh pink rose
- 1 Tbsp. of dried orange peel
- 1 tsp. of cinnamon
- 1 vanilla bean
- 1 tumbled rose quartz
- Mirror

You will need to pre-make your mirror wash. To do this, place the petals from one fresh pink rose for grace, one tablespoon of orange peel for vibrancy, a teaspoon of cinnamon for zest, the scrapings of one whole vanilla bean for sweetness, and one piece of tumbled rose quartz for beauty into a bowl. Boil water and pour it into the bowl. Let the mixture sit overnight on a windowsill that captures the light of a waxing moon. Enchant your infusion by drawing down energies of the moon into the water. Upon waking in the morning, strain the mixture into a bottle and—voilà!—your mirror wash is complete.

When it comes to enchanting the mirror, take a drop of the liquid on your finger and rub it into a mirror in a clockwise motion.

Look into your eyes and think about all of the qualities you wish to radiate from you. Repeat the following words:

Magic mirror of mine,
Let my confidence and glamour shine.
Reflect the best qualities in me
And magnify them for all to see,
For the good of all, but most for me.
As I will it, so it shall be.

Close your eyes and envision a sparkling light begin to engulf you, permeating your aura with an attractive glow. Give it a few minutes, and when you feel you are ready, open your eyes and move forward with your day, remaining cognizant of the glittering light that surrounds you.

Much like your black mirror we created in Chapter 6, it is best to have a mirror designated for your glamour efforts. It may be a good idea for you to invest in a small compact mirror as your glamour on the go tool. Luckily, many makeup products include a small application mirror that would work just fine. Otherwise, tiny travel mirrors are readily available at most drugstores and online. Carry a small vial of your mirror wash with you and apply whenever you need an enchantment recharge! In Chapter 11, I provide a additional mirror wash recipes to utilize for more specific glamour goals.

The Liner, the GLAM Witch, and the Wardrobe

On the surface, glamour is saturated in appearance—how you dress, style your hair, groom yourself, and paint your face. Vanity is an age-old feeling that puts an excessive amount of attention on appearance. The first makeups and cosmetics were not used to help achieve superficial advances like they are in many cases today. Created in ancient Egyptian times, they were used to align high-ranking women and men with the goddesses and gods. They believed wearing makeup impressed their deities, who in exchange granted them gifts in the form of protection and abundance. Today, makeup is applied to cover up flaws and enhance physical features. The ancient ways can still be applied to your daily beauty rituals today, though, particularly with regard to Lilith and her admiration for allure.

When I get ready every morning, I look at my day as if I am going to a costume party. I start with my persona and determine how I want the world to see me. What will I dress like today? Who do I want to be? What energies do I want to radiate? From this, I piece together my ensemble and pair it with accessories. This may include a pendant fashioned from a stone that embodies the energetic magnetism I wish to draw, or even something as simple as a color.

Many witches I know have adopted a more gothic approach to style, draping themselves in dark colors and makeups. Others take on a more renaissance-fair, bohemian style. Some dress completely casual, and others are more colorful. Regardless of your fashion style, it can add to your magic. Material objects like cosmetics, flashy clothes, and jewelry are objects that help accentuate glamour. These are tools of glamour. Much like an athame, candles, crystals, and herbs are used in spellcasting; glamour tools are the ingredients that are fused together in the oven of a witch's soul to create the exterior essence of glamcraft.

Enchanting an Item for Glamour

Any item can be charged with magical intent to help exude your glamour. You can draw symbols in your makeup or charge your supplies under the full moon to radiate with glamorous lunar luminescence, or in the sun to energize with vibrancy. When charging an item with magical intent for your glamour efforts, you can say something such as this little charm below.

Item of mine,
Radiate and shine!
Help me manifest glamour
And attract good favor.

As witches, we are adept in the meanings of colors and symbols and how to use them to our advantage in spellcasting; these same principles can be applied to the tools of glamour magic. You can cleanse and empower them just like any other object you would in the craft. Colors hold a great deal of power over our emotions. The correspondences associated with colors are a known sensation experienced by all and are something we as witches can manipulate with our glamour magic. The key is to identify your goals as a witch and develop a fashion sense around it. Now, let's take a look at some of the ways in which a GLAM Witch can level up their glamour!

Colorcraft

Your fashion is your magical armor, and it is through combining color magic with our wardrobe that we further emphasize our glamour. In Chapter 3, we discussed several colors associated with Lilith and how they connect to her primal energies. But those were just a snapshot of the plethora of colors and their various meanings. Whether you are slipping into colorful fabrics, painting them on your face as makeup, or even experimenting in interior decorating, here is a snapshot of how different colors in the everyday world can accentuate the intent of glamour magic.

⊛ ***Red***—Red is bold. There is no dimmer switch when it comes to red. It is always on! Red is a very direct color, fueled by the energetic electricity of fire. Think about the clichés of wearing red on a date, how the image of a red tie or suit appears, the stereotype of a red sports car, and the relationship between red and the bull. Red is not only the color for deep sensual love, passion, and lust but also for power, strength, and war. Red creates a presence. It is both commanding and demanding. Shades of red can be incorporated into your life when looking to enhance sexual suggestion, strength, or an all-around powerful persona.

⊛ ***Pink***—Pink is a wonderful color for attraction. It is happy and playful—both sweet and tart. Where red is more of a laser-focused color, pink pillows and flows like ethereal smoke. It is softer and more flirtatious. It takes the love of red and turns it inward to the self, creating an air of confidence and appeal. Wearing and surrounding yourself in pinks also helps create harmony in one's life. It makes you look more approachable. It helps the wearer pop like bubblegum and sizzle in sauciness.

✷ *Orange*—Orange is another warm tone with a fiery energy. Shades of orange help manifest confidence, vitality, and luck. This is a great color to incorporate into your life when you are looking for an extra boost of energy, whether emotional or physical. Orange is a fantastic color to incorporate into your workout routine and athletic endeavors. Where red is a color of strength, orange is a color of courage. Engulf yourself in oranges when you are up against the odds and need to channel the brave warrior witch within!

✷ *Yellow*—Yellow is loud. It screams, "look at me, look at me!" It's no wonder that this is a color of communication. Statistically, yellow is a color that is least liked. It is, for lack of a better term, annoying. Like the toddler that constantly asks "why?" yellow is curious and constantly thinking. It helps set the wheels of the mind in motion. It is inquisitive and inspiring, ruling over our thoughts. For this reason, it is a wonderful color to energize creativity. Anyone artistically inclined can benefit from including yellow tones in their creative space.

✷ *Green*—Green carries a very fertile energy, equivalent to that of the spring when the flowers and trees take bloom. Animals frolic and play in their mating rituals. It initiates a "go" response and symbolizes the movement of prosperity. This prosperity can incorporate materialistic wealth or the fertility of emotional success. Additionally, green is a symbol of health, connecting again to "green" vegetation and the healing properties of the earth. Dress in green when you want to achieve healthy abundance in life.

✷ *Blue*—Shades of blue harbor a calm and soothing energy. It is the dreamy color of water. It plays with our emotions and helps tranquility flow into our atmosphere. Blue is a peaceful color. It is commonly seen in places that exude relaxation, such as spas, salons, yoga, and meditation centers. When the world gets hectic and frustrating, splash yourself with blue to balance out heated emotions.

⊛ *Purple*—Purple is the most mystical member in the color family. It is representative of great wisdom. For this reason, it is deeply connected to psychic power and occult knowledge. Furthering blue's energies, purple is a calming force. Where blue rules the calming of our emotions, purple provides a calming of the mind. Purples are great to incorporate into divination practices to help energize the psychic mind.

⊛ *Black*—Black has long been associated as the witch's color. It is related to the darkness of the night sky and the unknown. Largely deemed as evil, black gets a bad rap but is an extremely powerful color for protection and night-related magic. Technically, black is not a color; rather, it is the absence of color. Black is also physically absorbing. On a hot day, anything cloaked in black will feel the effects of heat more intensely. Why do you think black is such a popular color in night clubs? Yes, it is slimming, sexy, and looks good on just about everyone, but it also absorbs. Wearing black to an exciting, sound-thumping night club will help you to draw in and absorb the energies of the environment and the others around you. Additionally, black is often associated with death and is the color one is expected to wear to funerals. I find that a lot of the witches who have predominantly black wardrobes work a lot with the spirit world and find comfort in the dark, since they deal with the shadows of life and death.

⊛ *Brown*—Brown is a grounding color and helps one to be centered. Different shades of brown are seen in sands, clays, soils, and woods. These materials are from the earth, our true home, and help build the foundations we reside in. Brown helps provide a homey sense of comfort. It is warm and cozy. Welcome brown into your life when looking to exude a down-to-earth persona.

✸ *White*—Where black is the absence of color, white embodies all colors. Scientifically, we perceive color due to interactions in wavelengths of light. White contains all wavelengths of light and embodies all colors. It manifests spiritual clarity and purity. White also reflects. It is a great color to dress in when in situations where others may project negativity onto you or may harbor envious feelings. White will reflect this back and prevent them from penetrating you.

✸ *Gray*—Gray is a combination of both black and white. It is a very balancing color and one that is wonderful to work with when trying to experience energetic equality.

✸ *Silver*—Silver is an enchanting color. It breathes a glowing luminance of lunar energies. Like the moon, it shimmers, sparkles, and is incredibly noticeable. Silver can enhance your life by adding a sensation of mystery and charm. It will make you stand out like the full moon in a sky of tiny stars.

✸ *Gold*—Gold is powerful. It yields success and status. Like the kings and queens of ancient times, gold is a royal color. It aligns with solar energy, helping us connect to the warm vitality of the flaming sphere we orbit. Shades of gold help manifest attraction and success and can be utilized when you are looking to be the center of attention.

✸ *Rose Gold*—I've saved the best for last! Rose gold is my absolute favorite and a supreme color of glamour and magic. It is the bubbly champagne of colors. It pops, gleams, and hisses with magical flare. It takes the flirtatious power of pink and fuses it with the successful sparkle of gold. It helps replenish confidence and self-love and attracts a wealth of good vibes.

✸ *Prints*—While not a color, prints are a major component to clothing. Prints are also very powerful ways of evoking whatever symbolism is behind the design. For example, animal and floral prints are very common representations in fashion. Wearing snakeskin patterns will help you embody the essence of serpentine energy. Leopard prints will welcome your wild side. Florals help reconnect you to the energies of the flower.

Crystalcraft

Remember that glamour is elementally aligned with earth, and one of the best embodiments of earth that can be incorporated into glamour magic is crystals. They are one of the many substances that witches use in their spellcraft, on their altars, during meditations, and as jewelry! Each crystal comes with an abundance of metaphysical properties and characteristics. Since it can be hard to memorize all of these, a good rule of thumb is to look at the color symbolism of the crystal. Red stones will yield more passion and strength, purple will denote wisdom and psychic power, etc. When it comes to attraction and beauty, the below crystals are excellent to work into your daily wardrobe for a bit of glamour magic.

✸ Amber	✸ Garnierite	✸ Pyrite
✸ Amethyst	✸ Jade	✸ Rhodonite
✸ Aquamarine	✸ Kunzite	✸ Rose Quartz
✸ Carnelian	✸ Labradorite	✸ Ruby
✸ Citrine	✸ Moonstone	✸ Sunstone
✸ Diamond	✸ Morganite	✸ Tiger's Eye
✸ Emerald	✸ Pearl	✸ Topaz

Scentcraft

Another glamorous appeal that helps cast a spell of enchantment is the power of scent. A powerful smell can take us back to a lost memory or arouse an appetite of hunger. It can also trigger disgust; for instance, scent tells us when something has gone bad and is no longer acceptable to eat. Witches can take advantage of the power of scent for their magical goals, especially when it comes to glamour.

Essential vs. Synthetic

There is much debate within the witch community on whether one should use essential oils rather than synthetics. There are many healing properties associated with essential oils, making them great to use as topical agents, bath additives, and sometimes even digestives depending on the type and usage. I tend to prefer synthetics, especially when dealing with glamour magic. With your fragrances, you are calling upon the *allusion* of scent. You are attempting to manipulate and elicit a mental reaction based on the fragrance in association to its natural state. Additionally, essential oils can be quite expensive and may not always be the most practical to use. There are some classic scents, such as musk and ambergris, that are from animal glands and are not particularly pleasant to obtain. If you wish to really call upon the herbal properties, you can infuse your fragrance oils with organic materials too. I will routinely add dried rose petals to my rose oils, orange peel to orange, etc.

Perfumery consists of blending a collection of fragrances together that are found in plants, resins, and other sources. Fragrances are readily available as either brand-name perfumes and colognes or through essential oils that can be mixed together to promote a magical intent. When doing so, it is important to use the basic formula of top, mid, and base notes to create a successful aroma.

The top notes in a perfume are designed to be the immediate burst that gives the first impression, like an aromatic appetizer for the nostrils. These top notes are commonly bolder scents, such as citrus and spicy fragrances. The full-fragrant goal is exposed through the mid notes, which, compared to top notes, are subdued and draw you further into the fragrance. Where the top notes fade quickly, mid notes are designed to be the main course and are the longest-lasting scent profile. Floral and earthy scents make for good mid notes due to their softer profiles. A fragrance is then closed by the base note. These notes are designed to be the lingering reminder for our noses. This last scent often does not expose itself until the others begin to wear off. These are deep, rich, and heavy scents like musks and resins. Regardless, whether you are whipping up an oil blend (see Chapter 11 for some recipes) or purchasing designer perfumes, below is a list of common scents used for attraction and allure.

- Bergamot
- Cardamom
- Clary Sage
- Chocolate
- Cinnamon
- Civet
- Dragon's Blood
- Frankin-
- cense
- Geranium
- Ginger
- Honey
- Jasmine
- Lavender
- Muguet
- Musk
- Narcissus
- Neroli
- Opium
- Orange
- Osmanthus
- Oud
- Patchouli
- Pepper (Black/Pink)
- Rose

✵ Sandalwood   ✵ Vanilla   ✵ Violet

✵ Tonka   ✵ Vetiver   ✵ Ylang-Ylang

The Magic of Body Language

Now that we have our persona and some kickass enchanted armor to stimulate our glamour, what's next? We still need to tie it all together with a form of communication. But this communication is not verbal. It is here that we will draw upon the corner of the Witch's Pyramid "to be silent" and merge with our Lilithian law of *flaunt it* through the application of body language.

What do you notice first when you see someone? You might notice a quality about them that you admire or desire. Their fashion or accessories might lure you in and speak to you on some level. But often these are not enough to really infect an onlooker's mind with your glamour goal. Your persona and style will get you noticed, but body language is the real talker. Our body language is a universal communication tool and the vessel by which glamour really becomes a GLAM Witch weapon. No words are needed—a simple glance, walk, arm placement, accidental brush, or flicker of breath is all it takes to communicate with others. While there are many different types of body language that can be used to enhance visual attraction, the main ones we will touch on here are eye contact and movement.

Witch Face

"Resting bitch face" is a pop culture reference to an inadvertent facial expression that displays annoyance, irritation, or lack of interest; however, with "resting *witch* face," witches can purposefully display their desires through facial expressions. When wanting to pull someone into your magnetism, you can call for their attention with something as simple as a smile, grin, or other flirtatious action that signals interest. If you want to repel, a blank, emotionless look will denote a sense of detachment, making you appear uninterested, mean, or simply unaffected.

An example I can use here is a previous work experience during which the head of my department lost their temper and dug into my colleagues and I in a meeting. My peers were all exhibiting signs of distress, some breaking out into hives, and others looking petrified. Instead, I closed myself off to the situation. I put on a resting bitch-witch face and appeared unaffected by the attempted belittling. It was very obvious that my demeanor was affecting our boss, as he eventually started to single me out further, expecting some kind of reaction. But in my glamour of facial expression, I built up a wall that deflected his negativity and sent it right back to him.

But there is another area of focus when it comes to facial sorcery—our eyes! Have you ever experienced an instance when you were able to talk to someone with just your eyes? I am sure some of us are familiar with this expression in relation to our parents—that "don't you dare do that" look. Or a mutual exchange of telepathic energy between two friends with a single glance. These instances do not involve facial gesturing or signals, winking, or shifting in a direction. It is a thought-provoking stare that commands attention.

Your eyes are said to be the windows to the soul. The emphasis of eye contact shows confidence in your demeanor. When it comes to public speaking, teaching, ordering something, flirting, dating, sex, job interviews, and really any social setting, you can work magic with your eyes. Proper eye contact will make you look more approachable, while also establishing poise and personal power.

Furthering the use of our eyes, we can also work with our pupils to perfect our witch gaze. While, again, we cannot change the color of our eyes at the bat of a lash, we can alter them at will to make ourselves more attractive. Our pupils naturally dilate in cer-

Eye Movement Codex

- **Direct eye contact** shows focus, interest, and an exchange of attention.

- **Glances** denote interest in the object that one is looking at.

- **Looking ahead** displays confidence and power.

- **Looking down** shows submission and gives the perception of being shy or timid.

- **Looking sideways** is a sign of distraction and lack of connection or interest.

- **Looking up** shows that you are thinking or perhaps creating a lie.

tain instances, particularly during sexual arousal, low lighting, and when focusing on small items. Dilated pupils are known to stimulate attraction and are something that any witch can use to their advantage when trying to gain the attention of an onlooker they are engaging with. This is a technique I was first introduced to in Fiona Horne's book *Bewitch a Man* and have since done additional research on. It has done wonders for me when trying to master job interviews, navigate dating, or work a sale. Essentially, when you maintain eye contact with another person, focus your attention on an eyelash or a tear duct, while using your mind to envision the desired outcome you are after. Your pupils will expand in this moment like an automatic lens of a camera, focusing in on a small subject. Test this out in a mirror a bit beforehand and see the subtle changes take place.

Position & Posture

Just as your eye contact can be used to assert attractiveness, your gestures can also help you get noticed. Any type of posture that is hunched or crossed will come across as closed off; use this only when you want to remain unbothered. The more expressive and grander you are with your gestures, however, the more attention you will grab. But we don't want this attraction to be comical. We want to be warm and inviting, mysterious, and coy. For example, to show interest in someone you are sitting next to, cross your legs in their direction or lean into them, giving a hint of attention.

Likewise, our movements give life to our persona and glamour tools. Your movements can draw others in or push them out as you wish. A commanding presence is one that comes with a commanding walk. One of my favorite quotes to illustrate the kind of walk I'm talking about comes from the glamourous fashion icon Miss J Alexander who says, "Walk like it's for sale and the rent is due tonight." I have since adopted this line as a personal mantra for any time I walk into a room, and I recommend you do the same. Every time you enter a room—every time you go out—the world is your runway, and you have to work it accordingly! Like the grace of a bird, the seduction of a snake, or the stealth of a cat, movement gets you noticed or can help to camouflage you.

When creating your walk and expressing yourself through movement, it is important that you own your space. A signature walk will be confident and fluid. The most graceful and attractive walks incorporate a rolling movement in your hips or shoulders. Think of your walk as a dance—a tango for one.

Masculine-style walks often include a rocking movement of the shoulders. Like a subtle dance, as your left foot steps out, your right shoulder moves out as well; return to center and then switch sides. Feminine walks use this same movement but with the hips instead of shoulders. In either approach, your body's movement creates what is called an "S curve." As the top of your body moves in one direction, the bottom half of your body moves in the other. This switching back and forth makes you appear to glide and is appealing to observe.

This type of walk is open and expressive. Keep your posture straight and your head up to make eye contact. You do not have to smile unless you want to. You can remain laser focused in front of you. Before field testing your glamorous signature strides, return to a mirror. Practice makes perfect, and the best way to develop the body language associated with attraction is to study yourself and your movements in the mirror. Follow this in public at events or when you are out and about running errands. Much like testing your persona, keep your eyes up and open to others' reaction to you.

The GLAM Witch's Doll

Growing up, I had a rather large collection of Barbie dolls. I was never interested in sports or cars or any of the stereotypical gender-normative toys for boys. Barbie dolls exuded a charm and enchantment that was extraordinarily bewitching to me. I would create magical worlds with them, mirroring the cinematic glitz and glam of the silver screen and getting lost in my personal valley of dolls. They were an escape, and the more I played with them, the more confident I became. Little did I know at the time, but my little witchling self was playing with one of the most powerful conduits for magic—a poppet.

Poppets are magical tools used to represent a person in magical workings and have been used in a variety of cultures throughout history. These dolls are traditionally crafted from various objects including sticks, leaves, corn husks, seeds, herbs, cloth, clay, wax, and/or sometimes even molded into dough that is later baked and buried.

Poppets can be used for just about any type of magic that involves a person, including healing, hexing, love, lust, and protection. Special herbs, oils, and crystals are placed inside the poppet, while sigils and symbols connected to the intended magic are drawn or sewn on it. Though crafting a poppet from scratch has its benefits, poppets are readily available at most department stores in the form of Barbie dolls. These are especially potent for glamour magic. Crafted in human form with many realistic characteristics that a witch can easily attribute to a physical person, dolls are magical vessels waiting to be tapped into. Barbie dolls are no different.

Barbies are often used to symbolize ideal beauty. For this same reason, negativity has been brought down on the dolls for portraying unrealistic expectations of attractiveness. Despite this, Barbie dolls have branched out in their appearance to represent a more diverse population in recent years. Different races, ethnicities, sexes, shapes, and sizes are now being produced. Barbie dolls are fantasy toys and a spitting image of glamour. While the other methods of poppet creation would be effective for glamour magic, using a tool that already sizzles with glamour will surely heighten your own glamorous appeal.

Witchcrafting: *A Glamour Poppet*

In the following spell, we'll be crafting a glamour poppet from a Barbie doll. The doll is going to represent you in your most glamorous form and further aid in your magical glamour efforts.

Materials Needed
* A Barbie doll (to represent you)
* A 4-6" round mirror
* 5 long-stem roses (orange or pink), cut in equal lengths
* 1 piece of labradorite
* 5 pieces of amber
* 5 pieces rose quartz
* 5 pieces of pyrite
* 5 pieces of aquamarine

✪ Personal effects (e.g., a strand of hair, nail clippings, or bodily fluids)

✪ Your favorite essential oil or blend

✪ 2 gold candlesticks

✪ 2 pink or orange candlesticks

✪ 2 silver candlesticks

Optional: A pencil or pen to mark up the Barbie with any tattoos or other distinguishing marks; doll stand; eco-friendly glitter

Timing and planetary hours are very important for this spell. It should be performed on a Friday in the planetary hour of Venus. The moon can be anywhere between the new and full phases. In my personal experience, the closer it is performed to the full moon, the better.

The preparation of this spell is my favorite part. While on the hunt for your poppet, I recommend selecting a doll that is similar in appearance to you but also accentuates the qualities you long for. Select a doll that you wish to create an allusion from. Get creative and have fun! Barbie dolls are sold at most department stores and are available in abundance online. There are many different brands, some very affordable and some extravagantly priced. You do not need to spend an arm and a leg on this, so do not feel that a more expensive doll will yield more successful results. That is not how magic works!

Once you have the doll, begin to customize it to fit your needs. Draw your tattoos on the doll, cut its hair if necessary, paint it, add scars and birthmarks, etc., anything that helps connect the doll more directly in physical appearance to you. When working with the poppet, we are setting our intention through the doll. The more the doll resembles you, the quicker the energetic bond between you will form.

I also highly recommend finding a fashionable outfit for your doll. In most poppet work, it is not necessarily required for your poppet to be dressed. Some feel that the nakedness of the doll create a stronger bond to the person; however, this is glamour magic and we are working on creating a more physical attraction. When witches create poppets from cloth, they will often select special colors of fabric to help assist in their working. As we have established, color and other materials possess their own unique magical essence and this kind of fashion magic will do just that! Dress the doll in something that you would wear in the color of your goal. If you are good with a needle and thread, perhaps you can even tailor your own doll clothing.

Once this is done, it is time to start bonding with the doll. The

doll's energy must interact with your own to establish a deeper connection. The most recommended approach is to sleep with the doll under your bed or on your night stand. This allows it to interact with your energies during sleep.

On the night of the spell, it is imperative that the moon be visible in the sky so that its reflection can be caught in the mirror. Unfortunately, if the sky is overcast, you will need to plan for another evening. The spell would be best performed outside in a private open space, but if you are unable to do this you can always do it inside at a windowsill where the moon is present. If neither of these options is feasible, start the spell outside and move it inside.

If you can take the day of your spell off, cash in that vacation time and celebrate yourself. Got to a spa or do something that is relaxing and helps your inner glamorous witch glow! Once night falls, set up your space with the materials above. If you need to travel outside, take the mirror with you, holding it in a position so that it captures the reflection of the moon. Recite the following:

Silver ball of glowing light,
I draw down your luminance on this night.
Glitter and sparkle, what a sight,
Reflect unto me, the radiance of moonlight.

Now, turn around and hold the mirror facing you so that both you and the moon are in the reflection together, and say:

Mirror, mirror, in my hand,
I'm the glam-est of the land.
Melted from tiny sand,
Reflect my glamour, make it grand!

Stare into your reflection and see yourself as the most beautiful expression that you can be. Place the mirror down on your altar. From here, you will start to create your glamour workstation. Take your five roses, cut in equal length, and construct a pentagram over the mirror. Each stem will touch the petals of the next so that every point of the pentagram is anchored by a bloom.

Next, you will place your charged crystals in the form of a crystal grid. Place the labradorite in the center—labradorite is a stone of transformation and magic; it carries a multicolored glow that helps accentuate glamour. Above the labradorite, create a line of crystals from it to the rose petals in the following order: amber, rose quartz, and pyrite. Amber is an ancient resin known for its beauty, rose quartz helps manifest beauty and grace, and pyrite is a stone for abundance and success. Create this same alignment of crystals at each point of the pentagram. In the space between each of the points, place a piece of aquamarine, a stone known for its effects on emotional harmony. While doing this, make sure that spacing is good for your doll to be placed in the center of the grid.

Hold your doll in both hands and look into its eyes. See yourself in the doll. Next, take your personal effects and place them into the open creases of the doll. By doing this, you are placing physical parts of you in the doll to magnify the energy. Once you are done, dab a bit of your favorite essential oil or blend on the doll's chest and say:

> *Mold my form and shape to be*
> *A living doll for all to see.*
> *I am you, and you are me,*
> *Together bound in beauty!*

Dress your doll and stand them in the center of the mirror, in the grid you have constructed. You can either stand it up using a stand or lay it out over the pentagram. Doll stands are easy to come by and will often be included with your purchase.

Now, you will brush yourself with each of your candles. To do this, take one of your candles and hold it above your head. Slowly trace it over your body as if it was a hand-held shower head. This helps connect the candle to your aura. Next, carve your name on one side of the candle (initials are fine if your name is longer than the candle you have), along with the Norse rune Wunjo, a powerful

rune for beauty, prosperity, and well-being. Once you have carved the candle, lick your thumb and trace over your name with your saliva. This helps bind the candle to your energies. Dress the candles in your essential oil and roll in glitter if you choose to use it. Repeat this process for each candle.

Once you are ready, you will place each candlestick in its holder above each point of the star, encasing the pentagram in a circle of candles. Light each of the candlesticks in a clockwise direction and recite:

Sacred flame inside of me,
Ignite and ebb from yours truly,
My aura aflame, for all to see,
Attraction is mine—as I will it, it will be!

Now, stand above your workstation so that your face is again caught in the mirror with the doll and say:

Fashion doll of fantasy,
Reflect glamour back unto me.
Together we are bound through beauty
And attract a state of ecstasy!

Further concentrate on your doll. Get lost in its beauty and envision yourself becoming it. Visualize all the glamour you could ever hope for spiraling around you and transforming you. Sit with your doll and meditate on this until the candles have burnt out. Leave your poppet and grid out overnight to soak up the energies of the mirror. It is best to leave your doll and grid as is, but sometimes this is not possible; in that instance, wrap your mirror in a silk cloth with the crystals for safety. Store them away until you need an extra boost of glamour. It is exceedingly important that the mirror never met another's reflection. This has the potential to draw away the glamour you have manifested for yourself.

Your poppet should remain in a place that you will interact with it daily. Some great locations would be your living room, bathroom, in your closet, or in your underwear or sock drawer for more privacy. Remember that this doll is an extension of you. It should never be played with or handled by anyone other than you.

During the spell, the doll changed from a toy to a magical tool for your glamour and for other spells down the line. It should be treated with the same respect you would want to be treated with. If the doll must ever be stored away, wrap it in the silk cloth with the crystals and mirror.

I dedicated a floating shelf to my poppet. I keep it standing or sitting on the mirror, with some flowers, crystals, and candle. I'll routinely provide it with fresh rose water and occasionally change his outfit, depending on the type of magic I need to manifest in my life. On the full moons, I will regularly recharge my mirror and poppet with intention. For me, this acts as my monthly energetic cleansing.

Lilith Poppet

As an alternative to a statue or photo representation of Lilith, you may also decide to create a poppet for her. The benefit of having a poppet dedicated to Lilith is that it serves as a vessel for her to take residency in during ritual. Being a shapeshifter, Lilith likes to take shape and form in objects. Because of this, a poppet is a perfect conduit for channeling her energies in ritual space. Choose any doll that you feel embodies Lilith's essence and decorate it accordingly. To charge it, follow the standard invocation outlined in Chapter 4, and welcome her into the vessel.

Glamcrafting: *A Lilithian Ritual for Glamour*

Throughout this chapter, we have explored some of the different ways to magically accentuate glamour in your life. By now, the connection between Lilith and mirrors should be well understood. Mirrors are portals to other dimensions and are also a compelling symbol of vanity and beauty. The black mirror we created in Chapter 6 is a fantastic vessel to connect with Lilith for all magical workings and will be the central source for this next ritual. It is here that we dedicate our persona and glamour to Lilith, embodying her essence and enchantment.

Materials Needed
- ✸ Lilith mirror wash
- ✸ Lilith statue or poppet
- ✸ Black mirror
- ✸ Hot pink pillar candle
- ✸ Offering (See Chapter 3 for a full list of examples)
- ✸ 2 silver candlesticks
- ✸ Pink roses or lilies
- ✸ Blood, saliva, or other bodily fluids
- ✸ Rose oil

Optional: Multicolor biodegradable glitter

Lilith Mirror Wash
- ✸ Cinnamon
- ✸ Feather
- ✸ Orchid
- ✸ Patchouli
- ✸ Red Roses
- ✸ Snakeskin

In preparation for this ritual, make a mirror wash combining the ingredients noted above. Follow the guide for this as instructed earlier in the chapter on page 176. Instead of putting the wash out to absorb the light of a moon, though, place it on your dedicated Lilith shrine to soak overnight. The next morning, strain and bottle.

Set up your space so that the Lilith representation is the object farthest away from you. Place the mirror in front of her. Place the pink candle in front of the mirror, and in front of the candle place the offering. On either side of Lilith's representation, place the candlesticks and put the vase of flowers behind her.

Once you have settled into your workspace, take your pink candle and carve the name Lilith on one side and your name on the other. Seal the carving of your name with your blood, saliva, or other bodily fluid. Dress your candle with rose oil. If you are using glitter, sprinkle it over the candle so that it sparkles with glamour. Light your candle and chant to Lilith. Rub your mirror wash into the glass of your black mirror. As you gaze into the mirror, come closer so that you can make out a bit of your reflection in the glass. Invite her to join you via the mirror with the invocation in Chapter 4. Begin scrying and calling forth Lilith's glamour in the following incantation:

From your black mirror I call on thee,
Lady Lilith, Dark Queen of Witchery.
I dedicate my glamour to thee
And evoke your enigmatic beauty!

Provide your offering to Lilith in exchange for her gift of enchantment. Talk to her freely about your aspirations and goals. Begin to stare into your black reflective vessel. If you can make out your reflection, visualize it taking the form of Lilith. When you feel the work has been completed, thank Lilith for her time and end the ritual. I recommend doing this ritual every so often to help recharge your glamour and strengthen your dedication to her.

Keeping the Confidence

Remember that you must continue to act practically with your magical activities. Keep your glamcraft alive with these tips for remaining the most confident expression of yourself.

1. **Regularly reflect on what makes you uniquely you.** Focus on your unique charms and how these help you stand out in a crowd. These are the stars that glitter and shine in the polarity of your shadow. By remaining focused on the areas you excel in and using your strengths to your advantage, you achieve greater confidence.

2. **Practice selfie sorcery.** As vapid and narcissistic as it may seem, selfies can help you become more comfortable in your skin. In our technologically savvy, social-media-obsessed world, selfies are one way to gain confidence and validation in your physical appearance. You learn which angles and lighting make you look your best, and you can integrate these practices in your glamour efforts.

3. **Visualize your goals.** Visualization is such an important part of life and a key concept when it comes to magic. Glamour magic is attraction based, and the universal law of attraction corresponds to the sympathetic principles of this mental metaphysic.

9

LUSCIOUS LUSTCRAFT:

*Indulgence of Self-Love with Sex Magic &
the Power of Orgasm*

"Sexual energy is natural, readily accessible, and incredibly
powerful. It's your birthright, a key to health, wealth, and
happiness—literally at your fingertips."
—Skye Alexander, *Sex Magic for Beginners*

S ex is a creative force and is the common element that links all
living things on earth. It stirs our carnal passions and desires,
fueling the fire within our loins. And just as we are alive, brought
to you in part by an act of sexuality, fire is a living element. It is
conceived from the vigorous friction between two things, or from
the blazing heat cast on an object. From this, a spark is born. The
spark must be nurtured, fed, and fanned to maturity. Fire breathes
oxygen. It consumes organic matter, expelling it as burnt waste. It
grows stronger and stronger and will eventually wind down. It dies

into charred embers, a soft glow of its original glory. Fire is life. It is the pumping, pounding power of our heart. It is the creative spark of our passions and desires. It is our sexuality, the life energy that feeds our primal appetite on a cellular level. And through this sexuality, it becomes a powerful form of energy that can be incorporated into witchcraft through the same transformative means of fire.

The Goddess is a divine representation of this flaming creative energy. Looking at the original aspects of the Mother Goddess, her role in sexuality is linked to fertility, procreation, and agricultural propagation. In the famous "Charge of the Goddess," this is emphasized in that "all acts of love and pleasure" are the rituals of the Goddess. If any goddess embodies this line, it is Lilith. Considered the handmaiden to Inanna's sex temples and later demonized as a seductive succubus, Lilith is a sensual goddess governing the powers of sex magic. It is through sexuality that Lilith relishes in power. When she fled to the cave by the Red Sea and was found fornicating with lustful demons, it was an echo to her previous incarnations as a sexual feminine force that governed the sacred sex teachings of the time. It was a time when people would learn how to harness their sexuality for spiritual purposes. As witches, we can do the same, and it is through Lilith that this power can be reclaimed.

In this day and age of advanced technology and apps for everything from bank accounts to dining, deliveries, and dating we have traded fertility for *flirtility*, as we worship the instant gratification of touch-screen erotic indulgence. Lilith is a sex goddess and one that governs this flirtility over the fertility of the ancient Mother Goddess. Her sexual prowess stems from pleasure over procreation and uses seductive means to feast on it. Biologically, sex creates life, yet in our modern age of contraceptives, we have culturally learned how to bask in the pleasures of sex without physical creation, calling forth the root of Lilith's lessons of lust. No, Lilith's magic in sex is not creative in the sense of breeding but rather in creating art, bliss, and joy from the ecstatic electrification of cellular impulses within us. Lilith's sex is creative through manifestation, and it is through this that we can transfigure the creation element of fire with sex into our desires as witches.

Visioncraft aids in establishing psychic power, shadowcraft welcomes our authenticity, glamcraft helps shape confidence, and here we reach a Lilithian point of passion, pleasure, love, and lust. With lustcraft, we travel to the point in the Lilithian Pentacle that Lilith is most at home in. It is through Lilith's re-emergence from the wilderness in modern times that we may reclaim her sexual teachings and become vessels for her power and love. In the pages that follow, we will explore several ways a GLAM Witch can integrate sexuality into their magical expression.

Journal Entry

Before plunging into the luscious lessons of lustcraft, make a new entry in your journal answering the following questions.

1. What are your definitions of sex and sexuality?

2. Do you feel comfortable in expressing yourself sexually?

3. What is your relationship to gender and sexual identity?

4. What areas of your sexuality need healing? Do you have any wounds? If so, what are they? How do you feel they can be best overcome?

5. What turns you on and in what ways? Do you have any fetishes or an appreciation for kink? Do you explore these or repress them?

6. How do you feel sexy? Do you seduce or prefer to be seduced?

7. Fire is representative of creativity, passion, and desire. What is your relationship with fire? How is your creativity fueled? What are you passionate about? What are your desires?

8. What is your relationship to the serpent? Does it fascinate you or ignite fear within? Do you dream of them often?

Sex Magic 1-Oh!-1

Sex magic is exactly what it sounds like—the integration of sex with magical activities. Sex magic is perhaps the most misunderstood, yet one of the simplest forms of magic to work with. This is due to the misrepresentation of sexuality and witches within pop culture, and the misogynistic and predatory actions in society. Nevertheless, when willingly explored, it can not only act as a conduit for magical pursuits but can be an enlightening and empowering act of divine love.

In practicing sex magic, we must make sure that our mind is focused on our desired outcome. Once you get the hang of it, you will notice tremendous leaps toward reaching your goals. Sex magic works because sex is pure energy, if not the strongest one a witch can employ. This is because acts of magic are best manifested through a trance state, and sexual activity can be trance-inducing in itself. By incorporating sex into the rising power part of a ritual setting, one creates a cone of power. If you recall from Chapter 4, a cone of power acts as a funnel in which your intent is pushed out of you and your space, and into the universe for transmutation.

Sex magic can be practiced alone, with a partner who practices with or without you, or in a group setting. Solo sex magic is the most prominent used by witches and is my recommended approach, especially for newbies. This is partially out of emotional comfort but also because it allows for a better way of maintaining focus on your intent. It is also possible to do this while engaging in sexual acts with other non-witches, so long as you remain focused on your goal.

Partnered or group sex magic with other witches has its place and can definitely be a powerful practice; however, I feel that things can get difficult with this, as the pairing or group might have difficulty remaining tapped into each other. When working with multiple magical partners, it is really important that you all have a mutual idea of what your goal is and that you are completely in sync with how you wish for it to manifest. I have found that trying to harness sexual energy in acts with others, magical or otherwise, can be very difficult, as your partner(s) can become distracting. Whether discomfort occurs or the experience is just plain awful and awkward, you may slip out of your trance state and thus spoil your connection to the sexual energy. Because of this, I feel solo sex magic is the most fruitful to engage in.

Considering the trance state of sexual acts, solo sex can be seen as a form of meditation. Masturbation is the ultimate expression of self-love. Due to Lilith's solitary nature, the sex magic practiced by the GLAM Witch is done so in solo sessions of magical masturbation. Think of it as *manifesturbation*! In the end, we are all masturbating anyway, and we know our bodies better than anyone else. We know where and how to touch ourselves and can get lost in the rapture of our personal bliss. After all, Lilith was said to be the hand of Inanna, and it is with this hand that we dip into Lilith's sexual mysteries.

GLAM Hexercise: *Lilithian Solo Sex Magic Template*

Here is a simple guide to performing sex magic. It can be practiced on its own or tailored into any ritual as an act of raising energies. To begin, think of your magical intention. What is it that you want to manifest in your life? A new job, a new lover, glowing radiant health? Whatever it is, make sure you have a very clear idea of it and how it will be beneficial for yourself or others.

Next, create an inviting and sensual atmosphere. You can perform your sex magic in the confines of a circle, following the Lilithian ritual template from Chapter 4, or you can set up shop in your bedroom. Most sex magic practices do not require a circle or formal ritual casting. It can simply be achieved through visualizing your goal at the point of climax. Nevertheless, full rituals can help provide aesthetic and additional energetic power to your working.

Start by taking a bath or shower to cleanse yourself and get in the mood. Once ready, head to your space and bring a red candle to stimulate manifestation and sexual power. Bring any other items you wish to incorporate with you. Carve your goal into the candle and cast a circle if you wish to. It is also a good idea to call upon Lilith here and channel her sacred sensual influence within you. Light your candle and begin to touch yourself and engage in personal pleasure—do not just limit yourself to stimulating your genitals. Engage with your body—all of it. Love yourself. While you do this, try to keep your mind's eye focused on your desired goal.

For some, it may be hard to achieve orgasm without thinking of sexual acts. Some may discourage this, but I feel that it is totally fine. As with many things in life, there are multiple ways to get to the destination! For the best possible outcome I recommend that you limit your arousal to your imagination and not the glow of pornography on a screen during your sex magic. When you are close to climax, it is important that you shift your focus and solely visualize your desired goal. Upon reaching the point of no return, begin to speak your desire aloud, repeating it over and over. Begin to chant to Lilith and offer your sensual energies as an offering to her.

In the post-orgasmic state, rub any sexual fluids onto the carving of the candle to align the goal directly to you. Watch the flame, envisioning your intent transpire. Reflect on your current state of bliss and joy. When ready, blow out your candle and say:

Through Lilith, Great Goddess of Sexuality,
My spell has birthed out of me.
It is done, and so has begun!

In blowing out the candle, the transformative element of fire turns to smoke and is absorbed into the ether. Here, your breath acts as a conduit and gives life to the spell. Continue to do this as often as you feel is necessary until your goal has manifested. Have faith in Lilith and the universal laws of attraction.

Orgasmic Gratitude

Sex magic practices do not always need to be done to manifest something in your life; they can be an act of gratitude to Lilith. Your orgasmic power can also be used as an offering to thank the Goddess and the universe for the blessings in your life.

Sexy Tools

As we know from Chapter 3, there are a variety of tools that witches can incorporate into their practice. One that was not previously covered in length and lends itself useful here, is the use of sex toys for sex magic ritual. Yes, that's right—anal plugs, cock rings, and dildos . . . oh my!

There is a plethora of sex toys on the market today for just about anyone looking to intensify their sex life—magical or otherwise! That said, I prefer the use of organic specimens over synthetic materials and battery-operated devices (at least for magical moments). Phallic fruits and vegetables can be used as magical sex ingredients for penetration. Likewise, round and robust fruits like melons and pumpkins can be carved for penile insertion, while banana peels can be used as masturbation sleeves. With this in mind, fruits and vegetables like bananas, cucumbers, zucchini, etc., should never be inserted vaginally or anally after being peeled, as their natural sugars may cause infection.

Aside from fruits and veggies, you can get your rocks off with crystals too! Not only are crystals sometimes polished to adorn certain sex toys, they are also now being carved into anal plugs, cock rings, dildos, and yoni eggs. Even crystal massage wands can be used for external self-pleasure in your rituals. That being said, it is very important to only use crystals that have been specifically designed for sex purposes. There are a variety of wands, spheres, and other carvings but not all have been properly polished or treated for use as a sex toy. Some crystals may have hairline fractures or sharp edges that were not buffed out when the stone was polished. Remember that if using crystal sex toys is an avenue you wish to explore, I recommend searching for vendors who specialize in these types of toys to prevent any adverse reactions. Although there are a number of different types of sex toys on the market today, common crystal forms include:

✸ *Anal Plug*—Anal plugs are designed to be inserted and held within the anal cavity. These can be inserted during sex magic rituals to assist in healing the root chakra or even to anchor energy within you, further enhancing your magic.

✸ *Cock Ring*—The cock ring is designed to be placed around the base of a penis, and sometimes also over the testicles. Its primary function is to restrict blood flow from an erect penis, thus creating a stronger erection. In some instances, it can even delay or intensify orgasm. Rings can also be used like a masturbatory sleeve that is slid up and down the shaft of the penis for pleasure.

✸ *Wand*—There are a variety of crystal wands on the market today for pleasurable experiences. Crystal sex toy wands can be substituted for an athame or wand in sex magic rituals and can become the energetic channel between you and your magic. As long as they are designed for sex, these can provide both internal and external pleasure. The physical thrusting movement utilized in this form helps to stimulate and stir up the energy necessary for your magical sex acts.

✸ *Yoni Eggs*—Yoni eggs are crystals carved and designed to be inserted vaginally and held in place by activating the muscles of the pelvic floor through Kegel exercises. The eggs can lend themselves wonderfully to meditation, ritual, and spellwork that correspond directly to the metaphysical properties associated with the type of stone.

I find using crystal wands in sex magic can add an extra energetic boost to my workings, and seeing as each crystal contains its own vibrations, try selecting one polished out of a stone that aids in sexuality and love, such as rose quartz. If in doubt, remember that clear quartz is always a go-to amplifier of energy and can assist in any magical working.

Your sex magic toys can be energetically cleansed and charged just like any of your other tools for witchery. They can also be placed upon your shrine to Lilith before your ritual to help accumulate your spiritual energies and thus welcome her further into your sex rites. When blessing your sex toys, you may wish to say something as simple as this:

May you provide me ecstatic pleasure and
further aid in my magical rites.

Photo: An example of a crystal sex toy.

Sex Ethics

As a friendly reminder, the following code of ethics should be administered when performing acts of sex, magical or otherwise:

1. **No means no.** It is a one-word sentence that harbors much power. Use it, respect it, and honor it.

2. **Consent is mandatory.** It is not freely given and can never be assumed. It also does not provide you with a special all-access pass to do whatever your loins desire. Have fun but be courteous and respectful.

3. **Protect yourself.** When dealing with matters of sex, it is important to take the appropriate precautions. Sex magic and magical sex are not immune to HIV or any other STIs. Talk to your healthcare provider to determine the best preventative means for you.

Sexual Pain & Shame

Unfortunately, many people are unable to enjoy their sexuality due to the infliction of pain and/or shame. As beautiful as sexuality is, and as pleasurable as it can be, it can also be the root of overwhelming pain for some. We live in a rape culture, where sexual abuse and violence are commonplace, often resulting in a lack of justice. Even when justice is served, the detrimental effects of the trauma can influence one's thoughts and sensitivities toward future sexual acts.

Likewise, the prejudice against members of the LGBTQ+ community may result in deep emotional burden. The hate crimes committed against LGBTQ+ individuals is also parallel with an alarming number of youth committing suicide to escape the pains associated with their sexual orientation and/or identity. The Trevor Project, a leading national suicide prevention organization for LGBTQ+ youth, notes on its website that those "who come from highly rejecting families are 8.4 times as likely to have attempted suicide as peers who reported no or low levels of family rejection." Also noteworthy is that "40% of transgender adults reported having made a suicide attempt. 92% of these individuals reported having attempted suicide before the age of 25." In other instances, some bury their negative thoughts and feelings deep within, locking them away in an inner emotional closet. As a result, some lead double lives or keep their sexuality in the dark.

Sexual shame can also be a learned behavior past down from society and orthodox religions. The practice of sex magic is not a sole solution by any means, nor will it completely erase or take back any of the traumatization that took place as a result; however, the practice of sex magic, particularly with a Lilithian twist, can offer much catharsis to sexual healing and liberation. Physically, sex is a natural anesthetic, and it is because of this that it can be used metaphysically as a catalyst for healing.

GLAM Hexercise: *A Spell for Sexual Healing*

As a homosexual and former victim of sexual assault, I have experienced my own emotional pains associated with my sexuality. Along my spiritual and magical journey, I found release through Lilith and was able to embrace my sexuality. Through her worship and the transformative power of sex magic, I reclaimed my sexuality for me. The following ritual is one I created years ago that uses the creative essence of sex magic to release pain, shame, and other negative qualities related to sexuality.

Materials Needed
- ✵ Representation of Lilith
- ✵ Black candlestick
- ✵ White rose
- ✵ Shovel

This spell is going to be best performed on a Saturday night during the waning moon. Saturday is ruled by Saturn and is a powerful day for reversals, especially when coupled with the fading lunar phase. Gather your materials and set up a space as you would for a sex magic ritual. Start by cleansing the area and placing a representation of Lilith as the focal point of the workspace. Take your black candlestick and chip away at the wax at the bottom of the stick to expose the wick. On one side of the candle, carve your name, and on the other side, carve the word "sexuality." Seal your name on the candle by licking your thumb and tracing it over the carving. Place your rose nearby, then light the wick and state the following:

> *By the power of fire,*
> *I release the pain inside of me*
> *And heal my sexuality.*
> *May I embrace my true identity*
> *And become forever free.*
> *Lilith, lend your wings and grace,*
> *Fill this room with your embrace.*
> *Lift me up and let me soar,*
> *Fearing my sexuality no more.*

Close your eyes and begin to touch yourself, following the sex magic template provided earlier in this chapter. As you masturbate, focus on your sexual pleasure, and how you wish to experience it.

Visualize and imagine the perfect lover, or activities you wish to engage in, without fear or shame. This is your reclaiming—claim your sexuality in whatever manner you wish that fills you with self-love and empowerment. Once you have climaxed, offer your orgasm as an offering to Lilith and dip the petals of the rose into your conjured sexual fluids. You may also rub any of your remaining fluids onto the carving of your name in your candle.

For the next part you will be going outside. If this is not accessible due to your living conditions, have a potted plant nearby. Dig a hole, place your rose inside it, and recite the following:

With the beauty and grace of this rose,
My sexual sadness shall find repose.
Rebound and bloom once more,
Healing my very core.

Visualize your body filling with a vibrant white light that dissolves the dark, rotten core of pain within. If outside, leave your rose to decompose naturally, to be carried away by the elements or a creature of nature. If inside, let your rose wilt and the petals fall. Once they have dried and fallen, you may collect them and release them in a nearby body of water as a symbolic act of emotional release.

The Sensual Serpent

The serpent is a sexual being, a symbol of Lilith, and a totem of the GLAM Witch. Largely associated to sexuality, serpent worship has existed in various cultures throughout time. Remember that serpents are a powerful representation of life, death, and rebirth. These three themes are also found within the act of sex. Our ability to have sex is manifested through our very life. Our livelihood is connected greatly to sexuality, and in sex we die. The orgasm has been called *la petite mort*, and translates to "the little death," in

Photo: Lilith (1892) by John Collier – Public Domain

connection with the momentary loss of consciousness experienced through it. And it is with this death that new life is created, as the male sperm (which also actually looks kind of like a little snake) is released in a labyrinth of love in search of the egg. In solo or homosexual acts of sexuality, this energy can be transmitted into the rebirth of ourselves symbolic of the magical ouroboros. The ouroboros is depicted as a snake or dragon eating its own tail. Symbolizing the endless cycle of life, it also becomes a combination of feminine and masculine forces, as a phallic object that wraps itself in the form of a circle.

Up until now, I have casually discussed the term kundalini, another powerful attributes of serpent power. In Eastern philosophy, the sacred serpent known as kundalini lies at the base of our spine and propels upward through our chakras, bringing enlightenment. It is a prevalent concept existing in tantra, *Kama Sutra*, and yoga practices. Through this energetic serpent, one can connect to their spirituality on a deeper level and meet the divine. There are many variations with which one may work with their kundalini energy. The kundalini is also seen as a representation of Shakti, a universal energy that is also worshipped as a goddess in Hinduism. In this regard, Lilith is a representation of Shakti as both an energetic source and variation of the Goddess herself. Within tantric practices, Shakti takes the form of kundalini, and it is by traveling up the spine to the crown of the head that she meets her mate, the great God Shiva.

Let's Talk About Love

Love is perhaps the most prolific of reasons why people come into magic. Whether it is to gain a love, call them back, or get rid of them, everyone is after love spells! It must be noted that Lilith is unlikely to grant any request for partnered love or marriage, however. This should not be seen as malicious—it is because the love manifested by Lilith is that of unconditional self-love. Any thoughts of wholeness or completion that are dependent on another person are thrown out of the window when it comes to GLAM. As New Age as it is, self-love and self-compassion are the building blocks of confidence and authenticity. In my GLAM Witch way, I focus on myself first and foremost. Without self-love, self-care, self-nourishment, and self-indulgence, there is no self—there is no identity. Acts of self-pleasure are the ultimate form of self-love and self-indulgence and further help to emphasize the power of sex magic within Lilithian Witchcraft.

This is not to say that romantic partnership is not possible or a beautiful, magical experience that anyone can partake in; it is just that love spells and the mindset behind them are not acts of liberation and empowerment for a GLAM Witch. Partnership is possible but should happen organically. I should note that in the event someone wanted to try a love spell to call a new lover into their life, they should speak from the heart and ask that Lilith bless it with equality; however, I would challenge you, in the same way Lilith will, to really think about why you are asking for external love and not working on manifesting it first within yourself.

Lessons in Lil-Lust

While Lilith does not have any correspondence to romance, her energies are saturated in a lexicon of lust, seduction, and magical sex. The very notion of lust has been wildly frowned upon in Western cultures as an embodiment of sin; however, it is here that Lilith's magic magnifies. For this reason, she was damned as the evil succubus, striking fear in heteronormative male minds. Though lust is primarily thought of as sexual in nature, it comes to describe an intense desire for anything one can indulge in. From material items like food and money to power or the entanglement of flesh, lust is the ultimate desire. And who shouldn't desire the rapturous bliss of sexual pleasure? Of all the animals in the world, only a select few experience pleasure through sexual activity. Humans are one of them. In this next section, we will turn from sex magic to magical sex, highlighting effective forms of GLAM Witchcraft to assist in the rapturous passion of erotic indulgence.

The Art of Seduction

Partaking in magical sex is different than sex magic. With sex magic, we use sexual activity to build energy and thrust it into the universe with our orgasms. Magical sex, on the other hand, is using your witchcraft to attract a partner with lust and enhance the sexual experience. They can certainly be combined but don't necessarily have to be. Taking what we learned from the previous chapter, we know that glamour magic is an application of confidence to attract. One of the areas that it becomes most fruitful is in matters of seduction. Here are some ways to lure in your loin's desire—by combining practical methods with glamour magic through the five senses—for a night of lustful bewitchment!

1. **Sound**—To start, "let's get it on" with a little bit of sexy music to put you in the mood! Music has a way of casting a spell by

itself and is an extremely effective tool for glamourous lust magic. For this sense, create a super sexy playlist by selecting songs that not only turn you on but evoke the presence of your inner Lilith. While making the playlist, fuel it with your sensual, magical intent. If you are planning on heading out, I suggest a lounge or other establishment with an ambient mood and setting.

2. **Sight**—As we learned in the previous chapter, glamour magic has a lot to do with appearance. While this is partially true, outer appearance works in tandem with your inner confidence and persona. For this sense, you will use your bewitchment to project your seduction goals. Begin by lighting some red candles in your bathroom and worshipping yourself. Take a sexy bath with your favorite bath bomb or body scrub and really indulge yourself. Light some incense, add some rose petals and maybe even a few tumbled stones that vibrate with sensuality, such as carnelian or garnet. Listen to the soft sexy beats from your mix in the background. Seduce yourself. It all starts within you.

Once your bath is finished, dry off and start getting ready. Take your time and don't rush through this part. Using color magic, dress yourself in rich reds or hot pinks. Select an outfit that really makes you feel confident in yourself, something that is really electrifying, that drips with sexiness. Wear jewelry fashioned from red-, pink-, or orange-colored crystals that exude sensuality and confidence.

In addition to your physical display, it is also important to remember the art of body language. When it comes to sight, also remember that "eyes are the windows to the soul." Make sure you maintain proper eye contact with your partner throughout the night. Eye contact is an important form of communication, highlighting confidence and affirming attention. Also ensure that your body language is not closed off.

3. **Smell**—A major component to seduction, smell can ignite a desire with the first whiff. The human body creates smells that both attract and repel. Some of these smells are pheromones that naturally make us more attractive and stimulate a sexual response from others. With glamour magic, we can enhance our pheromones to increase attractiveness through essential or fragrance oils. Something that is musky, floral, or spicy will entice the nostrils and send a wave of electricity through your mate's body. Various seduction oil blends are listed in Chapter 11 of this book. Peruse them and concoct your fragrant potion prior to the evening. Dab it behind your ears, your wrists and your clavicle/chest region and get ready to really attract some attention!

4. **Taste**—It has been said before that a way to a person's heart is really through their stomach! The next sense to highlight is the taste buds. Certain foods known as aphrodisiacs help to increase the libido when consumed. In this stage, you are going to fuse together a bit of kitchen witchery with lusty glamour by making a dinner that promotes sensuality.

    For the meat-eating witches out there, high-protein meats (particularly red meat) stimulate chemicals within our bodies that fuel excitement and accelerate our heart beat. Other foods known for their aphrodisiacal qualities include oysters, truffles, asparagus, dark chocolate, red wine, champagne, figs, and strawberries. With that in mind, a sample dinner menu may include a first course of oysters, a main course of steak with truffle sauce and asparagus, and a dessert with fresh strawberries, chocolate, and whipped cream. If you are unable to cook a meal, dining out is always a good option. Do a bit of research on different types of aphrodisiacs and select a restaurant or items from the menu that wet the passion-food appetite.

5. **Touch**—Touching is the grand finale to your night of Lil-lust. While touch may seem like a really easy sense to work with when it comes to lustful endeavors, there is a lot more to it than meets the eyes—or, rather, the skin in this instance! This is the sense that allows you to really weave your magic and cast your spell. Sensual touch initiates a slew of sexual responses in our brains and is a very effective communication tool. Erogenous zones are the areas of the body that have increased sensitivity. While the most commonly known areas are the genitals, there are several others such as the ears, lips, neck, and inner thigh. Learn about these zone—not only where you can touch your partner but where you can tell them to touch you as well.

    But there is much more to touch than this. It is a sense that you should use all through the evening. Make an effort to flirtatiously touch your partner throughout the night. Don't just go straight for the cookie jar either! Leave a lingering touch that has your partner craving more. This could be as simple as a soft kiss where your lips barely meet or a soft caress on the arm, barely touching, that commands the hairs on the back of the neck to jump up with excitement. Self-touch is an important element of this sense too. Use the art of body language to invite your partner and seduce them.

    Another element of touch to use is breath. Breath is a vital source of life, and you can touch someone indirectly through the use of your breath. This is a fun, effective way to ignite lust with touch. Breathing and blowing on your partner's fleshy erogenous zones are a surefire way to ignite passion between the two of you!

While each of the senses above plays a different role, it is important to remember that they should also act together throughout the entire night. Sound is not only sexy beats banging softly in the background while you get ready or engage in the grand finale. It is also using speech to communicate directly with your partner—your soft whispers and cries of ecstasy. It is not just how you look but also using eye contact to engage, encourage, and invite. It is your grooming and hygiene—the chemistry of your natural scent with your fragrance oil and tactfully placed drops of scent in the correct areas of your body. It is not just your dinner but also the salty taste of sweat on each other's bodies and the electrifying touches you engage in throughout the evening. It is the art of seduction, the work of red magic, your lustcraft that casts its spell here. Relax, improvise as needed, and most importantly, enjoy!

Witchcrafting: *A Bag of Lust*

For this spell, our goal is hot and steamy sex! This will be accomplished through constructing a mojo bag, a popular magical talisman used in folk magic that traditionally contains an odd number of ingredients found from animals, minerals, and herbs or roots. This spell should be performed on the night of the full moon.

Materials Needed
- ✸ Red candle for lust
- ✸ 1 dried chili pepper for spice
- ✸ 1 piece of snakeskin shed for sexuality
- ✸ 1 tsp. orchid root clippings for self-esteem
- ✸ 1 tumbled garnet for stamina
- ✸ 1 vanilla bean for sweetness
- ✸ Pinch of cinnamon for confidence
- ✸ Pinch of damiana for seduction
- ✸ Pinch of hibiscus for passion
- ✸ Red condom to use as a bag

✶ Sexual fluids to feed the ingredients and to align to sexuality

Construct your spell space as you see fit. Ground, center, and call upon Lilith. Carve your name into the candles, along with the word "lust" on the other side. Seal the carving as you normally would. Light the candle and say:

By the power of fire, ignite my desire.

Next, unroll your condom and place each ingredient out in front of you. Ask that Lilith bless each of your ingredients with the desired outcome of heightened lust and sexual magnetism. Now, you will take hold of each ingredient and speak your intention into it based on the qualities outlined in the materials list. See the example below for clarification.

Chili pepper, grant me spice, and aid me in achieving ecstatic pleasure.

Once this has been done, combine your dried herbs and snakeskin shed into a mortar and pestle and grid into a fine powder. While doing this, envision the hot, steamy sex you seek. Now, you will combine the remaining ingredients into the condom. Once stuffed, recite the following charm for Lilith to enchant the condom mojo bag:

Lady Lilith, I call on thee,
Sweet and spicy,
Love and lust,
Great sex is an absolute must.
Seduction, take hold now,
manifest a wham, bam, pow.
Saturate the sheets with sweat,

A night of lust is a guaranteed bet!

Now, using the sex magic formula from earlier in this chapter, begin to engage in solo sex to build energy and help fuel your spell. Once orgasmic energy has filled the space, add any fluids into the bag, feeding the other ingredients with your intent. Thank the ingredients for their work ahead of time. Now, you will breathe life into the bag. Holding the condom away from your mouth, position yourself so that the candle is between your mouth and the opening of the bag. Close your eyes and blow a sensual long blow into the opening. This will extinguish the flame of the candle and push its energy into the condom with the combination of your breath and smoke. Tie the condom shut, thank Lilith, and end your ritual. Your bag is enchanted and should remain potent for about a month. Place under your mattress or carry to your next sexual encounter, either in a bag or your pocket. After the month has passed, bury the bag as an offering and thank your ingredients for assisting in your magical sex efforts. Repeat this process as you see fit.

Sex Worker Sorcery

Criticized as objectifying and enslaving as often as it is praised for empowerment, sex work is frequently engulfed by stigma. Irish escort and sex worker advocate Laura Lee suggests, "To understand sex work, we must first define the term. My definition is simply two consenting adults exchanging sex for cash. This definition is important, because all too often sex work is conflated with trafficking, child sex abuse and rape—and it is these conflations that drive the scrutiny and negative attention we in the industry so often face." Sadly, this stigma often fuels violence. In a Huffington Post article from 2015, Sex Workers Outreach Project communication director Katherine Koster explains, "Globally, sex workers have a 45 to 75% chance of experiencing sexual violence at some point in their lives as a sex worker and a 32 to 55% chance of experiencing sexual violence in a given year." There are many hurdles to the profession, however some may embrace it as a means of empowerment despite the common dishonor of it being considered a last resort. For those who willfully engage in any form of sex work—from prostitution to exotic dancing, web cams to pornography, or phone sex to massage parlor "happy endings"—Lilith can serve as a powerful role model.

In her role as handmaiden to Inanna's temples of sexuality, Lilith has become the patroness of prostitution. Because of this, she can be called upon not only to offer fierce protection to sex workers but also to assist in granting successful pursuits. After all, all acts of sexual pleasure are her rituals, and an exchange of sex for cash remains an equal exchange of energy. Nevertheless, prostitution remains illegal in most of the United States and other countries of the world. The taboo nature of the work only helps appease the rebellious archetype of Lilith.

In my early 20s, I dabbled a bit as a sex worker to help make ends meet between jobs. During this time, I would call upon Lilith for protection, guidance, and aid in my endeavors. This next spell is inspired by the traditional hoodoo honey jar spell and will be used to assist sex workers in sweetening potential clients—particularly the wealthy ones! On top of this, the sweetening spell will aid in protection by defusing hostility and potential acts of violence. Whether you are actively working in the sex industry or simply looking to snatch up a wealthy lover, this spell is sure to make you come out on top!

Materials Needed
- A dollar bill
- Red pen
- Pinch of ground red roses
- Pinch of ground catnip
- Pinch of cardamom powder
- 1 small piece of jezebel root

- ✪ 1 small piece of snakeskin shed
- ✪ Your personal effects (such as hair, blood, or sexual fluids)
- ✪ 1 small owl charm to represent Lilith
- ✪ Honey jar with tin top
- ✪ Spoon
- ✪ Suc-sex-ful Oil (see page 275)
- ✪ Red candlestick
- ✪ Eco-friendly glitter

This spell is best per-formed on a Sunday or Friday during the wax-ing moon phase to aid potency for success, attraction, and sexual magnetism. Begin by gathering your materi-als and setting up your altar. Take your dollar bill and, using your red pen, write out "Good clients. Good sex.

Good money." in a continuous line as you twist the bill in a clock-wise motion while focusing on attracting kind, sensual, and wealthy clients. Once you have created a full circle with the three commands, write them on top of one another, creating three stacks in the center of the circle. Turn your bill clockwise and write this again, crossing over what you originally wrote. Do this for two more turns, as if you are creating a cross with your writings. In the end, it should look similar to the pictured petition above.

Now, you will place a sprinkle of each of the herbs in the cen-ter of the dollar. Each time you do, remember to speak your inten-tion into the herb, giving it life through the power of word.

1. Add the roses and say: *Rose, bless me with your beauty.*

2. Add the catnip and say: *Catnip, bring good clients to me.*

3. Add the cardamom and say: *Cardamom, ensure great pleasure and passion for all.*

4. Add the jezebel root and say: *Jezebel root, attract wealthy conquests to thrall.*

5. Add the snakeskin and say: *Snakeskin, add protection and sexual success.*

6. Add your personal effects and say: *A bit of me will seal this best.*

7. Finally, add the owl charm and say: *By the power of Lilith, night owl and handmaiden of sex, this spell will be bound and blessed.*

Once all of the ingredients have been placed on the bill, fold the bill toward you. Moving in a clockwise motion again to represent attraction, continue to fold the bill until it is unable to fold any-more. Set your petition aside.

Now, place your honey jar in a fireproof dish. Take off the lid and set aside. Using your spoon, eat three scoops of honey from the jar. Before eating each scoop say:

Sweet and sexy honey, show me the money.

Now, push your petition down into the honey, then add three drops of your Suc-sex-ful Oil to the jar and seal it.

Next, taking your candle, carve your name into the wax and anoint the carving with your saliva, blood, or sexual fluids. Then add three drops of your Suc-sex-ful Oil to the candle and massage it all over the wax. Once the candle is lubed up, sprinkle a bit of catnip and cardamom powder on a plate. Roll the candle into the mixture and shake off any excess herbs. Finally, sprinkle some of the gold glitter on the candle for added attraction and success.

Once your candle is ready, hold it several inches away from your genitals with the tip facing you to symbolically draw in sexual energy. Do this for a moment while you focus on infusing the candle with your sexual energy. When you are ready, melt the bottom of the candle using a match or lighter. Let a few wax drippings fall onto the center of the lid. Once the bottom is nice and melted, hold it firmly to the center of the lid and allow to cool.

Finally, you will be setting the energy of the petition in the honey free by lighting the candle. As you light the wick, repeat these words:

> *I'm the honey, and you are the bee,*
> *I attract wealthy clients with my sexuality.*
> *Fiery flame, I ask you to bless,*
> *As I call on the mighty temptress.*
> *Lilith, I ask that you watch over me,*
> *Aiding my sex work with protection and prosperity!*

Close your eyes and feel the essence of Lilith come alive within you, igniting you with her sexual power. Feel her wings fold over you, blanketing you in her protection. Sit and watch the candlestick burn out while you envision the most desirable sex work scenarios. Once the candle has burnt out, leave the jar on your altar or shrine for several months. If you feel the need to top the spell off, you can always fix another candle in the same fashion and repeat the second half of the spell. For added effect, when heading out to "work it," dab a bit of Suc-sex-ful Oil on your wrists, clavicle, and behind your ears.

Witchcrafting: *A Lil-Lust Potion*

What's a witch without a magic potion? It has been said that the way to the hear tis through the stomach, and in this next witch-crafting the sex witch's work will begin in the kitchen. Various foods and beverages are known to be aphrodisiacal, heightening sexual potency. I have adapted the following recipe from *The Sexual Herbal*, by the founding member of the American Herbalists Gild Brigitte Mars. It calls on you to create a damiana cordial, and while the process is a bit lengthy, it is a total treat and must-have for any GLAM Witch! Please note that while damiana is generally safe to ingest, it may cause potential problems for those with diabetes or who have recently had surgery, as it can affect blood sugar and glucose levels. Use with caution.

Materials Needed
- ✷ 1/4 oz. organic damiana
- ✷ 1/4 oz. organic rose petals
- ✷ 1/4 oz. organic hibiscus
- ✷ 1/4 oz. organic passionflower
- ✷ 2 c. brandy
- ✷ 1 ½ c. filtered water
- ✷ 1 c. organic honey
- ✷ 1 Tbsp. organic rose water
- ✷ 1 Tbsp. organic vanilla extract
- ✷ Cinnamon to taste

Optional: Shavings of organic vanilla bean

Prior to crafting your Lil-lust potion, charge your ingredients under the light of a full moon, calling upon the robust and fertile lunar energy to enchant and enhance your ingredients. Once charged, follow these steps:

1. Combine your herbs into a glass jar. Pour the brandy over the mixture and let sit for at least five days.

2. Strain the liquid into a new jar and set aside. The leaves will then need to be soaked in the filtered water for an additional three days. Pour the water on to the leaves, stir well, seal, and store.

3. Strain the liquid from the leaves and reserve it. Use your leaves as compost.

4. Place the water from the leaves in a saucepan and warm over low heat. Add the honey and stir until it has melted into the water. Remove from heat and cool.

5. Now, combine your honey water with the brandy. Add the rose water and vanilla extract. Shake well and let sit one to four weeks before using. When serving, use a frosted martini glass that has been rimmed with cinnamon and vanilla bean powder. Drizzle a small bit of honey in the glass. Shake your potion in a mixer with ice then pour into your glass and enjoy!

*Non-alcoholic: For those who do not drink alcohol, you can still enjoy this lustful libation by turning it into an iced tea. Simply skip step one and allow your herbs to sit in the filtered water for three days. Follow the rest of the recipe as is. The only other deviation is that since the herbs will not be soaking in alcohol, you can enjoy your recipe three to five days after all ingredients are combined.

Kinkcraft

Clearly, Lilithians are sex positive and have healthy attitudes toward sexuality. With sexuality, there is also a dark side—akin to our shadow self. Fetishes can be incorporated into sex magic practices and may also prove fruitful for magical sex. Many in the Pagan fetish community have embraced Lilith as a kink goddess, helping participants find liberation through sexual deviance, particularly BDSM (aka **b**ondage, **d**iscipline or **d**ominance, **s**ubmission, and **s**ado**m**asochism). It is here that shadowcraft and lustcraft merge together in the fifty shades of Lil-lust!

In Lilith's refusal to submit to Adam, a potent expression for feminine sexual dominance is created. Again, sexuality in this regard is not necessarily gender specific when considering non-heteronormative sexual pairings. Nevertheless, sexual dominance from a routinely submissive partner can be very liberating.

It has been argued by some that forms of kinkcraft, particularly BDSM are not enriching magical platforms; however, I disagree. Remember that everything is energy. Sex magic uses our pleasure to coax an energetic release. Kink activities of domination, submission, and pain carry their own unique elements in sex magic. Kink can be very creative and a compelling source of energy. The willful pain experienced can be channeled in ritual and spellwork as a sacrificial act. This pain becomes an energetic exchange between the Goddess, you, and your magical

magical request. If interested in further exploring this type of magical sex, I recommend the book *Dark Moon Rising: Pagan BDSM and the Ordeal Path,* by Raven Kaldera.

Lustcrafting: *A Sexual Dedication Ritual to Lilith*

Now that you have gone through the crash course of sex magic, it is time to apply it all in one big Lilithian lust-fest! In the following ritual of passion and pleasure, we will dedicate our sexuality to Lilith. In this ritual, you will be dedicating your body to her sacred sensuality as a temple, bestowing every orgasm as an offering to her power. Plan on having an entire night of pleasure with yourself and fully unlocking the doors to your self-love.

Materials Needed
✪ Lilith representation
✪ Mirror
✪ Lilithian libation
*Optional: Desserts (fresh fruit or something decadent); red candles; red roses; sex toys

You'll perform this ritual in your bedroom, ideally on the night of a full moon. This is because the full moon is when the moon's energies are at their peak—the climax of lunar energy! Splurge on full indulgence. Light your entire space with red candles and roses or any other accoutrements that you feel advocate sensuality.

Take a nice, sensual bath, soaking in flowers and herbs that radiate passion. Set up your space with your representation of Lilith and magic mirror. Position the mirror so that you will be able to look at yourself during the ritual. Dress yourself in silky lingerie, a robe, or nothing at all. Remember that this ritual is all about honoring your sexual indulgence through Lilith. Really let yourself go and welcome a night of exuberant self-seduction. You are going to love yourself. You are going to make love with yourself and channel this into the universe.

Set up your space so that a representation of Lilith and mirror can be viewed from your bed. Once your space is arranged and you are feeling lush with lust, pour yourself a bit of your Lilithian libation and settle into bed. Feel free to cast a circle around your bed, erecting an energetic temple to Lilith. Using the "Invocation of Lilith," (see page 76) call her into your space. Once you feel her presence and your body becomes electrified with sensuality, speak these words:

I walk the path of passion
And dedicate myself to desire.
I pulsate with eroticism
And burn with carnal fire.
I straddle love and lust,
For your worship is a must.
My body is your temple and
My sex is your gift,
My pleasure is your worship.
I give my body to you and in doing so, awaken me.
I conjure lustcraft and unleash it free.
All acts of love and pleasure, are your rituals from hereon.
I dedicate my body to you, Lilith,
For I am your sex witch, your priest(ess) of passion,
Forever flowering in your eyes,
Mastering the magic that manifests between my thighs.

Stare at yourself and the glorious display of sexuality that is you. Watch yourself performing in front of the mirror. Make love to yourself, and in doing so, make love to Lilith—the Lilith within and without. Mate with the energies of your surroundings. Get lost in your pleasure and eroticism. Love yourself and the moment. Wind your hips like the sex serpent that lies within you. Give birth to your bliss and happiness. Align with Lilith's energies as a sex goddess, dedicate your pleasure as an offering to her from this point forward.

Integrating Indulgence

I recently read that self-indulgence is essentially the act of feeling good without providing substance; however, I strongly disagree. Indulgence is a sympathetic feeling associated to the pleasures of life. Giving in to your desires and wants and doing something that makes you feel good is absolutely filled with substance. Our sexuality is only one form of indulgence that we can feed. As you move forward in your path, here are some tips to continue indulging in the pleasures of life, whatever they may be.

1. **Take time to do what you want to do.** If you want to stay home from work and sit on the couch and eat junk food—do it! Society often tells us that we should feel guilty for feeling good, but it is ok to yourself. It is ok to cheat on your diet, skip the gym,

and give up responsibility. Life is meant for living. Living your life and doing the things that make you feel good is an act of self-love, self-care, and empowerment.

2. **Masturbate as often as you'd like to.** Regardless of whether fueled with magical intent, sexual release and stimulation help relax you, so bask in your orgasmic power. After a rough day, give yourself the gift of self-pleasure. Just remember to turn off the porn and turn on your mind! Make love with yourself and focus on the healing properties of pleasure rather than visual stimuli for gratification.

3. **Treat yourself!** Sometimes, we may feel bad for buying ourselves something frivolous or splurging on a day at a spa, a blow out, or other activity. Who has time to feel bad about treating themselves? Not GLAM Witches! Take time to buy yourself that item you have always wanted. Pick up fresh flowers and dedicate them to how awesome you are. Eat cake and carbs! Be daring and try something new and adventurous. Take a nap. Take yourself to the movies or out to dinner. Date yourself. Nourish your well-being as you would a lover. Love yourself. Indulge in treating yourself because you are worth it, and you deserve it!

10

BIONIC BITCHCRAFT

Defending it with Protective Magics
for Flight or Fight

"A witch who cannot hex, cannot heal."
—Unknown

Witches are often cloaked in the mystery of curses, hexing, and that good old black magic. For some, the very idea of a witch will conjure up a vision of green-faced hags who stir their cauldron in preparation for their meal of children. From the Wicked Witch of the West to the Evil Queen, Maleficent, and the Sanderson sisters, witches have been portrayed as malicious, vengeful creatures of the night, in the same vein as Lilith.

Hexing is by far one of the most controversial topics of magic among witches. Many will tell you that it does not exist and preach a "do what you will as long as it harm none" rule of the craft; however, the practice of hexing is very real and can be very powerful and damaging. Baneful magics do exist, and there is a vast amount of ways to dip into them. When we look at nature, it is a loving, fertile home, but it also creates many destructive forces that kill and cause vast devastation. Witches honor nature, and with that, hexing and curses have their home in the craft as a pinnacle of willful chaos, justice, and resistance. That said, magic is not a game. None of the practices laid out here are anything to dabble in out of frivolousness, but this notion is magnified on a larger scale when it comes to matters of magical malice. There is a toll to pay when it comes to using magical manipulation for vengeful purposes.

Hexing today is an automatic and systematic habit for some witches. We are living in a pre-apocalyptic era of war, tyranny, hypocrisy, and injustice. The present world as we know it is a divine comedy of mass chaos. These dark times call for a dark force to neutralize and heal the lands, but in attempting to do so, some shoot from the hip with their hexing without considering, or even knowing, what witchery they are weaving. If not handled properly, a hex is the equivalent of a drunken night. Some of the largest regrets in life are caused by overindulgence in alcohol and the chaotic decisions made as a result. It is like getting drunk and pressing "enter," sending that text, email, or post that exposes your incoherent emotional wrecking ball. With the practice of hexing, all the emotion, all the rage, intoxicates you. When you cast that spell, you hit send. There is no delete or undo, no Ctrl + Z to set you free. There is great power and energy in rage but only when it is laser focused. Otherwise, it becomes a Pandora's box of nightmares, as you unleash your negativity into the ether, letting it spread and grow like a metaphysical cancer.

This is not meant to deter or frighten you but more so to educate you on the seriousness of this type of magic. Have I hexed? Yes. Do I regret it? Absolutely not. Did I get what I wanted? Yes, and then some! So what's the problem? Well, in doing this type of magic, I have learned just how much of a toll it takes on me. When you fight the wicked with wickedness, it starts layering one on top of the other, and one can start sinking into a cesspool of toxic energies that torment your well-being. Paranoia, fear, and misunderstanding take hold. As a result, I have learned that it is often better to remove myself from a negative situation than to use magic to manipulate it with vengeance. But, as with everything in life, there are exceptions. Hexing can be a cathartic practice as well, opening us to healing as we right the wrongs cast down upon us. Sometimes we are left with no other choice but to clutch our fists and fight back. Not out of malice but for survival.

At the end of the day, many different people will say many conflicting things about the practice of hexing. In the end, it is not my place to say if or when you should do it. The GLAM Witch has freedom of choice to do as they wish, as does Lilith. With this comes knowledge, though. You must be aware of the roles that magic plays in these circumstances, and the tolls that result from them, to better assert your choice.

Like "witch," "bitch" has become a versatile word. Once used as an insult, it has been reclaimed and used in an empowering sense. Lilith is a bitch goddess. Her qualities as a rebel and villain put her here. Today, "bitch" has shifted to also represent someone who is weak and unable to get the dirty jobs done. But it can still take on a harsher demeanor. So, here we are—at the Lilithian point of bitchcraft, presented with the dichotomy between society's representation of the coward and the villain. Like the element of air, bitchcraft is ruled by thought and mind. It is a tornado, a spiraling wind of chaos and destruction. Whether shielding the bitchcraft of others or deploying your own, this point of the Lilithian Pentacle calls forth the rebellious nature of Lilith and explores two avenues of witch bitchery—fight or flight.

Journal Entry

Grab that journal of yours and reflect upon the following questions.

1. What is your personal interpretation of hexing?

2. How do you handle adversity in your everyday life? Do you try to resolve the situation or point fingers and cast blame?

3. How do I define justice? What role should my spirituality have in applying justice?

4. What would Lilith do? How would she react to a negative situation that did not serve her in the fullest regard?

BITCHCRAFT FOR FLIGHT

Many in the magical community align Lilith with baneful forms of magic. One argument for this is that her rage is a powerful form of energy that can be manipulated and harnessed to aid in harming those who have harmed us. To a degree, this makes sense. If anyone should experience rage as a result of their treatment, it is Lilith. After all, she is all about equality. With this in mind, she can certainly assist in magics used to establish justice and position the karmic scales in balance.

Rule of Three

Some witches follow what is known as the Threefold Law, which states, "an it harm none, do what ye will." However, many witches question this and the ability to truly live life (magically or mundanely) in a way that does not cause harm. Every action has a reaction, and there is a price for every piece of magic you use. Perhaps your spell to get that new job you have been wanting works, but someone else who may have really needed it missed out due to your interference, thereby contradicting the Threefold Law. As a result, many witches today consider the rule of three to be outdated, and it is not a philosophy utilized in GLAM.

I have used Lilith in hexes and protective magics in my time and felt early on that this was something that she radiated with. But I began to think about it. When Gilgamesh killed the snake, Lilith ran into the wilderness. When Adam demanded she submit, she flew away. So I asked myself, did Lilith really fight back? Did she harm? No. She took refuge.

Have you ever noticed that when a large storm, earthquake, or other natural disaster is about to strike, animals tend to have the heads-up quicker than we do? The buzzing insects and bird chirps go silent. Cats retreat. These animals know something is brewing and take shelter. This is their survival instinct. They do not risk the dangers associated with waiting it out, nor do they attempt to challenge the storm. Why? Because they would likely die or get severely injured in the process, so instead they hide for survival.

When it comes to hexing, this can sometimes be the best situation—the art of doing nothing. In Buddhism, the practice of taking refuge means that a practitioner follows the steps of the Buddha. They follow the Buddhist path. Considering Lilith took her own refuge, fleeing in times of danger, GLAM reflects this same practice. Follow her steps. If negativity arises, you run. You run as far and as fast as you can away from a situation. This does not make you a coward. It makes you smart. It helps you survive.

The term "fight or flight" is associated with the psychological reaction of an individual in the presence of danger; this danger can be a direct, physical attack, emotional threats, or any situation that impedes upon our survival. Before we fight, let's examine how a GLAM Witch can learn from the application of flight in negative situations.

Neutralizing Negativity

Witches should always use protection, and, no, we are not reverting back to our chapter on lustcraft here! As we know, the world is made up of energy. We transmit energy and absorb it. Not all energy is filled with fluffy rainbows of love and light, nor should it be. But sometimes the hatred, fear, doubt, and jealousy from others can leak out of their existence and into your life, causing a myriad of toxic emotional tar. The thoughts and projections of others can leech onto you and syphon off your energy as well, leaving you feeling depleted and worthless.

Negativity has dangerous effects on our mind, body, and spirit. Rather than wielding a sword of witch bitchery and throwing out hexes left and right at possible sources of origin, one can take a proactive approach to get ahead of these situations by cleansing or shielding themselves from the influences of others.

Cleansing

Cleansing is an action that involves dissolving the negative energies that accumulate either within you or that have been cast onto you. Similar to the cleansing of any new tools or ingredients that you use in your magical workings, your body is also an important tool for your witchcraft and an extension of your magic; it is the shell of your energetic being. While dark, glamorous rituals can certainly be incorporated into your cleansings, they are certainly not necessary for all magical workings. Here are several ways to cleanse your vibration.

⊛ **Baths**—One of the most common practices used for cleansing involves submerging oneself in the healing waters of a ritual bath. Baths in general are a means of cleansing one's physical body. By incorporating other ingredients into the bath, such as crystals, herbs, and oils, you can strengthen the cleansing of your energetic vibrations as well. As you may recall, I often suggest taking a bath before doing any of the ritual work throughout this book, as it helps to dissolve negative energies and align you with your intentions. But these baths do not necessarily have to be a beginning piece to a spell or ritual. Sometimes, the bath itself can be the working.

My number one recommended tool for cleansing baths is black lava salt. This is a combination of mineral-rich sea salt and activated charcoal, which, when mixed, creates black cubic crystals of banishment. Salt in general is a natural detoxifier and dissolves in water, making it the perfect catalyst for dissolving toxic energies that have been clinging to you. When mixed with the activated charcoal, it can be used to absorb negativity. A simple recipe for a diffusing bath requires combining one tablespoon of black lava salt, a sprig of rosemary, a piece of black obsidian, and three drops of frankincense oil in a bath. All of these agents are revered for their ability to dispel negativity. While bathing, simply state, "May the negativity surrounding me be dissolved. I am free, I am free, I am free."

In addition to these ritualistic baths, one can also utilize the healing power of water in nature as well. Those who have access to the beach or ocean may decide to cleanse themselves by the power of the sea, submerging themselves in the salty, liquid velvet. Running out in the rain is another great source, as it symbolically washes over you in an act of cleansing.

✸ *Candles*—The transformative element of fire can be harnessed to purge negative energies from you as well. One of the techniques used for this is to brush yourself with a candle. This involves holding an unlit candle several inches away from you and tracing it over all areas of your body. By doing this, the candle becomes infused with your energy. Once this has been done, light your candle and state, "By the transformative element of fire, I purge the negativity that surrounds me. As I will it, it shall be."

Always use a black candle instead of white for acts of cleansing, protection, or banishment. Using a white candle for this will only amplify the negative energy, as white is a reflective color. Black is an absorbent color and will lock the negativity inside of it, purging it with fire when burned. For an extra oomph, use a candlestick, and chip away at the wax at the bottom, lighting it upside down to symbolize the reversal of negative energy. Also be sure to let these candles burn all the way down. You never want to reuse a candle for cleansing purposes.

✸ *Crystals*—Crystals are an abundant source of earth energy that help to ground one's spirit and energetic magnetism. Black crystals like smokey quartz, black tourmaline, and obsidian are great sources of purification and energetic detoxification. They can be incorporated into your wardrobe as jewelry or even held in a meditative ritual to assist in absorbing the unwanted energies. Aside from these uses, crystals can also help manifest energies when arranged in a crystal grid.

Photo: A personal crystal grid for protection. When constructing crystal grids, determine your intention and then select crystals and a geometric pattern that represents the desired energetic vibration. The above grid is constructed out of black tourmaline, smokey quartz, and two variations of obsidian. I arranged it in the form of a square pattern, to anchor the gird with the numerology of four for stability and foundation.

Witchcrafting: *A Body Crystal Grid*

A crystal grid is a combination of different crystals placed in a formation based on sacred geometry to assist in the manifestation of desired results. Once a goal is determined, a grid can be created through the symbolism associated with geometric shapes and crystals. They can be erected anywhere and used to charge any item, including yourself. A body grid is a crystal grid that is placed around or over your body to either energize or neutralize a desired energy.

All you will need for this grid is five pieces of black tourmaline. Lay down on a comfortable surface. Around your body, place the crystals in the following formation: one above your head, one below your feet, and one at each side, making a diamond shape around you. If any of the crystals make a pointed formation on the end, place the point so that it extends away from you; this motion helps draw energies out. (If it is pointed in, the point would help push the energies inward. But that would defeat the purpose here!) Place the last one on your belly button, so it acts as the focal point of the body grid and helps anchor the goal of the grid. Close your eyes and begin to ground and center yourself. As you relax, you will ask the crystals to absorb that which no longer serves.

✴ *Essential Oils*—Applied topically as fragrance oil, added to a bath, or even a diffuser, essential oils provide aromatic cleansing. Various religious and spiritual traditions have been known to use the power of fragrance to cleanse homes and spaces. Fragrances like frankincense, juniper, lemon, and sage are known for their purifying properties. For protective glamour, these can be adorned as fragrances or even through jewelry. Nowadays, it is rather easy to find beaded bracelets and necklaces that are designed hold onto essential oils.

✴ *Movement*—As we learned in the chapter on glamcraft, movement is a very powerful form of witchery, as it can aid in attracting or repelling attention. Similarly, movement can be a powerful method for cleansing as well. Physical activity like working out is a great way to work up a sweat and shake off toxic vibrations. A good run or a punch thrown in kickboxing is a transformative way to transmute built up negative energy.

Dance is also a very cleansing activity and is easily incorporated into ritual settings as an act of rising energy. Fire dancing in particular is an extraordinary cleansing technique, as it combines the transformative element of fire with movement to not only shake off the energies but burn right through them.

✴ *Plants*—Herbs and other plants are an essential element to witchcraft, as they are utilized in a variety of magical means to manifest results. Having a live plant in your space can assist in neutralizing negative energies by grounding them in the plant's earth energy. Simply hold your plant and ask that it absorbs and grounds the energies that are tied to you and which no longer serve a purpose.

✴ *Smudging*—Smudging is the ceremonious practice of cleansing through the burning of sacred herbs. This is often done with sage, but there are a variety of herbs that can be used for this process.

Some will use sage in a bundle with other herbs that better direct the energy. For example, smudging yourself with rose petals can assist in cleansing, purifying, and beautifying a space to establish harmony and splendor. The combination of the herbs' metaphysical properties and the purging element of fire create smoke that blows away toxic vibrations.

⊛ *Sound*—Bells, drums, gongs, and signing bowls are all tools that can be used to dissolve the vibration of energies with sound waves.

⊛ *Sunlight or Moonlight* —The sun provides courage, strength, and vitality, whereas the moon provides psychic stimulation and emotional recharge. When weather permits (unless you have wonderful windows), a very simple solution to use when you are feeling bogged down by the energy of others is to sit in the sunlight or glowing moonlight for a charge up and release.

⊛ *Teas & Tonics*—Tea is a literal detox that also works to clear away any unwanted energy—from inside and out. As we have already explored a bit in the chapters on shadowcraft and lustcraft, teas can be used for a vast array of magical applications. In more shamanic traditions, teas become especially healing.

Shielding

Shielding is a great method of protection. Like an energetic witch condom, the right shielding will protect you from others' toxic vibrations, deflecting the negative energies, either sending it back to the source or to another object. As discussed in the chapter on glamcraft, many witches drape themselves in jewelry or other flamboyant apparel—for attention, enchantment, seduction, or protection. The first thing someone notices can be a piece of jewelry or other part of your outfit. This is why I advocate for dressing "extra" with gaudy outfits. It might look cheeky, but by attracting the attention through an object you wear, you are trapping the initial energies into that piece. Again, wearing black is also a way to do this because, remember, black absorbs. Similarly, metallic clothing will deflect negativity from you. To shield with your attire, you simply enchant your objects with the power of word by telling it what to do. You can do this by simply stating a small spell: "Necklace of mine, spark and shine, deflect negativity, and do not let it penetrate me." Envision your accessory or piece of clothing blanketed in a blinding, sparkling white light that will either dissolve or reflect any ill will cast your way.

Another great way to shield negativity is to create a witch's ball of protection. This is an ornamental object that combines several ingredients to bring protection to your home or space. It absorbs the negative energies of a space so they will not linger or attach themselves to you. In this next witchcrafting activity, we will make one together and call upon the power of Lilith to protect your nest.

GLAM Witchcrafting: *Lilithian Ball of Protection*

A witch ball acts as a kind of energetic dreamcatcher that traps and neutralizes the negative energies of a property or other space inhabited by a witch. Dating back to the 17th century, these decorative balls were originally hung up to ward off evil spirits and acts of witchcraft. In modern times, witches have reclaimed these tools as a source of protection. Sometimes a witch ball is a simple decorative blown-glass ornament hung in windows. This variation can be very modern looking and inconspicuous so that the intention of protection is unknown to passersby. You can also make your own by filling a plain glass ornament ball with a variety of herbs and other ingredients used for protection.

Materials Needed

- ✸ Broken mirror shards
- ✸ Tumbled obsidian
- ✸ 1 tsp. of black salt
- ✸ 1 tsp. of mugwort
- ✸ 1 tsp. of sage
- ✸ 1 piece of snakeskin
- ✸ 1 Tbsp. of Spanish moss
- ✸ A photo of you
- ✸ Personal effects, such as blood, hair, and/or nail clippings
- ✸ Image of Lilith
- ✸ Square sticky note
- ✸ Black sealing wax stick
- ✸ Glass ornament orb

Perform this spell anytime between the full and dark moons. The reversal energy of the waning moon will assist in energizing your ball with protection. Cast a circle if you see fit. Once your space is ready, and you have cleansed yourself for the working, lay the broken mirror shards, obsidian, black salt, mugwort, sage, snakeskin, Spanish moss, and personal effects in front of you. Here, you will charge each of them by stating your intent and what you wish they for them to do for you (i.e. guard, protect, deflect, etc.).

Start by writing out a petition to protect the space. On the paper, write your address, the inhabitants of the home, and any other people or pets that you wish to also include in the protection. You will also need to write the phrases "absorb negativity" and "Lilith protect" on the paper multiple times so that the full page is completely covered by your writing. Roll the paper up and seal it with the black wax. Add it as the first material into the ball. Insert the photograph of yourself, image of Lilith, and the ingredients individually, telling each item that it is being included to aid in the protection of you and your space. Once finished, close your ball and state the following:

Lilith!
Protect me and this space,
Protect me with your dark grace,
Trap negativity, so that I may remain free.
Thank you Goddess, so mote it be!

Now, hold the ball and visualize your space being filled with Lilith's ferocious protection. Hang it in a spot that will not be disturbed and recharge as you see fit. You may even want to try burning some of the black sealing wax and pouring it over the opening to further seal the ball shut.

BITCHCRAFT FOR FIGHT

So, despite all your attempts to avoid the negativity, take shelter, and let things blow over, you may find a time when you have no other choice but to get your hands dirty and fight back. When faced with the potential of hexes, I lean on three main questions to help me ascertain if I should continue unloading my bitchcraft on the adversary:

1. **Is it warranted?** Did they do something intentionally, out of malice, or was the negativity the result of being a bystander? Did you have any direct influence in the situation? (i.e., If you called out your boss in a meeting and then got fired, you can't really hex them for firing you, since your action started it.) When working hexes for justice, it is very important to ensure that you played no part in the situation, otherwise you may end up hexing yourself in the process.

2. **Have I done everything in the mundane world to correct the issue?** Have I reported it to the appropriate channels? Have I expressed to whomever it is that has caused the pain that this is unacceptable? I truly believe that these practical acts must be achieved first before resorting to magical means.

3. **Do I accept any consequences that are associated with this?** If I employ my magic to curse the individual, am I ok with it causing unfortunate events to one of their loved ones? The universe may take this route to inflict them with harm. Am I ok with fully committing to the hex and letting the energies of hatred and anger fester deeper and deeper within me?

If I am not able to answer all three of these questions with an affirmative yes, then I know—for me, at least—that it is best to take flight rather than fight. But if I can give a direct yes to all, I move forth with my act of hexing.

Harnessing Hate

Remember that magic is built upon energy and you fuel that energy with our intent. Hate is a powerful emotion and the energetic source that is called upon for successful hexing. This is not bigoted hatred that comes from shallow misunderstanding and prejudice. It is the emotional havoc that plagues your well-being as a result of someone's intentional cruelty to you. This hate is a reaction to their malicious action, in which hexing becomes an act of justice.

To effectively hex, you really need to be able to harness your hatred for whomever or whatever it is that you are hexing. It must permeate deep within your bones. Hate is pure chaos and fury and can be a primal source of power for the hex to manifest. But the harnessing of this hatred is complex because, in most cases, people do not understand how to work with it.

We are often taught not to hate. To forgive and to let go. To grow. In some cases, this is possible, but there are others for which this philosophy is nothing more than a cheesy fairytale of love and light. We are told that we must end hate with love. But what many people don't realize is that hate and love are essentially the same type of emotion; they are just powered by a different source.

Hate and love are dual emotions, representative of extreme caring. Love is the attracting emotion that is born from happiness and joy, while hate repeals and manifests from anger, sadness, and rage. The opposite of hate is not love, and vice versa. Their opposite emotion is indifference. By choosing not to let the emotion take hold it becomes irrelevant and loses its power. Flight can be interpreted as this indifference. But hatred is a powerful reaction to anger.

When anger and sadness are intertwined, they culminate in rage. Hexing is an outlet for rage and a conduit for cathartic chaos. Like any other emotion rage must be released or it will boil within, taking over your being by bringing more negativity into your life. Remember that like attracts like. The sympathetic nature of magic is not limited to magical acts. It corresponds to energy and all of our emotions are fueled with energy. By remaining in a state of anger, hate, rage, wrath, fear, sadness, etc., you only attract other aspects of these emotions, be it through abusive behaviors of violence, addiction, toxic relationships, or other volatile actions.

If we think back to the lessons of shadowcraft, and the astrological application of Lilith, her wound manifests into rage, and from that there is rebirth. There is a healing side to these emotions; the difference is that our shadow manifests as suppression and the chaos ensues from that. The integration of your shadow helps acknowledge it and provide a means for it to coexist within your reality. It provides release.

You can elevate from the situation by unleashing the disdain for an individual who has wronged you into the world. But remember that spellwork is not often instantaneous, either; it requires vigilance and great concentration. The reason why most hexes fail is lack of concentration, lack of motivation, and lack of laser focus. Remember, a hex is your witch weapon. It is the astral bullet. If you don't have focus, you will not hit the target. If your hands are shaky from hesitation, you will not hit the target. When it comes to hexing, one must be committed to their hate and know how to control it properly, subsequently channeling it and directing it back to the initiator. This is not something that I can teach you from a book. This will take your own innate will and determination. That said, here are some ways to channel the chaotic nature of Lilith into justice work.

GLAM Hexercicse: *Mirrored Malice*

Mirror magic for protection or hexing purposes is a great way to help reflect the negative energies back to the source so they do not impede your vibrancy. Using mirrors for this type of magic can be a bit tricky, as it is best not to capture your reflection within the mirror. Because of this, I like to use a simple compact mirror which will be used for this next spell.

Materials Needed
⊛ Compact mirror
⊛ Item of individual
⊛ Black electrical tape

The associated item of the individual who is causing you grief can be as simple as a photo of them, their name written on a piece of paper, a piece of their biology, or something they have touched. Just make sure that it is thin enough to be sealed inside whatever compact you use. When purchasing a compact, make sure that it is purchased closed! For the spell, simply hold the opening of the mirror away from you and slide the associated item into the opening so that it does not catch your reflection. Once closed, state the name of the person, followed by saying:

I reflect the energy you send to me
Back to you. So mote it be.

Visualize the negativity that you feel from the person reflecting off you and back to them. Visualize chaos unfolding into their life. Now, take the mirror to a place that is near their home, work, etc. You will likely need to be a bit stealthy for this. Once you have figured out the place, dig a hole in the ground where you can as-sure it will not be disturbed. Bury the mirror. Once done, spit on the "grave" and say:

Spit for spite, I hex you with all my might!

Now, place a large rock on top of the grave to lock the curse into place and say:

Trapped you are in your wretchedness.
This rock holds you—bound, suppressed.
It sucks to be you, and with this spell it will come true.

Leave the space and never think of it again. When you notice things going wrong for the directed person, just chuckle and think to yourself "it sucks to be you!"

Unapologetic Rebellion

One of the most powerful attributes of Lilith is her sheer courage in the face of adversity. As a Dark Goddess, Lilith has no qualms about being unapologetic and exposing those who maliciously dis-courage fairness, equality, and justice. While in some cases, it is easier to remove yourself from a negative situation, or even be proactive and protect yourself from it in the first place, there are also times when your bitchcraft calls on the courage and strength of rebellion.

Rebellion is not necessarily negative. It can be justified when balancing the greater good of a situation. Rebellion can be toward political schemes, workplace toxicity, and even unjust relationships with a friend, lover, or family dynamic. Invoking the dark goddess during challenging times can be a necessity. It is through her that we can wield the sword of enlightenment and slice away at the nonsense surrounding us. This may seem chaotic, but it is ultimately for the greater good.

GLAM Hexercise: *Lilithian Ritual of Rebellion*

This invocation of Lilith is needed for times of oppression. It is a ritual for rising up to those that challenge you, oppress you, silence you, or lie to you. It is a means of unapologetic authenticity. The spell is going to call on you to use the lessons of persona from our chapter on glamour magic and take on the physical demeanor of Lilith as a rebellious adversary. A note of warning that I would like to give is that Lilith can be unpredictable, especially when it comes to her rebellious nature. Not only are you utilizing glamour magic to create this rebellious persona, but you are essentially invoking the presence of Lilith outside of a ritual setting. She has the freedom to stay with you as long as she chooses. Be aware of this ahead of time so as not to regret any rash decisions later on.

Materials Needed
- ⚝ 1 piece of High John the Conqueror root
- ⚝ 1 tsp. wormwood
- ⚝ 1 tsp. dragon's blood
- ⚝ 1 piece of snakeskin shed
- ⚝ 1 tsp. dried red rose petals
- ⚝ 1 tumbled bloodstone crystal
- ⚝ Red candle (to symbolize power, combat, and confrontation)

⊛ Image of Lilith
⊛ Mirror

First, make a Lilith mirror wash by combining High John the Conqueror root, wormwood, dragon's blood, snakeskin shed, and rose petals into a bowl with the bloodstone. These ingredients all yield courage and strength that are necessary for resistance while also calling upon the beauty and talents of Lilith. Pour boiling water over the ingredients and let them sit overnight under a waning moon to absorb the lunar qualities of release.

Upon morning, strain the ingredients into a glass vial. Gather your candle, image of Lilith, mirror, and wash. Using the Lilithian ritual template from Chapter 4, light the candle and invoke Lilith while asking that she grant you the strength and courage to stand up to whoever stands in your way. Rubbing a few drops of the mirror wash into your clean mirror, study your reflection and say these righteous words, calling out your inner Lilithian rebel:

No means no,
And my foe will reap what they sow.
I stand up to adversity
And welcome no apology.
By the power of Lilith, I challenge thee,
For the good of all oppressed, but especially me,
I invoke the Dark Goddess, Lilith, set me free!

Now chant the sacred names of Lilith from Chapter 4 (see page 70). Look deep into your reflection's eyes and feel the power of Lilith surge through you. Feel her mighty wings enfold you, embracing and nurturing you with her strength. As you gaze into your reflection, see yourself becoming Lilith, channeling her persona. Once you feel as though you have successfully slipped into your Lilithian skin, thank Lilith for her assistance and set forth into your day. Good luck to those who crossed you because they are in for a challenge!

Bitchcrafting: *A Lilithian Hexing Ritual*

While the original stories of Lilith were not malicious, in these spells and magical efforts we must call upon the side of Lilith that became feared. We must conjure her dark side as the villainous Goddess of rage and revenge. In this role, Lilith is the destroyer and a powerful archetype to conjure for magical acts of justice.

The following spell is reserved for the really nasty people of the world who have gone out of their way to hurt someone or something, who are the living cesspools of existence and are worthy of a hex! This is for the rapists, bigots, murderers, thieves, and those with slanderous tongues.

As a reminder, make sure that you are justified in your approach, that the proper everyday channels of justice have been instituted without desired result, and more importantly, that your hands are clean of any maliciousness from the event causing the anger. It is equally important to be sure that this spell is worthwhile for Lilith too. Make sure that this person and the harm that they have caused warrant her wrath. Based on her legends, would she see them as a worthy target? If yes, continue.

Materials Needed
- Rattlesnake shed (easily obtained online!)
- 1 tsp. dried chicory
- 1 tsp. jezebel root
- Pinch of bee pollen
- Image of the person
- Black figure candle to represent the person
- Fireproof dish
- Black Lilith Oil (See page 271)
- Nine sharp rose thorns

To begin, grind your snakeskin, chicory, jezebel root, and bee pollen into a find powder. While doing this, tell each ingredient what your intentions are and what you want them to do. Be specific. Take this powder to your altar or workstation with the other supplies. Now write the name of the person over their image. In the day of advanced technology, it is very easy to obtain an image of the person who has crossed you. In the instance you do not know the exact identity of the individual who has harmed, simply write "My Enemy" on a piece of black paper. Now, you will write "You are hexed" over the name in a cross-like detail.

Roll the paper into a thin and tight roll. Whittle out a hole in the base of the candle next to the wick to insert the paper. This can be easily done with a kebab skewer. Insert your petition into the hole. Take your black candle and carve three deep Xs into it. With each gash, state the following:

I hex your mind.
I hex your body.
I hex your spirit.

Now, you will place the candle on a fireproof plate. Sprinkle the powder around the base of the candle. Invite Lilith into your space. Anoint your candle with Black Lilith Oil. Light it and state the following:

I poison your soul and inflict pain
So that you will never cause harm again.
I kill the evil of which you reek
And ask this hex to peak.
Manifest deep inside of you,
Settle there and let it brew.

Taking your thorns, begin to press them into various positions on the candle. As you do this, recite:

> *Razor sharp thorns leave you unwelcomed scorn.*
> *May your treacherous mouth snap shut as your malice is undercut.*
> *The damage has been done, and your fears ignite one by one.*
> *As I plant this venomous seed.*
> *May the energy spread and magnify your ill will.*
> *A taste of your own medicine, I smite thee with magnified sin!*

Now, you will call upon Lilith for assistance. Call out to her and say:

> *Lilith's claws and razor wings*
> *Slice your insides and let them sting.*
> *As the candle burns, this will come true*
> *To benefit all from the malice you do.*

Now, visualize your desired outcome. Allow the candle to burn out completely. You may do this in one sitting or multiple times, each night at the same time until fully extinguished. If the latter, make sure you ground, center, and reach the point of rage each night, repeating the incantation above in its entirety.

When complete, you will bury the remains of the candle. If you know the person and have an idea of their habits, you can bury it in an area that they frequent. This is not always feasible, particularly if you are unaware of the person's identity; therefore, any forest or remote area will do so that your spell will not be unearthed. The only way the hex will be reversed is if the person finds your spell's remains and burns them. As long as it remains in the earth, it will continue spreading in their life. As it decomposes into the earth and is absorbed, it will magnify, growing stronger and stronger.

Practical Protection

It is important to safeguard yourself in the mundane world, just as it is important to do so magically. This includes remaining aware of your surroundings and the people around you, as not everyone you surround yourself with has good intentions. This does not mean that you have to be overly suspicious of every person you interact with, rather, it is more about being smart and feeling things out accordingly. That said, here are some practical tips to real-life fight or flight.

1. **Be unapologetic in the face of adversity.** If something does not feel right, chances are it isn't. Exercise caution and be prudent in your actions when you feel this. If something unjust has occurred, speak up! This is not only in regard to personal things but in life more generally. If you are witness to injustice, say something. Without speaking up and acting proactive in the face of adversity, nothing will change.

2. **Surround yourself with people who build you up.** This is perhaps the most important element. No matter what you do and how much you protect yourself or try to avoid negativity, there is no true way to do so completely. Like the darkness of night, this is a natural part in the balance of life. One way to help mitigate the situation is to remain in the presence

of those who inspire you to do your best and be your best self.

3. **Be true to yourself.** In the end, you are all you have. There is truly only one person who will get in your way and create obstacles for you, and that is you! Get out of your own way. While it is unlikely that you'll be able to completely avoid negativity, since darkness is going to eventually fall, try your best not to purposefully put yourself in negative situations.

PART IV

The Lifestyle of

THE GLAM WITCH

11

LOTIONS & POTIONS:

Formularies of the GLAM Witch

"Compounding incense, oils and brews is one of the easiest and most productive means to learn herb magic." —Scott Cunningham, *The Complete Book of Incense, Oils, & Brews*

Like a witch's spell, the magic potion is a fascinating and fearsome tool that the witch possesses. Spells are not always full-blown rituals or long incantations. They can be as simple as making a candle, crafting oil blends, or making beauty and bath products. From cosmic cosmetics to self-made ritual blends, many witches craft their own spells and ritual formularies to assist in their magical practices. While there is nothing wrong with buying witchy kits or other supplies from major retailers or at local occult shops, it can be very empowering to create your own lotions and potions. By creating your own, you can further fuel the product with your intent, amplifying its power. This is one reason why many witches get into the habit of creating their own candles, soaps, and other supplies. It enhances the essence of self-made witchcraft, helping to instill independence. It becomes an act of living witchcraft and further connects you to plant magic, or herbalism. In addition to the recipes already covered in the book, the following chapter provides some additional alternative recipes of GLAM Witchcrafting.

Note of Caution

Please exercise caution when creating your own products. It is always important to test oils and herbs to ensure allergic or adverse reactions do not occur. Additionally, unless otherwise noted, the formularies provided here are for external use only.

Bath & Body

These first sets of formularies are for the witches who enjoy pampering themselves with beauty magic.

GLAM God/dess Glow

The following recipe creates a luxurious and velvety body oil with a bit of sparkle to help you shine like an ultra-glamorous God/dess!

- ✸ 2 Tbsp. metallic mica (bronze, gold, rose gold, or silver)
- ✸ 3 oz. fractionated coconut oil
- ✸ 1 Tbsp. shea butter

✸ 6 drops preferred fragrance oil*

✸ A 4-oz. jar

*Vanilla, sandalwood, or rose are perfect pairings for this. Otherwise, feel free to add whatever oils you prefer, maybe even one of the recipes provided later in this chapter!

Using a funnel, pour the mica into the jar. Add the fractionated coconut oil. In a nonstick pan, melt the shea butter to liquid. Be careful not to overcook. Once the solid has turned liquid, pour into the mixture and shake well. Add the fragrance oil and shake for a good thirty seconds or so. Your oil is complete! For best results, apply to dry skin after a sensual bath. Allow it to set on your skin before dressing.

Beauty Body Scrub

This body scrub is not only going to hydrate and cleanse your skin, but the combination of herbs and oils will be used to scrub away impurities and let your radiant beauty shine!

✸ 2 c. raw sugar

✸ 1 c. coconut oil

✸ Handful of dried rose petals

✸ Scrapings from 1 vanilla bean

✸ 7 drops rose oil

✸ 4 drops sandalwood oil

✸ 4 drops vanilla oil

Combine the ingredients into a large mixing bowl. Stir well and transfer to a pint-sized jar. Apply to wet skin while taking a bath or shower. Keep covered when storing.

Aura-Cleansing Body Scrub

This body scrub is going to combine powerful cleansing herbs and fragrances to not only hydrate and cleanse your skin but to cleanse your energetic magnetism of any negativity that it has accumulated.

- ⊛ 2 c. epsom salt
- ⊛ 1 c. coconut oil
- ⊛ Handful of dried lavender
- ⊛ Spring of dried rosemary
- ⊛ Pinch of lemon zest
- ⊛ 5 drops lavender oil
- ⊛ 5 drops rosemary oil
- ⊛ 5 drops lemon oil

Combine the ingredients into a large mixing bowl. Stir well and transfer to a pint-sized jar. Keep covered when storing.

Zit-Zapping Mask

Here is a lovely little mask is great for fighting angry, stubborn breakouts. It combines three powerful ingredients, known for their assistance in battling zits, to ensure you have bewitching skin!

- ⊛ 2 Tbsp. *Aloe vera* gel
- ⊛ 2 tsp. dried chamomile
- ⊛ 3 drops organic tea tree oil

In a clean bowl, combine your ingredients and mix well. As you mix, recite: "Zit, be gone; zit, so long." Once your mixture is made, apply to a dry, clean face. Let sit for fifteen minutes and rinse.

Lilithian Lip Scrub

For a set of luscious Lilithian lips, use this simple scrub. It will leave them feeling like supple rose petals straight out of Eden! I love lip scrubs because they exfoliate the skin, ridding it of dead skin cells while also buffering the lips.

- ✪ 1 tsp. honey
- ✪ ½ tsp. olive oil
- ✪ 1 tsp. brown sugar
- ✪ 1 organic rose petal, crushed into a fine dust

Heat the honey so that it becomes liquid. Add the olive oil and mix well. Slowly mix in the sugar and rose petal dust. Continue mixing to avoid clumping. Transfer into a container and let cool. Once cooled, place a dab on your lips and rub them together before letting it sit for two minutes. Rinse, and enjoy your luscious Lilithian lips!

Mirror Washes

In Chapter 8, I introduced the process of making mirror washes for glamour spells. Here are several other recipes for washes that you can make to manifest alternative glamour goals. Simply use the ingredients listed under each intention and follow the instructions previously listed on page 176.

Invisibility

While many think glamours are for attracting, sometimes a glamour is needed to divert and promote the essence of invisibility. This mirror wash includes a variety of herbs known to cause confusion and invisibility. Mix and charge this mirror wash during the waning moon. When applying to a mirror, rub on counterclockwise and repeat "Invisibility, invisible me" over and over. It is important that you remain extremely focused on not being noticed.

- ✪ 2 c. boiling water
- ✪ 1 tsp. poppy seeds

- ✪ 1 tsp. amaranth
- ✪ 1 tsp. cherry bark
- ✪ 1 tsp. Devil's claw
- ✪ 1 tsp. sow thistle
- ✪ 1 Tbsp. fresh blueberries
- ✪ Sprinkle of parsley
- ✪ Fireproof bowl
- ✪ 1 tumbled bloodstone crystal

Success

This mirror wash is to attract success in all adventures. In the event you are interviewing for new jobs, you may also wish to burn your resume and apply the ashes to the wash, chanting "come to me" over and over.

- ✪ 2 c. boiling water
- ✪ 1 large piece of High John the Conqueror root
- ✪ 1 Tbsp. cinnamon
- ✪ 3 bay leaves
- ✪ 1 Tbsp. orange peel
- ✪ Fireproof bowl
- ✪ 1 tumbled golden tiger's eye crystal

Protection

In addition to the invisibility mirror wash, this wash gives overall protection to a location. I like washing mirrors that hang in the house with this blend to aid in protection of my home. Alternatively, you can carry a batch on you and use in reflective surfaces throughout the day to help manifest protection.

- ✪ 2 c. boiling water
- ✪ 1 Tbsp. sage
- ✪ 1 tsp. rosemary

- ✪ 1 tsp. elderberries
- ✪ 1 tsp. elderflowers
- ✪ Handful of oakmoss
- ✪ Fireproof bowl
- ✪ 1 tumbled obsidian crystal

Seduction

Looking to spice things up and seduce the object of your affection? Combine these ingredients into a mirror wash. When gazing into your washed mirror, repeat the phrase "I am desired" six times to manifest sensual glamour.

- ✪ 1 Tbsp. damiana
- ✪ 1 sprinkle of chili flakes
- ✪ 1 Tbsp. passionflower
- ✪ 1 tsp. cardamom
- ✪ 1 tumbled garnet crystal

Oil Blends

This list of oils can be used as fragrances, to dress candles, or to anoint on other objects for blessings or spellwork. They can be made in any size bottle, relying on proportions as indicated.

Black Lilith Oil

This oil blend can be fixed on anything to manifest fierce protection and aid in hexing.

- ✪ 1 part benzion oil
- ✪ 1 part black pepper oil
- ✪ 1 part oakmoss oil
- ✪ 1 part vetiver oil

Eden Oil

This oil blend calls upon Lilith's energy from her time in the garden. Combining the fruity scents of apple and pomegranate with the lush floral of rose, it is topped off with a hint of dirt for an earthy concoction that makes you smell like you just stepped out of Eden!

- ✪ 1 part apple oil
- ✪ 1 part pomegranate oil
- ✪ 2 parts rose oil
- ✪ Pinch of dirt

Enigma Oil

Enigmas are mysterious. To add a bit of mystery to anything you are doing, simply dab on a bit of this oil.

- ✪ 1 part vanilla oil
- ✪ 1 part opium oil
- ✪ 2 parts sandalwood oil
- ✪ 1-2 drops blueberry oil

Glow Oil

This glamour oil blend envelops you with a glowing aroma.

- ✪ 1 part jasmine oil
- ✪ 1 part neroli oil
- ✪ 2 parts white musk oil
- ✪ 1 drop sweet orange

blossom oil
Optional: Glitter

Follow Me

Fueling attraction with domination, this oil blend should be worn to obtain followers—socially, romantically, or otherwise!

- ✪ 1 part frankincense oil
- ✪ 1 part ambergris oil
- ✪ 1 part cedarwood oil
- ✪ 1 part patchouli oil

Lilith Oil

One of my favorite blends for evoking Lilith's presence.

- ✪ 1 part patchouli oil
- ✪ 1 part sandalwood oil
- ✪ 1 part rose oil
- ✪ 1 part musk oil
- ✪ 1 part lily oil
- ✪ 1 drop vetiver oil

Lilithian Trinity Oil

These three sacred floral scents are signatures of Lilith and create a lovely garden scent.

- ✪ 1 part rose oil
- ✪ 1 part lily oil
- ✪ 1 part lotus oil

Lunar Lilith

This Lilithian blend is good for full moon magic involving Lilith.

- 1 part gardenia oil
- 1 part peach oil
- 1 part white musk oil

Lust Oil

This oil ignites intense lust within yourself and those who smell your spicy seductive scent.

- 1 part pink pepper oil
- 1 part rose oil
- 1 part Egyptian musk oil
- 1 part sandalwood oil

Optional: 1-2 drops vanilla oil for a slightly sweeter smell.

Oracle Oil

Incorporate this oil into your divination practices to ensure maximum prophecy proficiency!

- 1 part wormwood oil
- 1 part lavender oil
- 1 part vanilla oil
- 2 drops clary sage oil

Shadow Oil

Used in work involving shadow magic.

- 1 part lotus oil
- 1 part lavender oil
- 1 part clary sage oil

Suc-sex-ful Oil

This oil is best used for those who work in the sex industry to assist in persuasion and bewitching wealthy sexual partners.

- ✸ 1 part bergamot oil
- ✸ 1 part patchouli oil
- ✸ 1 part rose oil
- ✸ A pinch of cardamom powder
- ✸ 1 piece of jezebel root

Ritual

This next section of formularies is for more ritualistic, ceremonious magic and spells. Many of these can be integrated into ritual worship of Lilith or used as incense or powders for magical bags in spellwork.

Attraction Powder

This blend of incense is used in beauty rituals. Grind the below into ingredients into a fine powder. Sprinkle on lit charcoal discs during your beauty rituals to summon the ultimate attraction.

- ✸ 1 tsp. catnip
- ✸ 1 tsp. cinnamon
- ✸ 1 tsp. granulated honey
- ✸ 1 tsp. orange peel
- ✸ 1 tsp. passionflower
- ✸ 1 tsp. rose
- ✸ 1 tsp. violet

Witchcrafting: *Homemade Candles*

For the really crafty witch, it can be very magical to create your own candles for spell and ritual use. I personally love candle making. It is a very therapeutic process and is relatively simple!

Materials Needed
- Pouring pitcher for candle making
- Container or mold of choice
- Beeswax or soy flakes
- Dye of choice
- Herbs of choice
- Wick

**Note:* I have found that soy wax is better for glass containers and beeswax works better in molds. It is important too that you have the correct wicks to match the type of wax you use.

Put your pitcher on the stove on medium heat. When determining how much wax to use, it is generally double the amount of the container. If you are using a mold, fill it completely with the wax chips, then add those to the pitcher. Repeat this one more time. Add the dye you wish to use and begin mixing with a nonstick whisk or spatula. Be cautious of the pan, as it will be hot. Be careful not to overheat the wax; it will start to burn and become no good if overheated. Mix constantly to break down the solid mass and prevent burning.

Once the majority of the solid form has melted, remove from heat and continue to stir. The hot liquid wax will continue to melt any remaining chunks and not burn the wax. Now, transfer into your mold or container. If using a container, place your wick in the center and, using a clothes pin, or even chopsticks, hold the wick in place on top of the container to ensure it sets correctly within the wax. When filling the container, I break down the process into three dispenses. Once the wax begins to harden in the container, I add a few drops of fragrance oil. If you add the fragrance too soon, the heat can alter or inhibit the aroma. Then I repeat this process two more times. I also incorporate some crushed herbs or tumbled stones in the drying wax on top. I recommend filling the mold halfway to begin. Once the wax begins to harden, set the wick in place and add any fragrances into the semi hardened wax. Then I add the remaining liquid wax to the mold. Treat your first candles as a practice round if you're new to candle making. Remember to fuel each batch with intent. You can time them around moon and seasonal changes to incorporate additional metaphysical properties as well. Have fun and enjoy!

Lilith Ritual Incense

The Lilith ritual blend can be used in any ritual or spell that honors Lilith. The product can be used in magic bags or sprinkled on candles or a hot charcoal disc to honor Lilith in ritual. Blend together a pinch of the following ingredients:

- ✸ Dirt
- ✸ Lily
- ✸ Orchid
- ✸ Patchouli
- ✸ Red sandalwood
- ✸ Rose

Red Goddess

This incense blend calls upon Lilith's lust and can be burnt in sex magic rituals or for magical sex. Combine the ingredients and grind into a fine powder. Light a charcoal disc and sprinkle on top to fill the room with this sensual smoke.

- ✸ 1 tsp. black copal
- ✸ 1 tsp. Damascus rose resin
- ✸ 1 tsp. hibiscus
- ✸ 1 tsp. red sandalwood

Rose Water

Rose water is a wonderful source of loving power that can be incorporated in rituals for self-love or glamour and beauty. Simply anoint yourself or any object with its lovely healing essence and watch beauty and magical unfold around you. You can store in a spray bottle and mist the room to encourage positive vibrations within your space or cleanse the area before ritual workings and spells. If you use organic edible roses, this can also be consumed.

I love rose water, but since the vast majority of store-bought roses are sprayed with chemicals, it is hard to make good-quality rose water with fresh petals unless you grow your own or are able to find some that are organically cultivated. Because of this, I prefer to use dried culinary rose petals. These pack a powerful scent and flavor to them and can easily be crafted into rose water.

- ✪ ¼ c. rose petals (organic fresh or dried culinary)
- ✪ 1 ½ c. water

To make these, simply add the rose petals to the saucepan of boiling water. Reduce to a simmer and cook until the petals have lost their color. Cool and store.

War Water

War water is great for acts of bitchcraft! Traditionally, it is used against enemies to cause discourse in their life.

- ✪ Mason jar
- ✪ Natural water (rain, lake, swamp, ocean, etc.)
- ✪ Enemy's name on piece of paper
- ✪ 9 rusty nails
- ✪ A handful of oakmoss

Fill the mason jar with the water and add the paper with the person's name to declare the work being done. Then add each of the nails, telling them to assist in the goal of your work. Follow this with the oakmoss. Seal the jar and let sit for a total of four weeks, shaking it once a week. Once the time has passed, strain the water into a different container and sprinkle it in an area that the enemy will cross.

Kiki's Flying Witches' Ointment

Flying Witches' Ointment is a psychedelic salve that was histori-cally linked to European witchcraft. It was used to help the witch leave their living body and travel to the astral realms, a practice that is commonly called astral projection. The original recipe for Flying Witches' Ointment contained an array of poisonous ingre-dients. Some practitioners continue to use recipes that contain the toxic herbals in hopes of experiencing hallucinated visions. As an alternative, my dear friend Kiki Dombrowski shared her modern-ized take on the classic recipe in her book *Eight Extraordinary Days*. I personally love this recipe and have used it in my divina-tion practices with Lilith.

- ✸ 8 oz. shea or cocoa butter
- ✸ 3 hazelnuts
- ✸ 3 star anise
- ✸ 3 cinnamon sticks
- ✸ 1 Tbsp. mugwort
- ✸ 1 Tbsp. dittany of Crete
- ✸ 1 Tbsp. cinquefoil
- ✸ ½ tsp. ground nutmeg
- ✸ ½ tsp. skullcap*
- ✸ ½ tsp. wormwood*
- ✸ 9 drops benzoin oil
- ✸ 9 drops jasmine oil
- ✸ 9 drops sandalwood oil

Optional: Can be an irritant

Bring the water to a boil and then reduce to a simmer using a dou-ble boiler. If you do not have a double boiler, bring water to a boil in a pot and fit a metal mixing bowl on top of the pot to create a double boiler. Slowly melt the base until it is completely liquid. Add the herbal ingredients (all but the oils) and simmer for at least thirty minutes, stirring frequently. At the end of the thirty minutes, turn off the heat and stir in the oils. Pour the concoction through a mesh strainer or cheesecloth into a measuring cup. Then, transfer the still-liquid ointment to selected containers. Allow it to cool and solidify before use.

EDIBLE ALCHEMY

We will finish this chapter with several consumable recipes. These potions are made into teas and alcoholic beverages that can assist in magical work and celebrations.

Teas

In addition to the tea from the shadowcraft ritual, here are four additional teas that can be worked into the four other points of the Lilithian Pentacle's magic!

At-tea-ction
- ✪ 2 tsp. white tea base
- ✪ 1 tsp. orange peel
- ✪ 1 tsp. rose
- ✪ ½ tsp. damiana
- ✪ ½ a vanilla bean scraping

Divini-Tea
- ✪ 2 tsp. chamomile base
- ✪ 1 tsp. mugwort
- ✪ 1 tsp. dandelion
- ✪ 1 tsp. rose hip

Lus-tea
- ✪ 2 tsp. red tea base
- ✪ 1 tsp. damiana
- ✪ 1 tsp. passionflower

⊛ 1 tsp. hibiscus

Pro-tea-ction

⊛ 2 tsp. black tea base
⊛ 2 tsp. elderflower
⊛ 1 tsp. mint

Alcoholic Beverages

As a follow-up to the Lilithian libation we made while exploring lustcraft in Chapter 9, here are a few of my favorite magical libations. Since alcohol has the ability to lower inhibitions and, in some cases induce visions, it can be a potent potion for magical work involving Lilith. Just remember to consume respectfully and responsibly.

Eden Sangria

Let's start with a Lilithian libation straight out of Eden! This lush sangria plays on a variety of red succulent fruits, creating a masterful potion with which you can honor and worship Lilith. In a large pitcher, combine the following ingredients and stir well.

⊛ 1 bottle red wine of choice
⊛ ¼ c. apple juice
⊛ ½ c. brandy
⊛ ½ c. pomegranate juice
⊛ 8 oz. frozen strawberries in syrup, thawed
⊛ 2 apples, diced into medium-sized chunks
⊛ Dash of cinnamon

Let sit for five to six hours in the fridge. The frozen strawberries will melt and add flavor and depth to the concoction. Once ready, stir well and pour into your chalice or other drinking vessel. Raise your glass in salute to Lilith and enjoy!

Full Moon Martini

This delicious martini is made to resemble the full moon and can be a great addition to any full moon celebration. It combines the loving, divinatory properties of the lychee fruit with white cranberries that assist in purification and cleansing. If you find canned lychees, you can use the juice from it for this. Lychee fruit is already sphere shaped and can certainly be added as a garnish, but the major part of this martini is a frozen lychee juice ice cube that will resemble a full moon and keep your drink cool!

- ✸ Lychee juice (from canned lychee is ok.)
- ✸ Sphere ice mold
- ✸ 1 oz. vodka
- ✸ 1 oz. white cranberry juice
- ✸ Splash of brut champagne
- ✸ Lemon twist for garnish

To begin, make sphere ice cubes by adding equal parts water and lychee juice to the mold. Mix well and freeze. Once frozen, place in a martini glass. In a shaker, combine ice, vodka, and white cranberry juice. Shake well and strain over the ice ball in the glass. Top with a splash of champagne to add splendor and a bubbly star aesthetic. Add lemon twist as garnish and—poof!—you have an edible full moon in your martini!

Purple Potion

This is a twist to one of my favorite cocktails—an aviation! The secret ingredient to this cocktail is crème de violette which is a type of liqueur made from crushed violets. The preferred brand to use is Rothman & Winter, which uses Queen Charlotte and March violets from the Alps. Crème de violette is known for its deep purple hue. When mixed with clear liquors such as gin it transforms into a gorgeous purple colored beverage that looks like liquid amethyst. With its strong floral taste, many feel that this drink tastes perfumey, however I feel as though it has a powdered sugary flavor. The traditional aviation is mixed with maraschino liqueur, but I prefer substituting lavender simple syrup to add yet another floral note to the mix!

- ✯ 2 oz. gin
- ✯ ½ oz. crème de violette
- ✯ ½ fresh lemon juice
- ✯ ¼ lavender simple syrup
- ✯ Garnish with violet blossom, lemon twist, or sprig of lavender

To make, add all liquids into a shaker with crushed ice. Shake well and strain into glass. Serve with a violet blossom, lemon twist or sprig of lavender as garnish.

Rose Quartz

For this final recipe, we will create edible crystal magic with a cocktail that resembles rose quartz. It will include grapefruit juice, honey, and pink champagne, all agents I feel contain uplifting, zestful energies that help ignite glamour. At the same time, we will be pairing it with tequila. Known to make clothes come off, tequila radiates with fire that will warm your soul and your loins. Combined, they invite the same magnetism as the charming rose quartz!

- ✯ Ice
- ✯ 1 ½ oz. grapefruit juice
- ✯ 1 oz. tequila
- ✯ ½ oz. honey
- ✯ Pink or rosé champagne

Fill a cocktail shaker with ice, grapefruit juice, tequila, and honey, then shake well. Add crushed ice to a tall glass. Strain cocktail over ice while also adding the pink champagne. The result is a glass of rose quartz to sip on while you celebrate your love for yourself!

12

SELF-CARE SORCERY:

Recharging with a Weekend of Witchy Wellness

"Magic is not a practice. It is a living, breathing web of energy
that, with our permission, can encase our every action."
—Dorothy Morrison, *Everyday Magic*

Growing up, birthdays were always important to me. They were my day—a day to celebrate me, my life, my accomplishments, and my journey through life. Despite this, many of my birthdays have not been as rewarding as I had hoped. Looking back, I can admit that I often got too caught up in the "importance" of a day that my expectations got the best of me. But with high expectations come dismay and disappointment. It wasn't until I decided to go away for my birthday one year—completely alone, by myself, in a foreign country—that this would change.

Growing tired of the disappointment, I wanted to reclaim my birthday for me and truly celebrate myself. I booked a flight to Puerto Vallarta and celebrated a week of solitude on the sandy beaches of the tropical paradise. I spent the day of my birthday on the beach alone, enjoying the surf, a playlist of my favorite songs, and the most delicious mojitos. In the evening, I took myself out for an exquisite dinner in the high hills overflowing with lush foliage and made a toast to me, myself, and I. The entire trip was exceptionally rewarding, as I explored and made acquaintances with other visitors and locals. And just like that, the week was over. Upon leaving, I cried an abundance of tears—tears of joy, tears of happiness. I had found what I was looking for—in ME. I had felt a shift, a sense of rebirth and excitement for life. By taking myself away, on my own terms, giving up responsibility and breaking tradition, I truly learned what it was like to celebrate myself. It was there that I learned the essence of self-care.

My definition for self-care is the conscious act of caring for one's identity in ways that lead to happiness and empowerment. The practice of self-care is considered a necessary part of mental and physical health, and in recent years has created a buzz as many people attempt to integrate the "mental health day" mentality into their everyday lives. But it is not just limited to these two areas. While not as widely discussed when it comes to matters of witchcraft, acts of self-care are just as important to our metaphysical well-being as they are to our mental and physical. Self-care rituals combine our energetic trinity of mind, body, and spirit while assisting in the replenishment of our magical self. Self-care is an attempt at honoring and establishing our own personal divinity.

One of Lilith's most vital lessons is importance of independence and identity of self. As noted throughout her lore, Lilith's individuality and freedom feed her solitary nature. She illustrates the importance of personal power and necessity of self. If you don't treat yourself right, who else is going to? You cannot expect to find this elsewhere. It all starts from within and flows out into your life. You have to reward yourself. Discipline yourself. Rest, relax, and rebirth yourself. There is no white horse coming to save you. You are your own white horse, and with self-care we take control of the reigns.

Self-care is very much subjective and can differ from person to person. While it might take form in acts of exercise or nutritious eating for some, it might be reality TV and lazy days on the couch for others. But it is important not to confuse self-care with coping—I made this mistake with alcohol for a while. I developed a drinking habit as a means to cope with work stress. But this soon turned into my coping mechanism for other stresses. Instead of dealing with them head on, I dealt with them through copious amounts of liquor. One glass of wine at night became two, two became four, four became a bottle, one bottle became two, and then the harder liquor hit. And before I realized it, I had completely abused the privilege to drink by falsely glamourizing alcohol as a self-care ritual. After much reflection and professional guidance, I make a conscious effort to establish boundaries with alcohol. I take periodic breaks from alcohol intake and have learned to pace myself. I may indulge in a glass of wine or a martini here or there, but I have learned my limits and how to reward myself with alternative indulgences that result in a healthier and happier me.

A great area of interest for many witches is the magical act of healing. In touching each of the points of the Lilithian Pentacle, and the magic directly involved, a healing and transformative process occurs. A GLAM Witch's self-care helps further bridge the gap between magical and mundane expressions of our metaphysical well-being while keeping the spark of Lilith alive within. Self-care is an act of self-love and dedication to your well-being. Self-care is not a selfish act. It is ok to like yourself and the things that you are doing. It is ok to give yourself a magical cat nap to disconnect, recharge, and reboot your esoteric essence. In fact, it is an essential part of witchcraft and only further magnifies the confidence called up for glamour magic and unconditional self-love.

I wish I could take you all on the extraordinary trip I took back in 2016, but alas, my time-traveling witch powers have yet to manifest! Nevertheless, this chapter is built on that principle and provides a weekend-long ritual template for self-care sorcery. Your self-care can be as magical or mundane as you wish it to be. It can be a daily practice or something you do as needed; however, I have found that taking a weekend off to disconnect from the stresses of the everyday life and reconnect with your most magical expression to be undeniably rewarding. It is an extraordinary step in initiating your independence and further saturating yourself in self-love, tapping into the indulgence of treating yourself. Self-care is like treating every day like your birthday. It is about celebrating and worshipping yourself like the divine expression that you are—in the eyes and image of Lilith.

It is best to schedule your weekend of wellness witchery anytime between the new and full moon phases to initiate rebirth and to welcome revitalizing energies. The template can be followed to a T or can be integrated with some of your own ideas. My recommendations are based on what has worked for me in my practice. This is a weekend for you, so feel free to switch things up as needed. Just be sure to limit your interactions with others and to disassociate yourself from the woes of social media. In fact, I also highly recommend taking a step back from news outlets too. Ignorance is bliss, if you ask me, and you don't want any negativity seeping into your soul's spiritual spa getaway!

Friday

Your ritual of self-care will begin on a Friday. Fridays are ruled by Venus, the planet of love, luxury, beauty, and harmony, therefore lending itself perfectly to the initiatory ritual of self-love. I try to do this in the evening after I come home from work, allowing my weekend of witchy wellness to begin early!

Crystal Phone Charger

Smart phones have become an extension of our well-being. Most of us are always connected to them—gossiping with friends, writing emails for work, curating Instagram photos, or sharing other posts. Phones are no longer just phones—they are personal data machines that transmit and radiate energy. As witches, we work with energy, and our phones are tools that sometimes need a good energetic recharge too—and I don't mean the kind where you plug your phone into a power outlet. For your weekend of wellness, I recommend you treat your phone to the same luxury and turn it off. Disconnect and distance yourself from your addicting technology of choice, from social media, and from news outlets.

Quartz crystals are a common component used in the makeup of cellular and other electronic devices. They can be energetically charged in a magical capacity in the same way a crystal would. For your weekend of witchery, try charging your phone with a crystal grid like the one discussed on page 245. Instead of placing yourself in the center of the grid, place your phone there and leave it for the duration of your weekend. Make sure that your phone is left off during this time too, as it will be doing the same R&R as you.

Materials Needed
- ✪ Picture of yourself
- ✪ Mirror
- ✪ Pink pillar candle (with 72-hour burn time)
- ✪ 1 rose quartz crystal
- ✪ Gallon of milk
- ✪ 1 Tbsp. honey
- ✪ Handful of pink Himalayan epsom salt
- ✪ A dozen roses (Any color will do. Look at the color meanings on page 51 to determine which energetic essence you wish to draw from)
- ✪ Rose fragrance oil

Begin with a detoxifying bath to banish negativity, heal your vibration, and enact the art of glamour! Light up your bathroom with candles as you draw a hot bath. Add the gallon of milk to the water, along with three tablespoons of the epsom salt. Since milk is revered for its rich nutrients to promote abundance and growth, saturating yourself in it will be beneficial for your recharge. Meanwhile, the salts will help to detoxify and dissolve your energetic impurities. Top this off with the honey, rose oil, and petals from one of the roses to bring in the loving energies of beauty and enchantment. Disrobe and slip into your lovely bath. Relax—enjoy a glass of wine, a martini, or an herbal tea to help calm your nerves—and detox from the past week.

Once finished, dry off and dress in something comfortable but luxurious. I'm an avid fan of silk robes and highly recommend them as an accessory for everyone's closet! From here, gather your remaining materials and construct an altar for yourself. Place your candle in the center of the workstation. Place your mirror behind it, and on one side you will place the remaining eleven roses in a vase. On the other, place your framed photo of yourself. In front of the candle, place a piece of rose quartz.

To begin, pick up your candle and brush yourself with it so that it can connect to your aura. Add three drops of your oil to the candle, along with your saliva to further harmonize the materials with your energy. The ideal situation would be to leave the candle lit the entire weekend. This requires a candle encased in glass. If you are worried it may be knocked over, you can place it in a cauldron or pot that contains an inch or two of water. In any event, ensure that it is away from flammable material with enough breathing room above the flame.

Ground and center yourself, then look at your reflection in the mirror. Light your candle and, while looking at yourself in the mirror, say:

I love myself.
Yes, I love myself.
For without myself, there is no me.
I am complete unto myself.
Powerful and free,
I do what I want, for myself.
It is just the way I be.
Like Lilith, I manifest self-love,
The only love I need.

Close your eyes and visualize a glittering pink glow encircling your heart, slowly embracing your entire body. Think about how much you like who you are, how much you love yourself. Reflect on how amazing it is to be you—the only you there is. Feel validated in your feelings, actions, wants, and desires. When you are ready, you may rise from your trance state and spend the rest of the evening doing something creative, such as reading a new book, make a playlist to celebrate yourself for the weekend, painting a picture, writing, etc. When slipping into bed, forego setting an alarm. Allow yourself a peaceful, restful night of beauty sleep.

Saturday

Saturday is ruled by Saturn, the planet of long-term goals, career stuff, and justice. But I also consider Saturday a day that is perfect for creating boundaries. An important feature of self-care is creating boundaries between you and your work, your friends, your family, your lover(s), etc. Additionally, we can use this day to recharge with a recommitment to long-term self-seduction. Not the seduction of a purely sexual nature but instead the self-seduction that creates a lust for life. To do this, you are going to date yourself for the day, becoming your own partner and thriving in independent outings.

Upon waking, take a solid thirty minutes to ground, center, and devote your day to yourself. While doing your daily devotion, draw upon the essence of Lilith's enchanting independence. Make yourself a nutritious and delicious breakfast. A bowl of plain Greek yogurt drizzled with honey and fresh berries is a great starter for the day. Another healthy option is to mash up an avocado and spread over a piece of toast with salt and pepper to taste. Top off with a poached egg for a powerful packing of protein. From here do some fashion magic by dressing up for yourself. Get ready and really dress to impress, like you would for a job interview or a first date. Really go all out. Deck yourself out for YOU! Take your time too; there is no rush.

Spend the afternoon doing something that inspires you. Go see a new movie you have been wanting to see or check out a new museum or art exhibit. Take a walk and listen to a new album, or one of your past favorites. You could also opt for just listening to the people, the wind blowing through the trees or ricocheting off signs and buildings. Pay attention to everything around you. Take your journal with you and record your thoughts and observations.

In Chicago, I always enjoy taking our public transit to the northern suburbs of Wilmette to the Bahá'í Temple. The gorgeous temple was constructed in the early 1900s and is the oldest of ten temples erected around the world in dedication to the Bahá'í faith, a religion built on the equality of all religions and people. I feel a strong connection to Lilith here due to the nature of equality on which the temple was founded, along with the ornate architecture and lush gardens. Walking through the gardens, I am often overwhelmed by a sense of supreme solitude and enriched love. The temple is also conveniently located across the street from a large park and beach of Lake Michigan which has a very old willow tree that I like to sit under as I watch the water ebb and flow.

Photo: The Bahá'í Temple in Wilmette, IL.

In the evening hours, take yourself to dinner. Splurge a little and make it someplace nice. Perhaps your favorite restaurant or a new place you have been meaning to try but have never had a reason to go. Try it out and celebrate yourself as if it were your birthday. Get a table for one and reflect on your solitude. Read a book or juicy gossip magazine or play a crossword. Bask in yourself and your confidence. When you get home, draw yourself another relaxing bath and finish the night with a bit of solo sex magic. Follow the template outlined on page 207 and use your orgasmic power to honor yourself and Lilith.

Sunday

In the Western world, Sunday is considered the first day of the calendar week. It welcomes new beginnings and rebirths. Additionally, Sunday is aptly named after the sun, welcoming vitality, success, and warmth. It is a perfect day to recharge through rebirth, to express gratitude to the universe, to Lilith, and to your inner divinity.

In both *Gilgamesh and the Ḫuluppu-Tree* and the *Alphabet of Ben Sira*, we see Lilith flee into the wilderness rather than meet the death of submission. Lilith's biblical appearance in Isaiah, says that she will "find herself a place of rest" in the wilderness. For this day, you will venture into the wilderness to meet with Lilith to offer a ritual of gratitude. This ritual will honor her but also connect you to her. You will be honoring yourself as a living extension of Lilithian energy.

Prior to venturing out, ground, center, and perform a morning devotion as you did the day prior. Have a light meal and determine your location. If you are a city witch, do not be discouraged by thinking you need a remote forest for this work. You can work your *hex and the city* magic in a local park, beach, or other natural setting of nature that is found within your concrete jungle. All you need is a quiet place in nature—a beach, field, forest—even a rooftop or balcony will do. It can be anywhere that provides solitude while being outside in the elements, somewhere you can avoid interruption. It is important to exercise safety when doing this. Be mindful of your surroundings.

The only thing you should expect to bring is one white rose. Most of the other materials you will use for this ritual will be obtained in nature, on your way to your desired wild space. You will be on the lookout for five fallen sticks or twigs, in addition to any other offerings you may wish to present. Here, you will use your intuition and look for signs. Pay attention to your surroundings along the way. Perhaps there will be flowers that stand out to you, a rock, or a dead branch, feathers, coins, or anything else that you connect with.

Once you have found the area that speaks to you, start erecting a natural altar based on the items you have collected. Make note of these and write them down in your journal. Identify why they stood out to you and what their energetic purpose is based on your feelings with them. Take the five twigs you found and create a pentagram in the center of your altar. Ground and center yourself. Relax into your wild environment and call upon Lilith. Welcome her to your space and present the rose. Place it in the center of your pentagram creation. Any other offerings that you have found along the way can be presented to her at this time. This temple, this space in which you are constructing an altar, is for nature. It is a decoration of gratitude. Create your own verse to Lilith and the universe, offering thanks for the lessons you have received and obstacles you have overcome. Turn your attention to yourself and declare your gratitude for you. Honor yourself. You may say something along the lines of this:

I dance for me,
I sing for me,
I live for me,
For I am free.

I am dark, beautiful, sensual, powerful, and wise.
I cultivate my confidence,
I bask in my sensuality,
I stand up to adversity,
I am unapologetically me.
I will never stop being me.
I give thanks for my freedom.
I give thanks to the Lilith in me.

Once the spell is spoken, engage in any activity that you feel compelled to do. You may bow your head and reflect upon your gratitude and self-love. You may feel the urge to dance and propel your energies into the space. Do what feels natural and comfortable to you. Enjoy your space and spend as much time there as you wish.

Once you are set, head home and spend the remainder of the day nesting in your home. Clean out a closet or relax on your couch. Bust out your at-home spa care and treat yourself to some glamorous beautification. Craft some of your own witchy cosmetics (see the previous chapter for inspiration) and treat yourself to a magical makeover. For dinner, order in or make your favorite comfort food.

Before you go to bed, return to your altar dedicated to yourself. As you sit there gazing at your reflection, take a moment to recall all the activities and thoughts you gathered throughout the weekend.

Upon waking Monday morning, feel free to call off work and have another day to yourself if you so desire. Relish in this time and means of self-care a little longer if it feels right. Regardless of whether you are committing to self-care with a dash of magic, these acts are a celebration of you with the mindful magic of intention and will. Treat each day as if it were your birthday, for each morning we arise is another day of life worth celebrating. Relish this time and remember that it is ok to take a pause to pamper your soul.

Alternative Acts of Self-Care

You should carve out as much time for self-care as you can and never feel guilty about doing so. This practice is an essential part of life as a GLAM Witch because you honor and nurture your "self" and your personal power. While the weekend template provided in this chapter is an example of what I would deem worthy, self-care is a continuous and individualized process. In addition to the template, here are some additional activities that promote self-care and soul nourishment that can be worked into your witchy wellness routine:

⊛ *Art*—Whether it is drawing, painting, or engaging in photography, flexing your mental muscles with creativity not only rouses passion but is therapeutic and relaxing. Engage in artistic activities that emphasize your witchy nature.

⊛ *Cooking*—Spells are very much like cooking. Set an intent, gather the ingredients, combine the two over a ritualistic process and—poof!—you have food. Cooking is a great alternative means for magic. Simply determine your magical intent with your hunger. Select spices and ingredients that connect to your goal, and engage in a bit of edible alchemy to bring comfort and nourishment.

⊛ *Dancing*—Fueling action with movement, dancing is a physical, artistic, and magical expression of transformation.

⊛ *Fitness*—For the fit witches who bask in fitness and body activities, working out is a wonderful act of self-care. I have found that both kickboxing and 5K races are not only fun, but they're also great ways to transmute pent up stress into release.

⊛ *Gardening*—This is a very therapeutic activity that also helps you connect with nature. For an extra dash of witchery, garden under the light of a full moon.

⊛ *Hike*—Another earth-based activity, hiking combines the elemental frequency of earth with physical movement. It is a fantastic escape and does wonders for the mind, body, and spirit.

⊛ *Movies*—A fantastic way to calm the mind and ignite creativity, movies provide fantasy, escape, glitz, and glamour. A bit of Hollywood magic in your weekend of witchy wellness can be a great way to recharge.

⊛ *Music*—Music is not only a delicious treat for our ears, but it is also packed with empathy. Lyrical language can be channeled into your spellcraft. When you cannot locate the "write" words and you're stuck in a writer's block, try using your favorite lyrics to convey the intention of your spell.

⊛ *Reading*—Reading is one of the best self-care methods because it encourages you to slow your pace and calm your mind. Nonfiction books are great for expanding knowledge, while fiction provides an excellent way to develop visualization skills that assist in meditations and rituals.

⊛ *Swimming*—Truth be told, I cannot swim. But that doesn't mean that I am not well versed in water witchery. Mine are mostly limited to luxurious baths, which are also self-care appropriate I might add! For those aquatically inclined witches out there, swimming can help you connect with the soothing, healing elements of water while also engaging in physical activity.

⊛ *Travel*—Ditch the broomstick for a plane and explore our planet with travel. There are many magical hotspots all over the world that can inspire you, whether they're found in lush tropical forests or concrete jungles of culture. Spread your wings and fly like Lilith!

⊛ *Writing*—As discussed on many occasions thus far, writing is a very healing outlet. It combines creativity with catharsis and can provide much soul nourishment.

⊛ *Yoga*—Yoga is a powerful moving ritual that combines mind, body, and spirit through physical poses.

13

LIVING LILITH:

Reclaiming Paradise

"Now is the time for the Goddess's return, for the return of
our lost souls."—Phyllis Curott, *Book of Shadows*

The power of the Goddess and the ancient art of witchcraft are
evolving in new ways today. Every generation continues to
add new elements to the nature of witchcraft and in doing so helps
to reinvigorate the world with magic. This book has examined
many aspects of witchcraft in correlation to Lilith as a goddess.
While there are many forms and branches of witchcraft, all with
their own codes of ethics, morals, and goals, the Great Lilithian
Arcane Mysteries define my personal practice of Lilith-based
witchcraft—one centered on self-empowerment, self-love, self-

compassion, and self-preservation. We are in an age where Lilith's power is growing more than ever. It is my hope that in sharing my path, more people can benefit from the delicious fruit Lilith has to offer. If nothing more, I hope to have helped inspire you on your own path to pursuing the magical life you deserve.

Witchcraft is ultimately a practice and it is through dedication that it becomes a lifestyle. A GLAM Witch lifestyle is rooted in the magic of Lilith—her archetype, myths, and mysteries. Though we have covered a great deal of rituals and spells within this book, living a magical life is not limited to the practices of ceremonial magic. Nor is it as simple as lighting a candle and reciting a prayer. There is a point where the practices of ceremonial magic and spell-casting take a backseat to other activities that shape the whole of your life.

Your magic will flow from your intention, be it big or small. In the process of cultivating your magical life make the conscious effort to do something daily that emphasizes your craft. It can be as simple as meditating in a peaceful place for a few minutes to help still your mind and stay grounded; looking up your daily astrology or pulling a morning tarot card to reflect upon throughout your day; curating a social media account with witchy imagery that inspires you; attending a workshop at your local occult store; or visiting a museum. Remember that it is also important to continue researching and exploring other avenues of occult practices to broaden your knowledge.

With GLAM, the Lilithian Laws are a blueprint for leading an empowered, magical life—to *see it, to own it, flaunt it, indulge in it,* and *defend it,* merge into empowerment through the enlightenment bestowed by Lilith. In turning the teachings of Lilith into a lifestyle, anchor the theory, practice, and crafts that we have explored with the following key points:

1. **Always trust your gut.** Visioncraft teaches the clear vision of spiritual sight. Not necessarily through clairvoyance but

through an inner vision. One must be open to receiving the blessings of the universe; they must pay attention to this. It is a reminder that life might not be the exact way you thought it would be, but if you have vision, if you have the sight, you can make it happen. It is the power of will and the willingness to see. This vision is that of spiritual ascension; it is your spiritual awakening.

2. **Darkness is beautiful.** Don't see the obstacles of life as depleting. Lilith encourages you to find the beauty in pain, the gratitude in light, and the ecstasy in the in-between. Shadowcraft represents healing. It is a magical practice that extends into the real-life reminder that that which does not kill you makes you stronger. Make the most of your inner darkness.

3. **Glamour is living your life out loud.** It is harmony and art. It is saturating yourself with beauty and the luxury of liberation. Glamcraft is the art of allure and fascination—the pure essence of a witch. It is the mystery of attraction through allusion and the pure personification of Lilith as the enchantress.

4. **Sexuality is an act of nourishment.** It is an act of love, though not romantic. It is expressions of both divine love and self-love through embracing primal and instinctual pleasure. Sex is life energy, and lustcraft is the magical application that creates a lust for life. Indulge in what gives you pleasure (physical or emotional).

5. **Protect yourself with unapologetic authenticity.** Bitchcraft is not solely an act of magical protection. Nor is it fighting adversity by being the adversary. It is authenticity and the mastery of choice. Like Lilith, you have the freedom to choose how to handle any obstacle thrown your way. You can be subordinate,

fight with rebellion, or you can simply move in another direction. The choice is yours and yours alone.

So as you progress on with your magical journey, nurture your own Lilithian garden within and reclaim your paradise—the secret and magical garden of the Goddess. Reclaim *your* Eden in the eyes of Lilith—she who was first—the red Goddess of passion, desire, love, and personal power. Consume her fruit, devouring her knowledge to awaken the power within. Break the chains that surround you. Sprout your wings and fly high. Welcome the wilderness within and find yourself. Attract awe. Know, dare, and will. Silence your mind and let your glamour do the speaking. Go forth on your path, whatever it may be. Breathe calmly, believe in yourself, and receive infinite possibilities from the universe. *Carpe noctem*—seize the night. Survive and thrive in your surroundings with inner vision. Love yourself and attract the life you want. In the end, the most powerful ritual you will ever perform is fully living your life for you—without any apologies or regrets. Enjoy your life. That is Lilith's lesson and ultimately fortifies the lifestyle of the GLAM Witch.

ACKNOWLEDGEMENTS

I want to give an enormous thank you to my literary coven at *Witch Way*, particularly Tonya Brown, for having allowed me the opportunity to be a part of your enchanting team. Thank you for taking a chance on me and helping make my vision a reality. You have become a sister to me, my Aries witch twin! A big thank you to Paul Flagg for your time and dedicated attention to editing this book—you are a wizard with words! Thank you, Kiki Dombrowski, for your tremendous support, guidance, and for sharing your Flying Witches' Ointment recipe!

There are many who have influenced me over the years, but I know for certain that I would not be where I am today if not for Fiona Horne. Thank you for igniting the spark of witchery in my soul and being a key element in my magical journey as a witch. I am proud to call you my *she*ro and honored to call you my friend.

Your contribution to, and support of, this book means the world to me. I am eternally grateful of your selfless generosity.

A huge, heartfelt thank you to my dear friend Jesse Gillespie for your incredible feedback and advice while writing this book.

Thank you, Dicle Uludağ of Spirit of Mine, for creating the gorgeous recreation of Lilith as *Queen of the Night* that graces the cover of this book. You are a talented and gifted soul.

Thank you to my extraordinary mother, Lynne Herkes who has supported me over the years and while pouring my heart and soul into this project. And to the fiercest batch of goddesses within my life who continuously support and inspire me: Christina Harris, Yazmin Ramos, Kay Traylor, Marcy Rae Henry, and Valerie O'Connor.

Tom Alcock, thank you for being an ear and voice of reason.

To Lilith, thank you for your guidance and blessings. Thank you for showing me the light in the dark, the ecstasy of pain, the beauty of rebirth, and the importance of being the most authentic version of myself. This book is for you.

And last but not least, thank YOU for picking up this book. I hope, if nothing more, that it inspires you on your magical journey in this life.

REFERENCES

by Chapter

Introduction

Adler, Margot. *Drawing Down the Moon: Witches, Druids, Goddess-Worshippers, and Other Pagans in America.* Penguin, 2006.

Brereton, Dan. *Buffy the Vampire Slayer: The Dust Waltz.* Dark Horse, 1998.

Horne, Fiona. *Witch: A Magickal Journey - A Hip Guide to Modern Witchcraft.* Thorsons, 2000.

RavenWolf, Silver. *Teen Witch: Wicca for a New Generation.* Llewellyn, 1998.

Starhawk. *The Spiral Dance: A Rebirth of the Ancient Religion of the Great Goddess – 20th Anniversary Edition.* HarperOne, 1999.

Chapter 1

Herkes, Michael. "Embracing Your Inner Glam Witch." *Witch Way Magazine*, Jan. 2018, pp. 28-33.

Horne, Fiona. *Witch: A Magickal Journey - A Hip Guide to Modern Witchcraft*. Thorsons, 2000.

Penczak, Christopher. *The Inner Temple of Witchcraft: Magick, Meditation and Psychic Development*. Llewellyn, 2002.

Starhawk. *The Spiral Dance: A Rebirth of the Ancient Religion of the Great Goddess – 20th Anniversary Edition*. HarperOne, 1999.

Valiente, Doreen. *An ABC of Witchcraft: Past and Present*. Phoenix, 1989.

Chapter 2

"Alphabet of Ben Sira 78: Lilith." Jewish Women's Archive, jwa.org/media/alphabet-of-ben-sira-78-lilith. Accessed 20 May 2019.

"Babylonian Talmud: Tractate Shabbath." Come and Hear, www.come-and- hear.com/shabbath/shabbath_151.html#151b_15. Accessed 31 Aug. 2019.

Blue, Mary. *Lilith: Keepers of the Flame*. CreateSpace Independent, 2015.

Chance, Harold J. The Worship of Astarte in Palestine During the Old Testament Period. 1932. Boston University, MA dissertateion.

Chilton, Bruce, et al. *A Comparative Handbook to the Gospel of Mark: Comparisons with Pseudepigrapha, the Qumran Scrolls, and Rabbinic Literature*. BRILL, 2009.

Collon, Dominique. *The Queen of the Night*. The British Museum Press, 2005.

Common English Bible. www.commonenglishbible.com. Accessed 16 Oct. 2018.

Crowley, Aleister. *The Vision & the Voice with Commentary and Other Papers: The Collected Diaries of Aleister Crowley, 1909-1914 E.V. (Equinox).* Weiser, 1999.

The Editors of Encyclopædia Britannica. "Lunar Calendar." Encyclopædia Britannica, www.britannica.com/science/lunar-calendar. Accessed 17 Jan. 2019.

Farrar, Janet, and Stewart Farrar. *The Witches' Goddess: The Feminine Principle of Divinity.* Phoenix, 1987.

Farrell, Nick. *The Hermetic Tablet: The Journal of Western Ritual Magic, Summer Solstice MMXVII.* Lulu.com, 2017.

Fries, Jan. *The Seven Names of Lamaštu: A Journey through Mesopotamian Magick and Beyond.* Avalonia, 2017.

George, Demetra. *Mysteries of the Dark Moon: The Healing Power of the Dark Goddess.* HarperCollins, 1992.

Goethe, Johann Wolfgang von. *Faust: A Tragedy, Part One.* Yale University Press, 1992.

Grey, Peter. *The Red Goddess.* Scarlet Imprint, 2011.

Herkes, Michael. "Goddess of the Month: Lilith." *Witch Way Magazine,* Nov. 2017, pp. 56-59.

Hurwitz, Siegmund. *Lilith the First Eve: Historical and Psychological Aspects of the Dark Feminine.* Daimon Verlag, 1992.

Koltuv, Barbara Black. *The Book of Lilith.* Nicholas-Hays, 1986.

Kramer, Samuel Noah. *Sumerian Mythology: A Study of Spiritual and Literary Achievement in the Third Millennium B.C.* Library of Alexandria, 1944.

Langdon, Stephen. *Tammuz and Ishtar: A Monograph Upon Babylonian Religion and Theology, Containing Extensive Extracts from the Tammuz Liturgies and All of the Arbela Oracles.* Oxford, 1914.

Lishtar. "Ninlil: Lady Air/Wind, the Avenging Bride." Gateways to Babylon, http://www.gatewaystobabylon.com/gods/ladies/ladyninlil.html. Accessed 5 Jan. 2019.

Olmsted, David. "Early Cuneiform Signs (2300 BCE) G - K." Nature Pagan, www.naturepagan.com/early-cuneiform-signs-f-k.

Accessed 16 Jan. 2019.

—. "Early Cuneiform Signs (2300 BCE) L - R." Nature Pagan, www.naturepagan.com/2300-bce-cuneiform-signs-l-p. Accessed 17 Jan. 2019.

Patai, Raphael. *The Hebrew Goddess.* Wayne State University Press, 1990.

Qualls-Corbett, Nancy. *The Sacred Prostitute: Eternal Aspect of the Feminine.* Inner City Books, 1988.

Rossetti, Dante Gabriel, and William Michael Rossetti. *The House of Life: A Sonnet-Sequence.* Ellis and Elvey, 1898.

Vernor, E.R. *Lilith From Ancient Lore to Modern Culture.* CreateSpace Independent, 2017.

Chapter 3

Collon, Dominique. *The Queen of the Night.* The British Museum Press, 2005.

Cunningham, Scott. *Cunningham's Encyclopedia of Magical Herbs.* Llewellyn, 2002.

Dombrowski, Kiki. *Eight Extraordinary Days: Celebrations, Mythology, Magic, and Divination for the Witches' Wheel of the Year.* Phoebe, 2017.

Herkes, Michael. "Goddess of the Month: Lilith." *Witch Way Magazine,* Nov. 2017, pp. 56-59.

—. "Serpent Magic." *Witch Way Magazine,* Mar. 2018, pp. 74-77.

Horne, Fiona. *L.A. Witch: Fiona Horne's Guide to Coven Magick.* Llewellyn, 2007.

Illes, Judika. *The Weiser Field Guide to Witches.* Weiser, 2010.

Melody. *Love is in the Earth: A Kaleidoscope of Crystals.* Earth-Love, 1995.

Penczak, Christopher. *The Witch's Heart: The Magick of Perfect Love & Perfect Trust.* Llewellyn, 2011.

Starhawk. *The Spiral Dance: A Rebirth of the Ancient Religion of the Great Goddess – 20th Anniversary Edition.* HarperOne, 1999.

Chapter 4

Adler, Margot. *Drawing Down the Moon: Witches, Druids, Goddess-Worshippers, and Other Pagans in America*. Penguin, 2006.

Cabot, Laurie, and Tom Cowan. *Power of the Witch: The Earth, the Moon, and the Magical Path to Enlightenment*. Delta, 1989.

Curott, Phyllis. *Witch Crafting: A Spiritual Guide to Making Magic*. Broadway, 2001.

Herkes, Michael. "Goddess of the Month: Lilith." *Witch Way Magazine*, Nov. 2017, pp. 56-59.

Horne, Fiona. *L.A. Witch: Fiona Horne's Guide to Coven Magick*. Llewellyn, 2007.

—. *Witch: A Magickal Journey - A Hip Guide to Modern Witchcraft*. Thorsons, 2000.

McCoy, Edain. *If You Want to be a Witch*. Llewellyn, 2005.

Penczak, Christopher. *The Inner Temple of Witchcraft: Magick, Meditation and Psychic Development*. Llewellyn, 2002.

Chapter 5

Fortune, Dion. *The Training & Work of an Initiate*. Weiser, 2000.

Penczak, Christopher. *The Inner Temple of Witchcraft: Magick, Meditation and Psychic Development*. Llewellyn, 2002.

Chapter 6

Alexander, Skye. *The Modern Witchcraft Book of Tarot: Your Complete Guide to Understanding the Tarot*. Adams Media, 2017.

Cabot, Laurie, and Tom Cowan. *Power of the Witch: The Earth, the Moon, and the Magical Path to Enlightenment*. Delta, 1989.

Dombrowski, Kiki. *A Curious Future: A Handbook of Unusual*

Divination and Unique Oracular Techniques. Phoebe, 2018.

Guiley, Rosemary Ellen. *The Art of Black Mirror Scrying.* Visionary Living, 2016.

Mueller, Mickie. *The Witch's Mirror: The Craft, Lore & Magick of the Looking Glass.* Llewellyn, 2016.

Wolfe, Stacey. *Get Psychic! Discover Your Hidden Powers.* Grand Central, 2001.

Chapter 7

Couglin, John J. *Out of the Shadows: An Exploration of Dark Paganisim and Magick.* Waning Moon, 2015.

Jacobs, Tom. *Lilith: Healing the Wild.* CreateSpace Independent, 2012.

Jay, Delphine Gloria. *Interpreting Lilith.* American Federation of Astrologers, 1981.

Jung, C. G. *Modern Man In Search of A Soul.* Harvest, 1955.

—. *The Portable Jung.* Penguin Classics, 1976.

Chapter 8

Herkes, Michael. "Embracing Your Inner Glam Witch." *Witch Way Magazine*, Jan. 2018, pp. 28-33.

Horne, Fiona. *Bewitch a Man: How to Find Him and Keep Him Under Your Spell.* Simon Spotlight Entertainment, 2006.

Huson, Paul. *Mastering Witchcraft: A Practical Guide for Witches, Warlocks, and Covens.* Backinprint.com, 2006.

Lady Rhea and Eve LeFey. *The Enchanted Formulary.* Citadel Press, 2006.

Morrison, Dorothy. *Utterly Wicked: Curses, Hexes & Other Unsavory Notions.* Willowtree Press, 2007.

Mueller, Mickie. *The Witch's Mirror: The Craft, Lore & Magick of the Looking Glass.* Llewellyn, 2016.

Schwartz, Howard. *Lilith's Cave: Jewish Tales of the Supernatural.* Oxford University Press, 1988.

Whitehurst, Tess. *Magical Fashionista: Dress for the Life You Want*. Llewellyn, 2013.

Chapter 9

Alexander, Skye. *Sex Magic for Beginners: The Easy & Fun Way to Tap into the Law of Attraction*. Llewellyn, 2017.

Blue, Mary. *Lilith: Keepers of the Flame*. CreateSpace Independent, 2015.

Camphausen, Rufus C. *The Encyclopedia of Sacred Sexuality: From Aphrodiacs and Exstasy to Yoni Worship and Zap-Lam Yoga*. Inner Traditions, 1999.

Couglin, John J. *Out of the Shadows: An Exploration of Dark Paganisim and Magick*. Waning Moon, 2015.

"Damiana."WebMD, www.webmd.com/vitamins/ai/ingredientmono-703/damiana. Accessed 15 Dec. 2018.

Herkes, Michael. "Lustcraft." *Witch Way Magazine*, Feb. 2018, pp. 50-53.

Horne, Fiona. *Bewitch a Man: How to Find Him and Keep Him Under Your Spell*. Simon Spotlight Entertainment, 2006.

—. *Witch: A Magickal Journey - A Hip Guide to Modern Witchcraft*. Thorsons, 2000.

Koster, Katherine. "17 Facts About Sexual Violence and Sex Work." HuffPost, 4 Dec. 2015, www.huffingtonpost.com/ 16-facts-about- sexual-ass_b_8711720.html. Accessed 7 Dec. 2018.

Mars, Brigitte. *The Sexual Herbal: Prescriptions for Enhancing Love and Passion*. Healing Arts Press, 2002.

Penczak, Christopher. *The Witch's Heart: The Magick of Perfect Love & Perfect Trust*. Llewellyn, 2011.

"Preventing Suicide: Facts About Suicide." The Trevor Project, www.thetrevorproject.org/resources/preventing-suicide/facts-about-suicide/. Accessed 14 Jan. 2019.

Ravishly. "Is Sex Work Empowering or Enslaving? 12 Experts Weigh In." HuffPost, 18 Oct. 2014. www.huffingtonpost.com/ravishly/is-sex-work-empowering-or-enslaving_b_5825882. html. Accessed 7 Dec. 2018.

Chapter 10

Cunningham, Scott. *Earth Power: Techniques of Natural Magic.* Llewellyn, 2002.

Horne, Fiona. *Witch: A Magickal Journey - A Hip Guide to Modern Witchcraft.* Thorsons, 2000.

Huson, Paul. *Mastering Witchcraft: A Practical Guide for Witches, Warlocks, and Covens.* Backinprint.com, 2006.

Morrison, Dorothy. *Utterly Wicked: Curses, Hexes & Other Unsavory Notions.* Willowtree Press, 2007.

Chapter 11

Cunningham, Scott. *The Complete Book of Incense, Oils, & Brews.* Llewellyn, 2002.

—. *Cunningham's Encyclopedia of Magical Herbs.* Llewellyn, 2002.

Dombrowski, Kiki. *Eight Extraordinary Days: Celebrations, Mythology, Magic, and Divination for the Witches' Wheel of the Year.* Phoebe, 2017.

Lady Rhea and Eve LeFey. *The Enchanted Formulary.* Citadel Press, 2006.

Chapter 12

Horne, Fiona. *Witch: A Magickal Journey - A Hip Guide to Modern Witchcraft.* Thorsons, 2000.

Morrison, Dorothy. *Everyday Magic: Spells & Rituals for Modern Living.* Llewellyn, 2002.

Chapter 13

Curott, Phyllis. *Book of Shadows: A Modern Woman's Journey into the Wisdom of Witchcraft and the Magic of the Goddess.* Broadway, 1998.

ABOUT THE AUTHOR

Michael Herkes (Chicago), also known as "The Glam Witch", has been a practicing modern witch for over 20 years. He is a devotee to the goddess Lilith and focuses his practice on crystals, glamour, love, moon, and sex magic. Michael is the author of *The GLAM Witch, The Complete Book of Moon Spells, Witchcraft for Daily Self-Care, Love Spells for the Modern Witch, Moon Spells for Beginners*, and is a contributing writer and graphic designer for *Witch Way Magazine*--a digital publication featuring curated articles about witch culture, craft, and daily life. Additionally, Michael hosts "Glam Fridays" on the Witch With Me IGTV channel @witch.with.tv, giving tips and tricks for magical makeovers. He is a professional tarot reader and nationwide speaker, having presented at festivals such as Gather the Witches, Hexfest, and WitchCon, in addition to being featured in an exhibit on display at the Buckland Museum of Witchcraft in Cleveland, Ohio. For more information and to follow Michael online visit www.theglamwitch.

WITCH WAY MAGAZINE

Witch Way Magazine is a Digital Witch E-Magazine that aims at helping our readers learn about topics from different perspectives growing their knowledge base and igniting new passions within their craft. Monthly digital articles feature topics on witchcraft, divination, Paganisim, and other acts of magical lifestyle. Printed limited edition specials are also available.

Get a free sampler issue when you sign up for the newsletter at www.witchwaymagazine.com.